A HISTORY OF
ACADEMICAL DRESS
IN EUROPE
UNTIL THE END OF
THE EIGHTEENTH CENTURY

Oxford University Press, Amen House, London E.C.4

GLASGOW   NEW YORK   TORONTO   MELBOURNE   WELLINGTON
BOMBAY   CALCUTTA   MADRAS   KARACHI   LAHORE   DACCA
CAPE TOWN   SALISBURY   NAIROBI   IBADAN   ACCRA
KUALA LUMPUR   HONG KONG

D.D. Chapel Dress

D.C.L. Festal Dress

D.Mus. Festal Dress

Nobleman

OXFORD ACADEMICAL DRESSES, 1792

A HISTORY OF
ACADEMICAL DRESS
IN EUROPE
UNTIL THE END OF
THE EIGHTEENTH CENTURY

BY

W. N. HARGREAVES-MAWDSLEY
M.A., D.Phil., F.S.A.

OXFORD
AT THE CLARENDON PRESS
1963

© *Oxford University Press 1963*

PRINTED IN GREAT BRITAIN

TO MY MOTHER
OLGA HARGREAVES-MAWDSLEY

PREFACE

THIS history is detailed, and contains all the facts gathered together during more than eight years of work. Supplementary information could be collected, but this would increase the size of the book for no commensurate gain. I trust that the essentials and all the necessary implications are here.

I have not pursued my history beyond the eighteenth century, for by that time not only was the formative period of academical dress over, but the forces which had since the Middle Ages bound all the institutions of Europe together had vanished. Nationalism entered the academical world; states made and unmade universities; in a moment the effects of the slow process of time were swept away; and the new universities founded in the iconoclastic nineteenth century gave scope for robe-makers to use their ingenuity in creating new robes for institutions without a past, sometimes borrowing freely and without true knowledge of the manner whereby the old universities had gradually acquired their costume through the years. What was devised in an age which ignored its inheritance is alien to a study which illustrates the historical continuity of the intellectual harmony of the Western world. This is also the reason why the Empires of Russia and Turkey find no place here. The Church, which inherited what Rome bestowed, is naturally the corner-stone of our Western civilization. Russia and Turkey lay beyond its bounds.

It may be asked why I have placed countries in the order they stand here. I have taken Italy first because the earliest true university in Europe was Italian and, as Spain and Portugal are naturally associated with Italy, they are included in the same chapter. France comes next, for the University of Paris is second in seniority. England follows, and the German-speaking and other nations come finally because universities were founded in those countries last of all.

It may appear that while Great Britain is very fully treated, some of the continental countries have not been similarly dealt with, but in fact this is not so, for Oxford and Cambridge have a longer and more elaborate sartorial history than any other

European universities. As is explained in the course of my book
the use of academical dress in many countries was greatly
curtailed during the first half of the seventeenth century, if not
earlier. Such dress as remained in use, generally only on important occasions, did not alter, but the dress of the English universities continued to evolve until the end of the eighteenth century,
as dress will if worn from day to day. Furthermore, in the case of
certain countries, after lengthy researches, sometimes made in
person, sometimes by correspondence, no more material could
be found, though some may possibly exist.

In order to shorten footnotes I have omitted 'op. cit.' wherever
possible, that is, when the same book is mentioned more than
once in the same chapter. When there are references to more than
one book by the same author in a chapter I have used a short
title to distinguish one from the other. I have only in one case
shortened the reference to mere letters, and that is B.M. for
British Museum.

The use of the terms 'amess' and 'amice' has caused confusion
among some who have read my manuscript, and the distinction
between the words has not been made in the *Oxford English
Dictionary*. The amice, which is an article of liturgical dress, a
square of white linen, is not referred to in my book, but the
amess (almuce) was the fur scarf used by men of dignity, and in
later times by canons; and to this I refer. This point of difference
is mentioned by W. B. Marriott in his *Vestiarium Christianum*.

Many scholars have aided me in several ways and know how
much I have appreciated their help. In the course of my work I
have corresponded with or met literary men of all European
countries, and it is pleasant to realize that in this distracted age,
when the bane of nationalism lies so heavily on us, in the
Republic of Letters there are no barriers. I regret that I must
refrain from naming all who have so kindly helped me, and
those not mentioned individually will, I am sure, understand
my confining myself to those who have given me exceptional
assistance, whom I name as: Dr. A. B. Emden, F.B.A., and
Dr. Czismadia Andor, to both of whom I am especially indebted,
Dr. F. Brittain, Dr. C. A. H. Franklyn, F.S.A. Scot., Professor
V. H. Galbraith, F.B.A., Dr. W. O. Hassall, F.S.A., Mr. W. A.
Pantin, F.B.A., F.S.A., Dr. August Roth, and Mr. P. S. Spokes,
F.S.A.   W. N. H.-M.

CONTENTS

LIST OF PLATES

INTRODUCTION

The Origin of Universities—The Origin of Academical
Degrees—The Origin of Academical Dress—Examples of the
Influence of Lay Fashion on Academical Dress—The In-
fluence of Forms of Association on Academical Dress

1. *The Origin of Universities*

By the twelfth century there had emerged two outstanding
seats of learning in Europe, Bologna and Paris. At the first the
jurist Irnerius between 1116 and 1140 introduced the *Corpus
juris civilis* to Europe,[1] and at the second a group of masters
with the blessing of the Church occupied themselves with the
liberal arts and theology. At Paris, by 1150, the theologians
occupied the cathedral area and the masters and students of
the liberal arts the left bank of the Seine.

The teachers in these two cities attracted audiences from all
over Europe, and both teachers and students, in different ways
in the two centres, formed voluntary associations for the purpose
of organization and protection. These recognized groups in
these two cities were known as *studia*, that is, schools of general
repute, but elsewhere, in fact wherever a cathedral chapter
had a school whose fame extended beyond its own locality,
studia existed.[2]

Only the *studia* of Bologna and Paris, and a little later
Oxford, reached the next stage in their development. As they
grew in size and scope faculties were organized and officers
appointed. The seal of their success was set upon them when
they were recognized by the Holy See, for they were then
accepted everywhere. They were, as *studia generalia*, free of the
threat of royal or civic interference, or from the undue influence
of the chancellor of the neighbouring cathedral. Paris gained
this distinction before Bologna, which the Emperor Frederick
Barbarossa had in 1158 taken under his wing in opposition to

[1] In this section and in Section 5 on the occasions when no other reference is
given I have relied on H. Rashdall, *The Universities of Europe in the Middle Ages*, ed.
F. M. Powicke and A. B. Emden, 3 vols., 1936, and S. d'Irsay, *L'Histoire des
universités françaises et étrangères à nos jours*, 2 vols., 1933–5.

[2] There is a general account of the development of the schools of cathedral
chapters in A. F. Leach, *The Schools of Medieval England*, chap. viii.

the pope's Paris. In this case the power of the emperor was almost equal to the prestige of the pope, and under his patronage Bologna flourished as it never did again.[1] In the course of the thirteenth century the term *universitas*, a word used in Roman law for any kind of corporation,[2] supplanted that of *studium generale* and acquired its modern sense of *universitas litterarum*.

The universities of Paris, famed for theology and the liberal arts and patronized by the papacy, and Bologna, notable for law and with a development under imperial auspices, were the models for the systems which were adopted by the other universities of Europe when they came into being. Paris, whose government was carried out by the masters, the masters constituting the university, was the prototype of the majority of the universities of northern Europe. Bologna, on the other hand, was rather a guild of students, who as a body possessed the supreme active power, while the professors formed themselves into a college of masters isolated from the students, and so outside the great university corporation which the students formed. This system was followed in general by the universities of southern Europe. The third great university of the Middle Ages was Oxford, which followed Paris. These three universities were the only ones founded *ex consuetudine*, that is they were already in existence as *studia generalia* in all but name when recognized by the pope. All the rest that followed were either founded by potentates and recognized in time by the papacy, or were founded by the papacy for the furtherance of its own influence, and as their origin was *ex privilegio* they never enjoyed the same glory.

2. *The Origin of Academical Degrees*

During the thirteenth century a system of degrees seems to have come into being at the universities then in existence. The three grades common to all were those of Scholar, Bachelor, and Master (sometimes called Doctor or Professor). The scholar attended lectures and argued on set questions in the schools, the bachelor was a student-teacher who was seeking to obtain a licence to teach in his own right. The mastership was

---

[1] C. H. Haskins, *The Rise of Universities*, as for instance on p. 13, deals with the rise of the *studia generalia*.

[2] F. K. von Savigny, *Histoire du droit romain au moyen âge*, iii. 295, § 154.

the highest grade in any faculty, and carried with it the obliga-
tion to lecture in the university for two years after inception.[1]

'Doctor', like 'Master' and 'Professor', originally meant no
more than 'teacher' or 'learned man'.[2] All three terms were
thus at first synonymous, but during the fourteenth century the
title 'Doctor' began, particularly in southern Europe, to be
used instead of 'Master' for the chief degree in the Faculties of
Canon Law, Civil Law, and Medicine, but not in those of
Theology and Arts.[3] Masters of Theology later became known
as doctors except in France where as late as 1584 they were still
called masters.[4]

The system of degrees in the three original universities was
accepted in more or less the same form by all universities subsequently founded. As time passed differences occurred in various
countries, a few of which are worth mentioning. Thus in France
the degree of Bachelor of Arts came to be little more than a
first public examination, and the Mastership of Arts was gained
after a mere two years study of philosophy.[5] In England the
Mastership of Arts became all-important and without it
membership of Convocation or Senate was impossible. In Italy
a doctorate became almost a necessity for success in the
academical world.[6] In Germany the Bachelor of Arts degree
vanished in the sixteenth century[7] and the Mastership of Arts
was incorporated in the new title of Doctor of Philosophy
which took its place.[8] Quite early the licentiateship became an
actual degree in the Faculty of Law at French universities.[9]

In all universities a distinction existed between Regents and
Non-Regents, that is those actively engaged in the teaching
work of their university and those who, having satisfied the
requirements of necessary regency, were no longer employed

[1] On the *licentia docendi* which, as at Paris, had originally always been sought from
the chancellor of the cathedral, since he had been the *magister scholarium* of the
cathedral school, see K. Edwards, *The English Secular Cathedrals in the Middle Ages*,
chap. iii. 3. The licentiate was one who had fulfilled the requirements of the course
for the mastership, but who had not yet qualified for it by necessary regency.

[2] F. K. von Savigny, iii. 151, § 77.

[3] J. Launoy, *Epistolae Omnes*, p. 801.

[4] P. Lénaudière, *De Privilegiis Doctorum*, p. 8, § xx (25–27).

[5] For example, J. C. Nadal, *Histoire de l'Université de Valence*, p. 228.

[6] G. Panzirolus, *De claris legum interpretatibus*, p. 77.

[7] F. Paulsen, *The German Universities*, p. 39.

[8] J. von Aschbach, *Geschichte der Wiener Universität*, i. 76.

[9] See Chap. II.

in public lecturing, either because they did not wish to or were considered unsuitable. Although non-regents had the right of the *ius suffragii*, the regents gained greater rights and wider powers.

Gradually a rule of precedence for faculties and degrees came into being and was practically the same in every university. An Act of the University of Vienna of 1389 gives orders for the precedence to be observed in processions. The banner of the university is to be carried first, then are to come Bachelors of Arts, then Bachelors of Medicine, followed by Bachelors of Law, then Bachelors of Theology, then Masters of Arts, Doctors of Medicine, Doctors of Law, and Doctors of Theology, Nobles walking with the Doctors. With Bachelors are to walk their group of Scholars, and with Masters of Arts and Doctors their Licentiates. This is a very clear example, and is particularly interesting as showing the position of licentiates.[1] Among the students the separate status of noblemen, scholars, and commoners was commonly recognized at all universities.[2]

3. *The Origin of Academical Dress*

The evolution of academical costume is complicated by the secular and ecclesiastical contacts which characterized the universities at the time of their earliest development.

In the early days of the *studia generalia*, which owed their beginnings to the chapter schools, the masters and scholars, being at least in minor Orders, wore, as befitting secular clerks, some sober form of dress, loosely termed a *vestimentum clausum*, something closed.[3] Even in those countries such as Italy in which scholars were not necessarily regarded as clerks,[4] they were forced in the interests of discipline to use a uniform of some kind, which in fact would be much the same as that of the secular clerks.[5]

---

[1] *Conspectus Historiae universitatis Viennensis*, i. 49. For precedence at Oxford in 1432 see S. Gibson, *Statuta Antiqua*, p. 239, and for that at Paris in 1491 see J. Launoy, op. cit., p. 62.

[2] For the distinction at Paris between undergraduates who were scholars (*Boursiers*) and so lived on the foundation of a college, and commoners (*Pension-naires*) who paid their own way see A. Franklin, *La Vie privée d'autrefois*, x. 30.

[3] A. Renan, *Le Costume en France*, p. 30.

[4] H. Rashdall, iii. 386, n. 1.

[5] See the reconstruction of students' dress in D. R. Hartley, *Mediaeval Costume and Life*, p. 15, pls. A and B, and p. 17.

The dress which the secular clergy wore was in general character no different from that worn by the laity of all classes of the community. Everyone from highest to lowest wore, as did the clergy, a hood to protect the head in bad weather.[1] If priests wore their *pluvial*, a loose cape with a hood and with a hole for the head to pass through and a slit in front for the passage of the arms,[2] it was no different from the outer garment worn by any citizen.[3] There was only one exclusively clerical non-liturgical garment, the *cappa clausa*, and even this was really no more than a development of the *pluvial*. In 1222 at the Council of Oxford Stephen Langton, Archbishop of Canterbury, ordered clerks to wear the *cappa clausa*,[4] and he thus introduced into England the clerical outdoor dress already in use on the Continent. The result of this was that at Bologna, Paris, and Oxford and at subsequent universities the *cappa clausa* came to be regarded as the academical dress, at least for formal occasions, for Doctors of Theology and Masters of Arts, who as priests—nearly all Masters were in Orders—wore this garment before any particular form of academical dress had come to be established. Further, when in due course Langton's rule about the use of the *cappa clausa* was more and more neglected by the clergy in general, the garment came to be regarded as an exclusively academical one.

As regards clerical head-dress also, its origin is to be found in lay fashion. Thus the *pileus*, which became the typical clerical head-gear and, by the same process as that of the *cappa clausa*, the head-dress of the universities, was simply adopted by the Church at the Synod of Bergamo (1311), on which occasion clergy were ordered to wear it 'after the manner of laymen'.[5]

At first the lay minority at the universities, found for the most part in the Faculties of Civil Law and Medicine, must be supposed to have worn some dignified form of dress according to the lay fashion of the time. It is noticeable that the earliest statutes of universities concerning dress are rather sumptuary

---

[1] R. A. S. Macalister, *Ecclesiastical Vestments*, pp. 254–5.
[2] F. Cabrol and H. Leclercq, *Dictionnaire d'archéologie chrétienne et de liturgie*, iii, cols. 370 and 376.
[3] W. B. Marriott, *Vestiarium Christianum*, p. 167; C. D. Du Cange, *Glossarium*, s.v. Pallium pluviale.
[4] D. Wilkins, *Concilia Magnae Britanniae et Hiberniae*, i. 589, 'Council of Oxford', § xxviii.
[5] H. Norris, *Church Vestments*, p. 161.

regulations than anything else. In time, however, the authorities succeeded in obliging members of these faculties to wear a form of *cappa*, the *cappa manicata*, at least on formal occasions.

After the first stage during which the statutes concerning costume were somewhat vague, we find the authorities of all universities beginning to adopt a new and deliberate policy, that of accepting lay fashions in a modified and particularized form into the canon of academical requirement, thereby creating a true 'academical dress'. A special *shape* and *cut* was what by the fourteenth century had become the essential feature of academical dress, but the significance of *colour* in such dress was not recognized until later.

From the late fifteenth century onwards the whole movement of everyday fashion was towards a shorter, less cumbersome dress in keeping with an active age, and the wide modifications of academical and legal costume were a mirror of that age. More than ever before the universities were open to outside influences. The *Epistolae Obscurorum Virorum* (1516) well illustrate the change in the intellectual climate in the universities of the day.

Then came the Reformation, resulting in upheavals which lasted for a hundred years, during which period the discipline of collegiate life broke down everywhere except in England, France, Portugal, and Spain, and in a few universities in south Germany and Austria where the Old Church was more secure. In all other countries legislation about dress occurred less and less, and even when orders were published they were less than half-heartedly observed; until by the eighteenth century, when France was beginning to fall a victim to the anti-clericalism of the *Philosophes*, only in England, Spain, and Portugal was a recognized academical dress worn by members of universities on all occasions. An insular conservatism was the cause of its preservation in England as well as a determination to keep the strongholds of the Establishment in Oxford and Cambridge intact, while in the other two countries a powerful church discipline, which had scarcely been questioned, preserved it.

4. *Examples of the Influence of Lay Fashion on Academical Dress*

The hood was originally merely a useful head-covering. Long before it had been given up in ordinary dress, that is by about 1450,[1] it had become a recognized feature of the dress of academical persons. It is typical of the growth of specialized costume that a fashion abandoned in everyday life is appropriated by institutions, themselves strongholds of conservatism. The hood thus worn was small and close to the neck, and was joined to its 'shoulder piece' which covered the shoulders and the upper part of the arms, the two together in reality forming one article. For the most part in continental and English legal dress it remained unchanged, but in academical dress both in this country and elsewhere it was greatly modified during the sixteenth century. In England the academical 'shoulder piece' was abandoned during this period and the hood was worn alone, greatly elongated by 1592 as can be seen in an oil-painting of that year by an anonymous artist of the founding of the Vicars' Close at Wells.[2] The liripipe on the English hood, which first appears in the reign of Henry III,[3] was an appendage of it, and originally served a useful purpose, being used both to pull the hood on and off the head and to hold the hood in position by binding it round it and fastening it under the chin.[4]

On the Continent both hood and 'shoulder piece' were generally abandoned during the sixteenth century except in rectorial dress, but an equivalent of the English hood had by this time appeared. This was the scarf worn on the shoulder, variously called *chausse*, *chaperon*, and *Sendelbinde*, and was in fact a liripipe. It originated in an everyday fashion for head-dress which was in vogue between 1420 and 1470, and which consisted of three parts, the *roundlet*, a ring of thick rolled material which fitted the head, the *gorget*, a piece of stuff sewn on to the inside of the *roundlet* and which hung down from it, and a liripipe (later to become the *chaperon* when the other parts of the dress were given up) like a long scarf to which *roundlet* and *gorget* were attached.[5] Originally worn on the head the *roundlet* and *gorget* after the middle of the fifteenth century were usually cast on either of the shoulders and hung down behind from the liripipe.[6]

[1] C. W. and P. Cunnington, *Handbook of Mediaeval Costume*, p. 111.
[2] H. Parnell, *The College of Vicars Choral, Wells*, pp. 6–8, and ill., p. 7.
[3] C. H. Ashdown, p. 56, fig. 72.   [4] C. H. Ashdown, p. 143, fig. 175.
[5] W. M. Webb, *The Heritage of Dress*, pp. 114, figs. 122–3, and 115, fig. 125; C. W. and P. Cunnington, pp. 113 and 115.
[6] For example, the citizen of Bruges who appears in an illumination in the

When in the later fifteenth century this fashion began to disappear from ordinary dress, it was retained by men of official standing and particularly by professional and learned men.[1] Thus in France legal and court officials and academical persons wore the *chaperon*, the *gorget* sometimes being cut up so that several ends appeared hanging down, in which case it was known as the *cornette*.[2] The *chaperon* was also used in Germany where it was known as the *Sendelbinde*. In England, since the use of the hood was well established as part of academical costume long before the fifteenth century, the shoulder-scarf was not employed as a symbol of degree at the universities.[3] It was, however, used by great officials of the Crown.[4] Survivals of it are to be found in the little gathered piece of cloth on the lower left-hand corner of the 'bridge' yoke of the barrister's gown, attached to which is a streamer coming over the left shoulder and hanging down in front,[5] and in the little tippet of Oxford and Cambridge proctors. The latter seems to have been worn by them in their capacity as officials.

The use of the *pileus* in the early Middle Ages has already been mentioned. Other varieties of head-dress for academical use were the result of fifteenth-century lay fashions. Thus the academical bonnet, much more full and looser than the original *pileus*, was derived from an ordinary fashion which first appeared in France in 1449.[6] Another variety, rigid and somewhat square with a tump, known in later times as a biretta, appears as early as the middle of the fifteenth century worn by a figure on a choir stall in Ulm Cathedral.[7] The introduction about 1520 of a square cap at the University of Paris, which seems to have originated in Italy,[8] was a development of the true *pileus*, but

---

manuscript (1475–1500) of Vasco de Lucena's edition of Quintus Curtius executed at Bruges in the von Essen Collection, Skokloster, Sweden (illustrated in *Gyllena Böcker*, *Nationalmuseum*, Stockholm, pl. xxii).   [1] D. R. Hartley, p. 91.

[2] E. Pasquier, *Les Recherches de la France*, pp. 382D–383B; J. Malliot and P. Martin, *Recherches sur les costumes*, iii. 88.

[3] It appears on certain English brasses, but is worn by laymen, or clergy in ecclesiastical and not academical costume. For examples see H. Haines, *A Manual of Monumental Brasses*, pp. lxxviii and cciii.

[4] See the portrait of Lord Burghley (d. 1598) in the National Portrait Gallery, London, No. 362.

[5] W. M. Webb, op. cit., pp. 163, fig. 141, and 164.

[6] D. Diderot and J. le R. D'Alembert, *Encyclopédie*, ii. 324 a–b, s.v. Bonnet.

[7] W. Lübke, *Ecclesiastical Art in Germany during the Middle Ages*, p. 218, fig. 157.

[8] C. D. Du Cange, s.v. Birretum.

the results of this development were very different. It was known as the *pileus quadratus* or *bonnet carré*, and our own square cap is a particular form of it.

By 1500 the general tendency in academical dress was to become more simple and comfortable, with the result that the heavy outer, closed dress being left off, the sleeved or sleeveless tabard, or some form of sleeved *tunica*, or other such dress, now the outer garment, assumed a new significance.

At the same time as this was happening, lay fashion was rapidly changing. There were two main features of this change; one was the opening of dress in front from about 1470 onwards, the other the elaboration and increase in size of the sleeves. After 1490, not only was the over-garment open in front, but it was thrown widely open, so that the lining of fur, which was afterwards placed in front in the form of two facings, could be seen.[1]

Various forms of sleeve appeared in lay fashions during the fifteenth century. There was the bag-sleeve, a tube of material through which the arm passed, sometimes called the glove-sleeve. This tube increased in length during the sixteenth century.

An example of the bag-sleeve showing embroidery in two places on the lower part of the thigh-length sleeve is to be seen in the brass of one not connected with a university, Lawrence Colston (1550), at Colston, Staffs.[2] A bag-sleeved gown is worn in his portrait by Cardinal Granvella (1517–86), minister of the Emperor Charles V.[3] Such is the origin of the England Master of Arts gown's sleeve.

On the Continent the bell-sleeved gown, with a flap collar joined to the facings, from the sixteenth century onwards worn in nearly all countries by doctors, was derived from a late fifteenth-century Italian lay fashion.[4] The same gown, worn academically, appears in the monument of the great Italian humanist Ficino (d. 1499), in the church of Sta. Maria del Fiore, Florence.[5]

---

[1] H. Haines, pp. cciv and ccxxxix, e.g. brass of John Colman (1506) at Little Waldingfield, Suffolk.   [2] C. H. Ashdown, p. 231, fig. 318.
[3] W. von Seidlitz, *Allgemeines historisches Porträtwerk*, portrait of Granvella in pt. 3–4.
[4] For an example of this gown worn by a rich Italian gentleman of 1494 see I. Brooke, *Western European Costume*, i, coloured plate opp. p. 102.
[5] M. Z. Boxhornius, *Monumenta illustrium virorum, et Elogia*, p. 45.

From a fashion of the later fifteenth century is also derived the winged-sleeved gown, which appeared as a feature of academical dress in England and elsewhere during the sixteenth century. It was an elaboration of a popular lay fashion of 1483.[1] It covered the upper part of the arm, and was used greatly in Germany and the Low Countries, and by graduates of the lay faculties at Oxford and Cambridge. The panel-sleeved (or false-sleeved) gown was a degenerate form of the winged-sleeved gown. This type, familiar to us from the Oxford commoner's gown, was used also by continental students from the later sixteenth century, as can be seen from a print of a student of one of the theological colleges of Rome, which were founded as a result of the Counter-Reformation.[2] No more clear example of the lay character of this form of gown could be given than the brass of a gentleman of 1607 at Dersingham, Norfolk.[3] The winged-sleeve seems to have reached England later than elsewhere, for it does not appear to have become fashionable until the reign of Elizabeth.[4]

Lastly there is the cloak-gown, allied to the gown with 'streamers', but originating in a Spanish fashion of the sixteenth century. It did not reach England directly, but the flap-collar on the English academical lay gown and undergraduate gown may have been influenced by it *via* Italian fashions. It was the last proper academical dress used by German students.[5]

5. *The Influence of Forms of Association on Academical Dress*

Three forms of association grew up in universities. The first of these was the Faculty, less strong in the English universities than elsewhere, the second the College, strong at first at all universities, but later only really so in France, England, Spain,

---

[1] C. Martin, *Civil Costume*, no. 28.

[2] P. Bonanni, *Ordinum religiosorum in ecclesia militanti catalogus*, iii, no. xxxvi, 'Student of the College of Fuccioli', and see also nos. xxxiv, xxxv, and xlii.

[3] J. S. Cotman, *Sepulchral Brasses*, ii, p. 88. John Aubrey proves the lay character of this gown when he writes: 'When about 1632 I learnt to read of John Brome the Clark of Kingston St. Michael, his old father (above eighty). . . daily wore a gown like an undergraduate's at Oxford, with sleeves pinned behind, etc.' (A. Powell, *John Aubrey*, p. 31).

[4] See, for example, the portrait at Emmanuel College, Cambridge, of Sir Walter Mildmay (d. 1589) in court dress.

[5] It was even used by clergy, both Roman Catholic and Protestant, as an out-of-door dress.

and the Austrian Netherlands, and the third the Nation, strong at first in France and Italy, and in due course in Germany.

The first of these kinds of association was a result of the gathering together of those who taught the same subject and who found that only by a united effort could their common aims be made known to their university at large. It also secured them against the unqualified, who might try to set up for themselves at the university. The second was a corporate body, which enjoyed the benefits of an endowment; and the third was an association based on nationality to defend the rights of an alien in a foreign land.

The faculties, which developed at Paris in the course of the thirteenth century, played a more or less conspicuous part in the affairs of subsequent universities, particularly that of Arts, membership of which at Oxford and Cambridge as well as abroad was necessary to full membership. The other faculties were those of Theology, Canon Law, Civil Law, and Medicine.

Although the first Paris college, the *Collège de Dix-Huit*, was founded as early as 1180, it was not until the foundation of the *Collège Sorbonne* in 1257 that a college became an organization independent of an ecclesiastical corporation other than the university. Of this latter type were all the colleges of Oxford and Cambridge and those of Paris which were founded after this time.[1] In Spain and Italy the college system, though in being, played a much less important part in the life of universities.

Nations appeared at Bologna at the beginning of the thirteenth century as subdivisions of the *Collegia*,[2] but at Paris they emerged at the same period as masters' associations within the large Faculty of Arts.[3]

It is natural in view of the practice of the great guild movement, the movement towards association in every trade and profession, which affected town-life in Europe at this time, to

---

[1] Thirty-seven Paris colleges are named in a list of those existing in the fifteenth century (Oxford, Bodl. Libr. MS. Twyne 2, fo. 101). One Oxford college, University College, is known to have been in existence in 1249, but it does not appear as a true corporation until after the *Collège Sorbonne*.

[2] Not to be confused with colleges. They were more like halls (hostels) for foreign law students.

[3] For a full account of the nations see P. Kibre, *The Nations in the Mediaeval Universities*.

expect that members of faculties, colleges, and nations, as the case might be, should wear some particular dress of uniform shape and colour betokening the group to which they belonged.

Some examples of faculty colours will show that no exact code of colours was observed at all universities, but there were certain tendencies. Thus black at Paris, Oxford, and Cambridge, and white at Salamanca, Coimbra, and Perpignan were the colours of the Faculty of Theology. Green, yellow, or sanguine were at various universities the colours of the Faculty of Medicine, while blue of various shades very often denoted the Faculty of Philosophy, and in such differently placed universities as those at Perpignan, Coimbra, and Ingolstadt. The most constant of the colours was scarlet for Canon Law, but even this by no means always held good. Indeed, as can be seen from inventories[1] such as those of Oxford regents, all kinds of colour were used by academical persons as late as the middle of the fifteenth century.[2] Yet it was in the course of this century that faculty colours appeared, a significant symbolism of association.

In some countries, in England and Spain especially, founders of colleges ordered certain kinds of dress to be worn by members of their foundations.

As far as the nations were concerned a special dress was discouraged by the authorities, who with good reason feared that sartorial distinctions might encourage the rivalries and antagonisms which these divisions tended to promote. It was, however, worn by the various nations at the University of Prague until the sixteenth century at the appropriate national festivals.

[1] For example, H. E. Salter, *Registrum Cancellarii* (O.H.S.), i. 44 and 70.

[2] That it was still cut rather than colour which was significant even in 1434 as betokening the wearer's degree can be understood from a papal letter of that year in which a regular priest, an Augustinian, was allowed to wear the habit or costume wont to be worn by secular Masters of Arts and Doctors of Divinity of Oxford provided that it was of the colour of the habit of the priest's Order (*Calendar of Papal Registers*, ed. J. A. Twemlow, *Papal Letters*, viii. 504).

1

I. ITALY

I. BOLOGNA (twelfth century)

THIS ancient university had originally only a Law School with the students by the first part of the thirteenth century divided into two nations, the *Citramontani* (the Italians) and the *Ultramontani* (the rest).[1] It was not until long afterwards that Schools of Medicine and the Liberal Arts appeared, and when they did appear their members desired to form a special university of their own with their own rector. In 1295, not wishing to see the university thus divided, the magistrates of Bologna condemned this pretension of the students, who as was general in Italy had their full say in affairs. Thus for the time these two bodies were forced to remain simply as appendages of the old Law School; but having had a taste of independence the new schools still clamoured for at least partial recognition. In 1316 this was granted and the Faculties of Medicine and the Arts were at last recognized. In the second half of the fourteenth century a School of Theology was founded by Pope Innocent VI and was placed by him under the authority of the Bishop of Bologna. The theological students had no rights of their own, and as the artists were not satisfied with their privileges the two joined forces in their discontent.

The various schools were so loosely attached to one another that in reality under the title of the University of Bologna there was indeed more than one university.[2] As time went on these differences of foundation and the resultant rivalry between the schools which formed the university threatened to destroy its unity, and it was not until 1584 that the authorities, finally bowing before the arbitration of the Church when ancient civic

[1] F. K. von Savigny, *Histoire du droit romain au moyen âge*, iii. 132, § 67.
[2] F. K. von Savigny, iii. 133.

liberties had been brought low by the power of Spain and the
Counter-Reformation, put all quarrels to an end by an enactment fortified by a papal decree of 1570.[1]

The foundation of the Law School in the twelfth century by
the Emperor Frederick Barbarossa gave it an enviable and
royal character. It has been suggested that from its very beginning Doctors of Civil Law took to scarlet cloth robes dressed
with ermine as if they were nobles, and from what remains in
the university library of the frescoes depicting the pupils of
Irnerius this seems to have been the case.[2]

Doctors of Canon Law out of regard to their sacred calling
did not wear scarlet, but had by the middle of the fourteenth
century a blue *cappa manicata* reaching to the ankles with elbow-
length sleeves. Their head-dress was sometimes a small 'turban'
cap lined with miniver,[3] but there is also an example of their
wearing a round *pileus* over a small coif.[4] Doctors of Civil Law
at the same period continued to wear their scarlet, and Boccaccio in a letter of 1348 describes their robes as of scarlet cloth,
full, dressed with miniver, and with large hanging sleeves. This
was exactly the same as the dress of nobles.[5] In a Bologna
manuscript of 1354, the *Speculum Juridicae* of G. Duranti, the
author, a Doctor of Civil Law, appears in a miniature kneeling
on a light green floor wearing a vermilion gown with a red
hood and a long red fur-lined mantle with a fur collar (Pl. 1a).[6]
In another Bolognese manuscript of 1378, *Novella de Regulis
Juris* by J. Andreae, the author in the initial N wears the same
dress as Duranti.[7]

In 1432 the rector was ordered to wear a black cloth *cappa
manicata* or a sleeveless tabard. In either case this dress was to
be buttoned up close to the neck. In his public capacity he was
to wear no other fur but miniver on his head-dress, which is

[1] F. K. von Savigny, iii. 137, § 70.

[2] E. D. Glasson, art. 'Les Origines du costume de la magistrature' in *Nouvelle
Revue historique de Droit français et étranger* (1884), p. 114.

[3] R. Bruck, *Die Malereien in den Handschriften des Königreichs Sachsen*, pl. 210,
no. 66—Leipzig, Stadtbibliothek MS. CCXLIII (*Decretum Gratiani*, Bl. 81').

[4] *Studia Gratiani*, ii, tav. xxviii—*Decretum Gratiani. Causa Prima. Cesenae* (Bibl.
Malatestianae, Cod. 3. 207, fo. 76, figure in foreground with hand on boy's head).

[5] C. Meiners, art. 'Geschichte der Trachten' in *Göttingische akademische Annalen*
(1804), pp. 217, 218, and 250–1; E. D. Glasson, art. cit., p. 113.

[6] H. J. Hermann, *Italienische Handschriften*, ii, Taf. lxxv, text p. 186.

[7] H. J. Hermann, op. cit. ii, Taf. lxxvii, 2, text p. 190.

PLATE I

a. Two Doctors of Civil Law of Bologna (kneeling), 1354

b. Rector of the University of Padua, 1576

mentioned as being generally a hood, but he might wear an unfurred hood on informal occasions. If, however, he chose to wear a *birretum* (*pileus*) this was not to have on it any miniver, which was to be confined to the hood. In summer he might substitute a thin cloth (*sindon*)[1] lining for that of miniver if he so wished. Later he was allowed a silk *cappa* instead of a cloth one.[2]

An excellent example of the dress of a Doctor of Both Laws of the first half of the fifteenth century is to be found in a Bolognese miniature in Antonius da Butrio's *Commentariorum super Libro II Decretalium*.[3] Da Butrio, who became a Doctor of Civil Law in 1384 and a Doctor of Canon Law in 1387, both of Bologna, wears over a blue *supertunica* a scarlet *cappa clausa* with a scarlet 'shoulder piece', the hood of which is on his head. His outer dress including the 'shoulder piece' is lined with miniver.

In spite of the fact that officially the university still demanded that Doctors of Both Laws or of Canon Law or Civil Law separately should wear a *cappa*, and a 'shoulder piece' and hood,[4] the tendency among Doctors of the Faculty of Law towards the end of the fifteenth century was to give up such dress and so allow the *supertunica* to become the outside garment. Thus on his monumental effigy in San Benedetto, Bologna, Pietro Ancharano, Doctor of Both Laws (d. 1493), wears over a *subtunica*, a loose full gown, which is what by development the *supertunica* had already become. This is the *vestis togata*, which is called the dress of Bolognese doctors in Rawlinson's transcript of the *Constitutions of the College of Civil Law, Bologna*, and is described as having very full tapering bell sleeves.[5] Ancharano has a miniver 'shoulder piece', but its hood, which he wears on his head,[6] is of cloth or silk and is not furred. The back part of the hood with its liripipe can be seen falling over his shoulders behind.[7]

---

[1] Martial, the Latin poet, uses the word.

[2] C. Malagola, *Statuti delle Università e dei Collegi dello Studio bolognese*, p. 55— Stats. of 1432, Univ. of Jurists, rubric viii; *Statuta et privilegia . . . universitatis . . . Bononiensis*, p. 5; Oxford, Bodl. Libr. MS. Rawlinson D413, fo. 68.

[3] Rome, Biblioteca Angelica MS. 569, fo. 1; M. Salmi, *La Miniatura Italiana*, tav. xi.

[4] C. Malagola, p. 196—Stats. 1459-98, rubric xxv; *Statuta et privilegia . . . univer-sitatis . . . Bononiensis*, p. 93.

[5] Oxford, Bodl. Libr. MS. Rawlinson D 413, fo. 7[b].

[6] Cf. the wearing of the hood as a head-dress by the rector according to the statute of 1432.   [7] M. Z. Boxhornius, *Monumenta illustrium virorum, et Elogia*, p. 137.

When in the fourteenth century the Medical School began to stand on its own, Doctors of Medicine took to the dress of Doctors of Civil Law as they did at Oxford. Thus Boccaccio in 1348 describes Doctors of Medicine as also wearing a full scarlet cloth robe dressed with miniver, and with large hanging sleeves.[1] In 1378 they were ordered to wear with a dress that was decent and befitting their standing either a furred hood or a miniver *pileus*.[2] By 1410 they appear to have been allowed silk (*sirichus*) hoods, perhaps as a substitute for fur in hot weather, as at Oxford twenty-two years later.[3] The *biretta* (*pileus*) was by this time common to all doctors.[4]

Thus we may say that as early as the fourteenth century the dress of Bolognese doctors and those of other Italian universities, except of Theology, had come to consist of a round scarlet *pileus* and a long *supertunica* of the same colour.[5] Such a bright dress trimmed with miniver and even ermine was worn by doctors of Bologna as late as 1595 as can be seen from the two figures at the bottom of the fresco-memorial to Camillo Baldo in the *Biblioteca Comunale dell' Archiginnasio* at Bologna. Their round *pilei* with a border of miniver are the same as that worn by a doctor of Bologna in a miniature, *Il maestro e gli scolari* in a fifteenth-century manuscript, *Libro dell' Università dei Notai*.[6] But during the latter sixteenth century Italian doctors gave up scarlet dress and took to black, and to square caps instead of round ones.[7]

In 1347 all the university statutes promulgated from 1317 onwards were collected, and what is mentioned in them of dress makes it clear that the costume of non-doctors and under-graduates was strictly regulated. Whatever their dress, whether some form of *cappa* in the case of masters for formal occasions; whether as bachelors they wore a tabard; or whether as students they wore a cloak (*gabanus*), all were to be made of black 'statute cloth'. In each case an under-dress (*subtunica*)

[1] C. Meiners, art. cit., p. 217.
[2] C. Malagola, p. 432, rubric v.
[3] C. Malagola, p. 505, rubric vi.
[4] *Chartularium Studii Bononiensis*, i. 337.
[5] A. Scappus, *De Biretto Rubeo*, p. 5; G. Panzirolus, *De claris legum interpretatibus*, p. 95.
[6] Bologna, Museo Civico, n. 95, reproduced in D. Fava, *Tesori delle Bibliotheche d'Italia: Emilia e Romagna*, p. 360, fig. 208.
[7] G. Péries, *La Faculté de droit dans l'ancienne Université de Paris*, p. 47.

was also to be worn, and was to be closed at the sides and buttoned up in front right to the neck. Hoods were to be worn by all.[1] In 1372 scholars of the Gregorian college were to be provided each year with two of these cloaks.[2] Members of the Faculty of Medicine not doctors were in 1378 and 1395 forbidden the use of miniver.[3]

By the end of the fifteenth century certain changes had occurred in these habits. Thus in a marginal drawing of 1491 appearing at the end of the *Acta Nationis Germanicae Universitatis Bononiensis* of that year a master, who is holding back a student from attacking the rector, wears a sleeveless tabard, while his head-dress—no head-dress for the masters is mentioned earlier —is an apexed *pileus*, and the student on the right wears an open *supertunica* reaching only to the knees with short glove-sleeves, a recent innovation. As in other universities of Europe at this time he had assumed a form of head-dress, in this case a tight skull-cap with a 'stalk' apex.[4] In 1514 students wore a *pallium*, a much longer dress than that worn earlier; it is referred to as the *toghe lunghe*.[4] Bachelors in the later fifteenth century began to wear a small plain bonnet.[6]

It seems certain that by 1491 the rector never wore the *cappa manicata* mentioned as one form of his dress in 1432, but always its alternative, the sleeveless tabard, together with a long broad *chaperon* which hung over his right shoulder.[7]

By the latter part of the sixteenth century the rector's dress had beome magnificent. The scholar Ulisse Aldrovandi (1522–1605) in his *Diario* writes of the rectorial robe as being stiff with gold braid and worked with gold and silver thread.[8]

The dress of the proctor of the German nation in 1497, according to a striking picture in the Act Book of this nation,

---

[1] H. Denifle and F. Ehrle, *Archiv für Litteratur- und Kirchen-Geschichte des Mittelalters*, bd. iii, p. 366, rubric lxxxv.

[2] F. K. von Savigny, op. cit. iv. 481 ff. *De Vestibus Scholarium: Chartularium Studii Bononiensis*, ii. 291; D. Fava, p. 360, fig. 208.

[3] C. Malagola, pp. 446, 460, and 473.

[4] E. Friedlaender and C. Malagola, *Acta Nationis Germanicae Universitatis Bononiensis*, p. 425.

[5] *Statuta et privilegia . . . universitatis . . . Bononiensis*, p. 15.

[6] D. Fava, p. 360, fig. 208.

[7] E. Friedlaender and C. Malagola, p. 425; C. Malagola, *Statuti*, p. 55—Stats. of 1432, Univ. of Jurists, rubric viii.

[8] C. Malagola, *Storiche sullo Studio Bolognese*, p. 62.

in which a group of students are being sworn in by their
proctor, consisted of a scarlet sleeveless tabard and a crimson
'turban' bonnet.[1]

As early as 1400 the wearing of academical dress by students
at Bologna does not seem to have been strictly observed if we
are to judge from Laurentius de Voltalina's miniature of a
university lecture at Bologna which appears in the fragmentary
Liber Ethicorum in the *Kupferstichkabinett* in the Berlin Museum.[2]
The students wear hats of ordinary lay fashion and their other
dress is of the same character. The lecturer, Henry of Germany,
wears no recognizably academical costume; but this is perhaps
because he was a visitor and was not a member of the university.

Although it seems that for a long time after this the tendency
of students to wear lay costume was checked, during the sixteenth century they gave up all pretence of wearing academical
dress.[3] The rector and the regents continued to wear their
proper habits on ceremonial occasions.

The Spanish College of Bologna, dedicated to St. Clement, was
founded in 1377, but its full statutes were codified only in
1536–8. At this time all members were ordered to wear over
black cassocks black cloth gowns reaching to the ankles with
sleeves. This is said to have been the original dress of the college
and was the same in shape as that worn in the past by doctors of
the University of Bologna. Besides this gown they were to wear
a purple cloth hood (*exhyacinthus, morellus*) gathered close at the
shoulders.[4] The open gown (*pallium*) was absolutely forbidden.
The rector's dress was on all occasions to consist of a long,
ankle-length gown and a silk hood,[5] but by 1564 he had come
to wear a silk gown as well as hood.[6] In 1570 Doctors of Theology were ordered to wear the 'priestly *pileus*', that is the
horned cap.[7]

In the statutes of 1660 it was ordered that candidates for

---

[1] E. Friedlaender and C. Malagola, col. pl. between pp. 4 and 5; D. Fava,
p. 360, fig. 208.
[2] P. d'Ancona and E. Aeschlimann, *Dictionnaire des Miniaturistes*, pl. lxx.
[3] C. Meiners, art. cit., op. cit.
[4] *Statuta almi et perinsignis Collegii maioris Sancti Clementis Hispanorum Bononiae conditi*,
pp. 29, 30, and 70; on p. 30 it is said to be of silk.
[5] Op. cit., *Tertia Distinctio*, Stat. 12.
[6] Op. cit., Extra Stats. XL.
[7] Op. cit., Extra Stats. XLIII.

admittance to the college should wear a long dark cloak of baize or flannel with a plain collar and facings, together with a hat with a simple cord round it.[1] The collegian when accepted was to substitute a gown for the cloak.[2] The rector was allowed a cloak and a gown of smooth black velvet. In summer he might wear a tawny-coloured cloak.[3] When important personages visited the college all the members were to wear a gown and *beca*.[4] At mass in the chapel *becas* were not to be worn, and gowns were to be worn closed.[5] The rector's *beca* was to be of velvet or stuff like velvet.[6] This is the only reference to the wearing of a *beca* by a Spanish rector and was probably used by him in this case in order to distinguish him from the other heads of colleges in Bologna.

II. PADUA (1222)

All that we learn of dress at Padua before the fifteenth century is in a stray reference which occurs in 1331, the date of the earliest surviving statutes. In that year all members of the university except canons and priests regular were told that they might spend only a certain amount on the cloth used for their dress.[7]

The most important university statutes referring to dress are those of 1465 and 1531 and concern the Faculties of Medicine and Arts. In the first of these the rector is ordered to obtain in time for his May installation a hooded robe, as *caputeum* in this case means, and if he fails to do so he is to incur the penalty of a fine of £50.[8] This robe is to be of silk on the occasion of his installation, but otherwise of cloth, thin for summer and thick for winter.[9]

All members of the university of whatever nation or degree were in the statutes of 1531 ordered to wear on all occasions a long black silk gown fastened at the neck with a band (some

---

[1] *Ceremonias y costumbres usadas y guardadas en colegio mayor de S. Clemente, Bolonia,* p. 9.

[2] Op. cit., p. 12. [3] Op. cit., pp. 16–17.

[4] A sash, op. cit., p. 21. For *beca* see below under Salamanca.

[5] Op. cit., p. 27. [6] Op. cit., p. 30.

[7] H. Denifle and F. Ehrle, op. cit., p. 497—Lib. 5, § 12 (*De vestibus scholarium*).

[8] *Statuta almae universitatis Patavini,* p. 9*a* [Bk. I, § xviii].

[9] Op. cit., p. 9*a* [Bk. I, § xix].

form of morse), closed in front, and having wide sleeves, which is presumably the *clericalis habitus* enjoined upon all members in 1486.[1] Members of religious Orders did not wear this, but their own habit.[2]

Doctors were distinguished from non-doctors in the fifteenth century by the Doctors of Theology wearing a violet amess (*almutium violaceum*) and by doctors of other faculties having a gold collar (*torque aurea*) and using miniver on their dress.[3]

By the middle of the sixteenth century two forms of dress for summer and for winter had developed for the dress of the rector. This is illustrated in C. Vecellio's collection of woodcuts first published in 1590, a new edition of which, sometimes better than the original, was produced in 1598. The rector's summer dress was a brocaded robe reaching to the ground with tapering bell sleeves, the lining and facings being of silk. The collar had a square flap, which was joined to the facings, and was edged with fur. In a water-colour of 1576 in an album a furred *chaperon* hangs on the rector's right shoulder[4] (Pl. 1*b*). His black cap is rigid, of the Tudor type with side pieces in the Vecellio woodcut, but is small and soft in the album. The rest of his dress was ordinary lay garb including a ruff, and he wore a double chain with a medallion suspended from it. The winter dress consisted of a soft black velvet square biretta, and a robe of gold brocade with full-hanging bell sleeves. The robe was worn closed and the whole of it was lined with miniver, while the hood which fell on the shoulders and down the back was of marten's fur.[5] According to another woodcut in the same collection, the reproduction of which appears to most advantage in the 1598 edition, Doctors of Law and Medicine from the sixteenth century, if not before, shared the same dress. This was a full robe with an upright collar and ample bell sleeves, the whole robe richly braided and with the device of a pineapple on the mid back, and a round bonnet bound with a cord.[6] Marco Bevilacqua, rector in 1595, during his term of office seems to have been zealous to preserve the dignity of doctoral dress. In

---

[1] J. Facciolati, *Fasti Gymnasii Patavini*, p. xx.
[2] Op. cit., p. 57*b*, Bk. IV (*De Scholarium habitu*).
[3] F. M. Colle, *Storia scientifico-letteraria dello Studio di Padova*, i. 104.
[4] B.M., MS. Eg. 1191, fo. 72ᵛ.
[5] C. Vecellio, *Habiti Antichi e Moderni* (1590), p. 156ᵇ.
[6] C. Vecellio, *Habiti Antichi* (1598), pl. op. p. 122.

that year he ordered Doctors of Medicine and Doctors of Philosophy to wear the proper dress, as described above, even if they were members of a religious Order. It was to be full-length, and short cloaks were not to be used. At the same time he ordered members of the Faculty of Theology to wear a black clerical biretta with the ridges forming a cross.[1]

Our information during the seventeenth century is particularly interesting as there is some excellent illustrative material.

First, there is a well executed woodcut of the dress of the rector and pro-rector which appears in J. P. Tomasini's *Gymnasium Patavinum*, a laudatory description of the university published in 1654. The rector wears a full and open bell-sleeved robe of damasked silk, with over the left shoulder a gold brocaded *chaperon* reaching almost to the bottom of the robe. The robe was scarlet in summer and purple in winter. His head-dress consists of a very tall cap like a *mortier*[2] with piping running along the bottom of it in the form of two snake-heads intertwined. He wears red sandals. The pro-rector has no head-dress. He wears a small turned-down white collar, a girded cassock, and over this a flap-collared, sleeveless full-length gown with very long 'streamers' running from behind the shoulders, like that of the gown of an Oxford commoner.[3]

Then there is the print of Quintilio Carbo which is pasted at the end of his diploma of the Doctorate of Law granted to him in 1627. This print, which has been coloured with water-colour paint, is of a date later than 1627 and was probably executed after he had become famous.[4] Carbo as a Doctor of Law wears an open gown with a broad flap collar and under it a cassock. The gown and cassock have been coloured dull plum-blue or dull violet. Unfortunately, since the print is only bust size the type of sleeves cannot be seen, but no doubt they were, as in 1590, of the bell-sleeved variety. He wears white bands with band-strings decorated with large pompons.[5]

---

[1] J. Facciolati, pt. 2, p. 221.
[2] This was tall and cylindrical.
[3] J. P. Tomasini, *Gymnasium Patavinum*, pp. 55–56, and pl. p. 57.
[4] London, Victoria and Albert Museum, MS. Drawer 53.
[5] It is interesting to notice the following extract: 'The maroon-coloured gown of the President of the Royal Society of Medicine is said to have been copied from the robe of a Doctor of Medicine of Padua of the eighteenth century' (W. J. Bishop, art. 'Notes on the History of Medical Costume', in *Annals of Medical History*, N.S. vi, No. 3 (1934), p. 205ª).

Lastly there are the series of portrait engravings illustrating a biographical account of contemporary professors of Padua, C. Patinus's *Lyceum Patavinum* (1682). According to these, three kinds of gown were at this time worn by regents. The first, which was probably the festal dress, is glove-sleeved, the arms appearing through a gash in the sleeves, and has a square flap-collar. The facings of the gown, the collar, and the gash in the sleeves are furred.[1] It would appear from the fact that these gowns are lightly engraved that they are intended to be represented as scarlet. The next type is voluminous, slightly gathered at the shoulders, with ample sleeves, a square collar, and narrow facings of fur.[2] This seems to have been the black undress gown worn for all formal occasions except when the festal robe was worn. But the most generally worn garment in this collection is a simple cloak, which was merely an informal garb for men of learning.[3] Sometimes a skull-cap is worn, but this is of no particular significance. Clerical professors wear a narrow white turned-down clerical collar, lay professors white bands. Sometimes braid or silk is used on the first two kinds of dress instead of fur, and this was very likely for summer use.[4]

At the beginning of the eighteenth century this cloak seems to have become so popular that professors wore it more and more instead of the formal full-sleeved gown; for in 1703 it was ordered that they must overcome their dislike of the gown (*toga*) and must wear it and not the cloak (*penula*) when lecturing and when taking part in university functions.[5]

Evidence for the dress of a professor in the eighteenth century is furnished by T. Viero in his collection of coloured prints issued in 1783–5. The costume consists of long white bands, a black court suit with a black apron (short cassock) over it reaching to the knees, and an open, ankle-length black gown with full, pointed bell sleeves. The sleeves are doubled back, and the gown has lapels and a collar with a flap.[6] With this was worn on formal occasions a full miniver 'shoulder piece'

---

[1] C. Patinus, *Lyceum Patavinum*, portraits of Montagnana and Scotus.
[2] C. Patinus, portraits of Scarabicius and Calliachius.
[3] C. Patinus, portrait of Pighius.
[4] C. Patinus, portraits of Frigiomelica, Albanensis, and Calafatti.
[5] J. Facciolati, pt. 2, p. 63.
[6] T. Viero, *Raccolta*, i, No. 45; G. Morazzoni, *La moda a Venezia*, tav. xviii.

open in front.[1] The head-dress was a rigid round *pileus*, the upper part of it wider than the lower.[2]

In the sixteenth century students ceased altogether to wear academical dress in spite of the order of 1531 mentioned above. In the late sixteenth century they wore ordinary lay dress of Spanish style, the latest fashion in Italy,[3] and in the seventeenth century they aped the dress of courtiers.[4]

III. THE SAPIENZA, ROME (1303; refounded 1431)

No early records dealing with the Sapienza, founded by Pope Boniface VIII in 1303, have been preserved, and not even after its real life began with its refoundation by Pope Eugenius IV in 1431 is there any mention of dress for a long time. This university is not to be confused with the university of the Roman Curia, directly governed by the papal court.

In 1552 *Punctators*[5] in the exercise of their office were to use a violet robe and a biretta of clerical shape.[6]

Not until the eighteenth century is anything more mentioned about dress. By this time the ceremonial of the university as well as many of its institutions had fallen into decay, and in 1751 Pope Benedict XIV introduced reforms, in the course of which he ordered professors to resume in the schools and at lectures the traditional biretta and black gown,[7] or rather a chimere (*zimarra*), which was long and sleeveless.[8]

Collegio de San Pietro. In the eighteenth century the dress of students at this College of Theology consisted of a cassock and over it a blue sleeveless gown with a streamer hanging from each shoulder, the left-hand streamer being adorned with filigree

---

[1] Oxford, Ashmolean Museum (Hope Collection)—Print of J. B. Morgagni, dated 1719.

[2] Oxford, Ashmolean Museum (Hope Collection)—Print of J. Capivacci, 18th cent.

[3] A. Rosenberg and M. Tilke, *The Design and Development of Costume*, ii, pl. clvii, fig. 10.

[4] C. Meiners, art. cit., p. 247; J. P. Tomasini, op. cit., p. 212.

[5] Examiners (H. Rashdall, *Universities*, i. 226, n. 1, and 482, n. 1).

[6] F. M. Renazzi, *Storia dell' Università di Roma*, ii. 253.

[7] F. M. Renazzi, iv. 247-8.

[8] G. Moróni, *Dizionario dell' erudizione*, ciii, s.v. Zimarra, where this dress is mentioned as being the recognized dress of the professors at Rome. Cf. M. von Boehn, *Modes and Manners*, ii. 160, where the '*Venetian zimarra*' is described as a wide-open gown of black silk.

work, a tiara, two keys, and the bees from the arms of the Barberini family, all done in braid.[1]

IV. PISA (1342)

The University of Pisa after entirely perishing was set up again by Florence when the latter city conquered Pisa in 1472, after which time it became famous.[2] Records about dress are scanty, and we know nothing of it before the university's resuscitation.

In the statutes of Cosimo I Medici of 1543 and again in those of Juliannus Lupius of 1621–2 the rector's dress was mentioned as consisting of a brocaded silk robe interlaced with gold and a hood to match. The shape of the robe was the same as that of doctors, which appears to have been closed and with full hanging bell sleeves.[3] In the Lupius statutes of 1621–2 the vice-rector's dress was described as of the same shape as that of the rector, but it was plain and was made of fine cloth instead of silk. With it he was to wear a red silk hood.[4]

V. FLORENCE (1349)

In 1397, as was the case at Bologna and Padua, only plain black cloth was to be used for the outer dress of members of the university whether as doctors they wore the *cappa* or as bachelors and students the *gabanus* (cloak).[5] Even the rector was to have the same cloth for his dress, although he was to be distinguished by having a special head-dress, a *pileus* lined in winter with miniver or squirrel and in summer with silk.[6]

If we are to believe that this is not the artist's exaggeration it would seem that the dress of professors in the fifteenth century became very rich indeed. Guarino da Verona (1374–1460), the great humanist and Professor of Greek at Florence,

---

[1] P. Bonanni, *Ordinum religiosorum in ecclesia militanti catalogus*, iii, no. li. The great Barberini family, of which Pope Urban VIII was a member, was in the seventeenth century the leading family in the papal domains. One of its members, Taddeo, founded this college and the Barberini Library.

[2] S. d'Irsay, i. 239–40 and 245.

[3] *Statuta almi Pisani studii* (*Annali delle Università toscane*, tom. 30), cap. xi, p. 12; A. Fabronius, *Historiae Academiae Pisanae*, ii. 8.

[4] *Statuta almi Pisani studii*, cap. xi, p. 13.

[5] A. Gherardi and C. Morelli, *Statuti della Università Fiorentina*, i. 97, ann. mccclxxxvii, rubrica cviii; C. Meiners, art. cit., pp. 234–5.

[6] A. Gherardi and C. Morelli, i. 15, ann. mccclxxxvii, rubric v; A. Corsini, *Il Costume del medico nelle pitture fiorentine del Rinascimento*, p. 6.

in the illumination in which he is depicted presenting his translation of Strabo to his patron Antonio Marcello, wears a full-sleeved scarlet *roba* and a light violet *chaperon* over both shoulders. He is bareheaded. The man standing behind him, no doubt an academical person, perhaps a Master of Arts, wears over a black *tunica* a silk plum-coloured *roba* with short sleeves hanging a little and doubled back, edged down the front with a narrow facing of red. His head-dress is a black *pileus* with a loose top, and slung over the shoulders is a red *chaperon*.[1]

VI. PAVIA (1361)

Originally a Law School, later of university status, Pavia had collapsed by 1421, in which year the Milanese, having conquered the city, rehabilitated its university.[2]

There is no information whatever about dress in the short statutes, but thanks to the *Memoirs* of Carlo Goldoni, the famous eighteenth-century dramatist, who was at one time a student at the *Collegio de Ghislieri*, one of the constituent parts of the university, we know what the costume was like there.

Clerical dress and the tonsure were required of all foundation scholars and exhibitioners, this being a papal college, whether the students were preparing to become priests or not, and in fact by this time few were. Their dress consisted of an abbé's court dress, i.e. a black cloth suit faced with black silk, and over it a short cape-gown with a flap-collar. On the left shoulder of the suit, not of the cape-gown, was worn a *chaperon* called at Pavia *sovrana*, of black velvet embroidered with the Ghislieri arms in gold and silver, surmounted by the pontifical tiara and the keys of St. Peter.[3]

VII. FERRARA (1389)

This university never flourished and was notorious for selling degrees. There are no records of it to be found which deal with its dress. There is, however, an interesting detached miniature belonging to a lost manuscript of the school of Ferrara painters which very likely shows the kind of dress worn by regent-

---

[1] P. Neveux and E. Dacier, *Les Richesses des Bibliothèques provinciales de France*, i, pl. vii, left (Albi MS. 77—*Strabo, de Situ orbis geographia* (fifteenth cent.)).

[2] N. Schachner, *Mediaeval Universities*, p. 286.

[3] C. Goldoni, *Memoirs*, pp. 30–33. The Ghislieri family had been patrons of the college. It was founded by Pope Pius V in 1569.

doctors of this university shortly after its foundation. Two Doctors of Medicine are talking together in a portico. One wears a crimson lake tight-sleeved *roba*, a red *chaperon*, and a rigid 'pill-box' *pileus* with a 'stalk' apex. The other wears a red *roba*, a violet *chaperon*, a black tabard over the *roba*, and a red Ulysses cap.[1]

The other medieval universities of Italy had only an ephemeral existence.[2]

II. SPAIN

1. SALAMANCA (1254)

In default of information about dress in the early days of Salamanca, for the statutes before the sixteenth century do not aid us in this way, we are dependent upon two stray illustrative sources.

Of these the most outstanding is the bust-portrait of a Doctor of Canon Law which appears in the first initial of an Orosius's *History*, a manuscript executed in Spain in 1442.[3] The doctor wears a crimson skull-cap which covers his ears except the lobes,[4] and a crimson lake *cappa clausa* with side slits lined with green. He has a blue 'shoulder piece' lined with ermine, and a flat blunt-ended blue hood which can be seen hanging down a little way behind. Under the *cappa* he wears a plum-coloured *tunica* (Pl. 2*b*).

In view of the fact that in 1442 Salamanca was by far the greatest of the few Spanish universities existing, and of what H. Rashdall[5] and N. F. Robinson[6] say about the colours of the Faculty of Canon Law at Salamanca at this date being red or crimson and green, there seems little doubt that a Doctor of Canon Law of this university is intended in this initial.

[1] M. Salmi, tav. lvii (*b*) (Turin, Biblioteca Nazionale MS. I. 1. 22–23, fo. 22).

[2] S. d'Irsay, i. 129, 242, and 243.

[3] Cambridge, Fitzw. Mus. Maclean MS. 180. For the colours of the Faculty of Canon Law here depicted see H. Rashdall, op. cit. iii. 389, n. 3.

[4] Such a cap had been worn by some doctors who attended the Council of Constance (1414–18) (*Concilium Constantiense*, pp. 48–49).

[5] Op. cit., loc. cit.

[6] Art. 'The *Pileus Quadratus*' in *Transactions of the St. Paul's Ecclesiological Society*, v, pt. 1 (1901), p. 9, n. 3.

PLATE 2

a. Doctor of Salamanca, 1497

b. Doctor of Canon Law of
Salamanca, 1442

c. Tail-piece showing Round Bonnet,
Biretta, and *Bonnet carré*, 1666

The 'shoulder piece' can be seen, together with other dress of the same character as that worn in the *Orosius* initial, in the recumbent statue in the cloister near the entrance to the chapel of Sta. Barbara in Salamanca Cathedral, of the canon treasurer Don García de Medina, Doctor of Canon Law, and a professor of the university (d. 1474).[1]

As for other dresses, before the sixteenth century we have no definite information, for although Constitution VII of the University of Salamanca forbids the admission to an Act of anyone not in the dress of a master, we are not told what this was.[2] Students as yet had no specified garb, but wore whatever they chose provided it was not too rich.[3]

By the earlier part of the sixteenth century, however, a certain amount of information begins to accumulate and enables us to form an idea of a full system of academical dress which had come into being.

First of all, on the panels painted by Gallegos preserved as part of a retable in the cloisters of the Old Cathedral of Sala-manca appear Saints Cosmas and Damian dressed as Doctors of Medicine, wearing black bell-sleeved gowns and skull-caps each with a small yellow tassel.[4] Yellow was the colour of the Faculty of Medicine at Salamanca,[5] and throughout the Middle Ages these two saints were often depicted in the dress of doctors of this faculty.

Then there are the statutes of 1538, which although they are silent about the dress of graduates, probably because the question of their costume was as yet left to ecclesiastical authority, contain much information about the dress of students. They had the choice of either a short pleated cassock (*loba sotana*) or a long cloak with a flap collar (*manteo*), but they were not to be worn together.[6] They were also to wear a particular academical cap (*bonete*) of the square type like a biretta as opposed to such a lay head-dress as the *gorra*. Only servitors (*Capigorristas*) were to wear the *gorra*. If they were in mourning, students might wear cloaks with hoods with long liripipes attached drawn over the head.[7] Students were as yet allowed

---

[1] V. de la Fuente, *Historia de las Universidades de Enseñanza en España*, i. 177.
[2] V. de la Fuente, i. 178.   [3] V. de la Fuente, i. 177.
[4] V. de la Fuente, i. 178.   [5] N. F. Robinson, loc. cit.
[6] A. Vidal y Diaz, *Memoria Histórica de la Universidad de Salamanca*, p. 94 (Stats. of 1538, Tit. LXII).   [7] A. Vidal y Diaz, loc. cit.

only short cassocks in order to distinguish them from the clergy,[1] but in 1587 at the request of the university Philip II revoked this clause and allowed all students to wear the full cassock,[2] as they do in the woodcut frontispiece to the *Estatutos hechos por lo muy ensigne Universidad de Salamanca* (1625).

By the end of the sixteenth century the dress of all students except *Capigorristas*, who wore a black cloth cassock, a small cape, and a round cap (*gorra*), had become more elaborate.[3] This elaboration was due to the necessity of distinguishing between the members of the many colleges which had recently arisen. All except *Capigorristas* wore a long brown cassock and a long brown cloak (*manteo*), but members of the College of Santa María de Burgos wore a yellow cloak instead of the brown one.[4] The distinguishing mark of the various colleges was the *beca* which was of a different colour for each. The *beca* was a strip of cloth 11 ft. 3 in. long. It was worn doubled over the chest, passed over the shoulders and fell behind in two strands which reached the heels. Students received their *beca* at the ceremony of their matriculation. It was brown for the College of San Bartolomé, blue for that of Oviedo, violet for that of Cuenca, and violet also for the College of Santa María de Burgos, but in that case it was worn with the yellow cloak.[5] The use of the *beca* was not confined to Salamanca. A blue *beca* of cloth was worn at Seville.[6]

In 1643 students were ordered to wear their caps (*bonetes*) on all occasions, not only in the schools, but outside them also.[7] Doctors at this time wore the same whether secular priests or laymen except that the clerics wore an upright, rigid variety of the *bonete*, but the laymen wore an ordinary bonnet or hat in accordance with contemporary fashion. All doctors wore a tuft of the colour of their faculty on their head-gear of whatever

---

[1] A. Vidal y Diaz, p. 96.   [2] A. Vidal y Diaz, p. 111.
[3] G. Reynier, *La Vie universitaire dans l'ancienne Espagne*, pp. 41–42.
[4] G. Reynier, p. 19.   [5] G. Reynier, pp. 17, 18, and 19.
[6] In his correspondence Joseph Blanco White, writing in 1796, describes the *beca* in full. 'This slip of cloth,' he writes, 'is about 1 ft. in breadth, and between 8 and 9 ft. in length. Folding it in the middle, so as to form an angle, and holding the fold on the breast, the two halves are thrown over the shoulder so as to fall on the back nearly reaching the heels.' At Seville a white kid glove was worn in the fold of the *beca*. The *beca* was held in position by a circular rim of wood (*The Life of the Rev. Joseph Blanco White written by himself*, i. 61).
[7] V. de la Fuente, iii. 93.

variety it might be.[1] An excellent example of the dress of a clerical regent appears in the woodcut frontispiece of 1625 mentioned above. The lecturer wears a hard horned biretta and has a cloak over his cassock.

The faculty colours on the tuft of the caps of doctors of Salamanca were for Theology, white; for Canon Law, red; for Civil Law, green; and for Medicine, yellow.[2] In 1592 this tuft reached its greatest size at Salamanca and also at Coimbra, for the birettas of Doctors of Theology were in that year covered by an enormous bush of white silk fleece which issued from the apex.[3] This was called the *floccus*, and appears to have been worn at Salamanca as early as 1497 if we are to judge from a woodcut executed in the city in that year. A doctor seated at a table writing wears a tall *pileus* with a button-apex, and from this rise many long pieces of material to form a bush[4] (Pl. 2a).

II. LÉRIDA (1300)

The University of Lérida had a short life.[5] The only reference to dress is to be seen in the statutes formulated at the time of its foundation, and is simply a collection of sumptuary rules to be observed by students.[6]

III. VALLADOLID (1346)

Valladolid, although important during the Spanish Renaissance of the sixteenth century, soon afterwards fell away and was refounded in 1773.

In the statutes of 1505 students were ordered to wear the short, pleated cassock (*loba sotana*) or the flap-collared cloak (*manteo*) and a 'Castilian cap'. No other dress was allowed. Servitors, however, might by special permission of the rector wear pointed caps (*caperuza*), which appear to have been in shape like fishermen's stocking-caps.[7]

By 1547 the colours of the faculties as used on the tassels of

---

[1] V. de la Fuente, iii. 237.   [2] N. F. Robinson, loc. cit.
[3] A. Scappus, p. 64.
[4] J. P. R. Lyell, *Early Book Illustration in Spain*, p. 71, fig. 55 (Livy, *Las Decadas*, Salamanca (Segundo grupo gótico), 1497).
[5] S. d'Irsay, i. 174.
[6] J. Villanueva, *Viage Literario a las Iglesias de España*, t. xvi, p. 230.
[7] *Estatutos de la Universidad de Valladolid* (1651), § 30, p. 91; *Historia de la Universidad de Valladolid*, i, pp. xcvii and xcviii (Stats. 1505, § 30).

the head-dress of doctors and masters were as follows: for Theology, white; for Canon Law, green; for Civil Law, red; for Medicine, yellow; and for Arts, blue.[1]

The Colegio de Santa Cruz was closely connected with the university. From the fifteenth century onwards collegians wore a dark red *beca*, a drab-coloured cloak fastened at the neck with buttons, and a black cap.[2]

IV. HUESCA (1354)

The early history of the University of Huesca is obscure, and such records as remain before the sixteenth century contain no mention of dress. During this century and later, in spite of the fact that it had declined so much that it had become no more than an academy with a local reputation, there is much information about dress.

In 1569 the *pileus flosculus*, a round cap with a broad, vertically ridged edging of wool, is described as the doctoral head-dress.[3] This head-gear, which later spread to other Spanish universities except Salamanca, was originally an Italian lay fashion of the fourteenth century as can be seen from an example in a Bolognese manuscript of Petrarch's *Canzone*, in which in a miniature an old man wears such a cap.[4]

Until the end of the seventeenth century all students, whether in orders or not, seem to have worn the clerical collar (i.e. a small white turn-down collar with a division in the middle) and a cassock or buttoned cloak (*loba cerrada*), but about this time the authorities of Huesca ordered lay students to wear, as they had done earlier, a circular ruff and a long cloak (*manteo*) with a flap-collar and with an opening down the front but held closed by a belt, while only those students who held ecclesiastical office or benefice were to wear the clerical collar

---

[1] V. Velázquez de Figueroa, *Anales universitarios,* i. 150.

[2] *Constitutiones et statuta collegii majoris Sanctae Crucis oppidi Vallisoletani,* p. 8A, Const. xxx.

[3] R. del Arco, *Memorial de la Universidad de Huesca,* ii. 309.

[4] Cambridge, Fitzw. Museum, Maclean MS. 173 (Petrarch, *Canzone*), fo. 51. It was also worn in Germany in the seventeenth century (F. Hottenroth, *Handbuch der Deutschen Tracht,* p. 763, fig. 218, No. 6). A cap with sloping sides and decorated with large tufts is worn by Canon Bonaventura who is depicted as a doctor in the seventeenth-century oil-painting by J. de Valdés Leal of Seville (1622-91) formerly in the Cook Collection, Richmond. I cannot find any other example of such Spanish doctoral head-dress.

and the cassock. These last might wear the cassock open or closed as they wished, but were forbidden to have loose tails hanging behind from the cincture.[1]

Clerical doctors wore in the seventeenth century a *bonete* (a biretta of Italian style), while secular doctors wore a wide-brimmed hat, which from the sixteenth century onwards was worn indiscriminately by clerics and laymen, professors and students. The tassel of the appropriate faculty colour was worn on both kinds of head-dress.[2]

In the early eighteenth century it was enacted by royal decree that the brims of these hats should be turned up at the edge, and this was half-heartedly enforced among the students of Huesca, Alcalá, Valladolid, Toledo, and Salamanca. It was not long, however, before these hats were superseded at Huesca and elsewhere by a new fashion, the Schomberg hat, which had a downcurving brim.[3] The authorities of Huesca seem to have taken a particular dislike to it, and in 1770 at a Convocation of the university it was forbidden, and surprisingly enough it was ordered that a three-cornered lay hat should be worn by all members of the university except clergy. The clerical members were to wear hats covered with black gummed taffeta, with the brim rising on both sides.[4] Such a hat can be seen in Goya's oil-painting 'The Bewitched' in the Spanish Room in the National Gallery, London.

At the *Colegio de Santiago*, Huesca, which was incorporated in the university in the sixteenth century, the same dress was worn as at the Colegio de Santa Cruz, Valladolid, with the addition of the cross of St. James worked on the breast of their cloaks. The cross of the rector was larger than that of others. The Inquisitor of Aragon in 1561 ordered that these crosses should be removed.[5]

v. BARCELONA (1430)

The only collection of statutes of the University of Barcelona, that made in 1629 by P. Lacavalleria and entitled *Constituciones de la Universitate de Barcelona*, contains no mention of dress.

---

[1] R. del Arco, i. 21.   [2] R. del Arco, i. 22.
[3] It is to this form of hat that Joseph Baretti refers when describing his amusing encounter with the students of Cervera in 1760. He mentions at the same time their 'ample black cloak' (J. Baretti, *A Journey from London to Genoa*, iv. 52–53. Letter LXXII, 26 Oct. 1760).   [4] R. del Arco, i. 41–43.   [5] R. del Arco, i. 22–23.

VI. ALCALÁ (1499)

According to the reformed statutes of 1665, the first systematic collection of Alcalá's statutes, the academical dress for all members of the university was fixed as a cloth gown (*ropa de paño*), also known as a *balandran*.[1] In 1716 gifts of biretta and gloves during the doctoral ceremony are mentioned.[2] There is in the Old Cathedral at Madrid a picture of about 1640 in which the Rector of Alcalá bestows a *pileus quadratus* upon a new doctor. Doctors seated beside the Rector wear silk 'shoulder pieces' coloured according to their faculty.

VII. MALLORCA (1698)

Although for long a college, Mallorca did not become a university until the seventeenth century. In its statutes for 1698 the dress of all, both doctors and collegians, was ordered to consist of gown and hood (*borla*).[3]

III. PORTUGAL

The University of Coimbra, founded in 1288, was moved backwards and forwards between that place and Lisbon, until in 1537 Coimbra became its permanent home.[4] It remained the only Portuguese university until the twentieth century.

Although it is said[5] that the doctoral *pileus* (*barrete*, *biretta*) and ceremonial dress is as old as the university it is not until the fourteenth century that we have any definite information about the academical costume worn here.

In 1321 graduates were ordered to wear *tunicas* reaching to the heels, and undergraduates to wear them reaching to the middle of the thigh.[6] This is repeated in the statutes of 1431, and is then particularly directed at the Faculty of Theology.[7]

In the statutes of Don Manuel (1504) the dress of bachelors is considered to be a gown (*pello*), a development of the *super-tunica*, a hood (*borla*), and a round cap (*cabeça*).[8] This *cabeça* was lower and softer than the doctoral *barrete*. At the time of

---

[1] *Reformacion en la Universidad de Alcalá de Henares*, p. 13, Tit. VIII, § 4.

[2] *Constitutiones Collegii Ildephonsi ac per inde totius almae Complutensis academia*, pp. 67, § xlii and 76, § xlviii.

[3] *Constituciones, Estatutos, Privilegios de la Universidad Luliana de Mallorca*, pp. 114–15.   [4] S. d'Irsay, i. 140.

[5] T. Braga, *Historia da Universidade de Coimbra*, i. 66.   [6] H. Rashdall, ii. 113.

[7] M. E. da Motta Veiga, *Esboço Historico-Litterario da Faculdade de Theologia da Universidade de Coimbra*, p. 41.   [8] T. Braga, i. 299.

taking their degree bachelors were to make presents of a *barrete* and gloves (*luvas*) to the 'Father' (*padrinho*; praelector) who presented them, and to the rector.[1] In the same statutes the doctoral ceremony is mentioned as a well established tradition. Doctors are to wear on this occasion, and at other times when festal dress is required, a trailing cloth robe (*hũa roupa roçagante*) with a little cape (*capello*; 'shoulder piece') over it, a hood (*borla*), a biretta (*barrete*), and a ring (*anel*).[2]

In later times the everyday dress for graduates and under-graduates alike was a long plain sleeveless cloak decorated at the back with bands of stuff of the same material and colour as the main cloak. On the sides at the front ran from neck to foot two rows of buttons descending vertically and set on very thickly. The distinction between graduate and undergraduate lay in the fact that only graduates had a head-dress. This was a square black cap, whose upper part was stuffed in such a way as to form two small domes. Between these domes was a tassel.[3]

From the later sixteenth century onwards the full dress of doctors was a black silk gown with close sleeves, with for Theology a white hood and white tassel on the cap and a ring with a white stone; for Canon Law a green hood and tassel and a ring with a green stone; for Civil Law a red-crimson hood and tassel and a ring with a stone of the same colour; for Medicine, yellow hood, tassel and stone; and for Philosophy, dark blue hood, tassel and stone.[4]

In the Marqués de Pombal's statutes of 1772 Doctors of Canon Law were ordered to continue to use green and Doctors of Civil Law red.[5] Pombal in this year created a new faculty, that of Mathematics, the dress of doctors of which subject was to be a black cap with a light blue tassel, a light blue hood with white loops, and a black silk gown with an armillary sphere embroidered in white on the left breast of the gown. Doctors of other faculties who were also Doctors of Mathematics might wear the device of the armillary sphere in white embroidery on their respective gowns.[6]

[1] T. Braga, loc. cit.   [2] T. Braga, i. 301–2.
[3] W. Bradford, *Sketches . . . in Portugal*, ill.—'Bishop of Guarda'; W. M. Kinsey, *Portugal*, p. 397.
[4] D. J. Cunningham, *The Evolution of the Graduation Ceremony*, p. 46; A. Steger, *Dissertatio de purpura*, p. 31.   [5] *Estatutos da Universidade de Coimbra*, ii. 629.
[6] *Estatutos da Universidade de Coimbra*, iii. 147.

Later elaborations were made in the dress of doctors. Not only the tassel but the whole cap came to be of the colour of the faculty to which the doctor belonged, and doctors of two faculties wore rings with stones of the two colours. The velvet of which the hood was made was of the colour of the superior faculty, and the loops of the hood which lay above the velvet was of that colour also, but the satin lining of the hood and the lower loops were of the colour of the inferior faculty. Further, the cap of a doctor of two faculties had the two faculty colours alternating on it.

The Faculty of Theology was the exception, for if the Doctor of Theology were a doctor of another faculty also, the ring and hood were of the colour of that other faculty, but the cap was plain white. With these insignia a black silk gown with close sleeves was always worn.[1]

IV. MALTA

THE ROYAL UNIVERSITY (1769)

In the original statutes (1769) of the Royal University of Malta various costumes were prescribed. The rector, who was an ecclesiastic, was to wear a rochet and a short purple gown with an eight-pointed Maltese cross of white stuff embroidered on it. To this gown a small hood was seemingly attached. Professors, if ecclesiastics, wore from the same period a surplice and biretta at all solemn academical functions, while lay professors wore a black academical gown, but the shape is not specified.[2] No official distinction in academical costume for the various degrees appears to have been laid down in the nineteenth-century statutes, but there is preserved in the university archives a manuscript of the 1830's to the effect that at that time Masters of Arts wore a woollen gown, bachelors of higher faculties a woollen gown with a silk stole, doctors a silk gown with a biretta,

---

[1] D. J. Cunningham, p. 46.
[2] *Costituzioni per i nuovi Studi dell'Università e per il Collegio de Educazione di Malta*— Malta. Valletta, Royal University Libr. MS. 1343, Tit. XVIII, § x; Tit. XXII, § iv; Tit. XXIII, § v.

and doctors of seven years' standing a black silk gown with
black velvet sleeves 'like that of Councillors'. Graduates who
were ecclesiastics were allowed to wear their religious habit if
they preferred.[1] These costumes may well have been worn in
the latter part of the eighteenth century.

[1] Correspondence with the University of Malta, 12/9/55, Reg. No. 389/54.

2

FRANCE

I. PARIS (twelfth century)

The Thirteenth Century

THE earliest mention of academical dress at Paris is that to be found in the order of Pope Innocent III in 1215. This papal order and others of a disciplinary character were carried out by Cardinal Robert de Courçon in that year.[1] According to this Regent Masters of Theology and Regent Masters of Arts are both to wear a *cappa rotunda*, black and ankle-length, while as a less formal garment they are allowed the *pallium*, that is, a loose *supertunica*.[2] The less formal dress is worn by Pierre de Carville, Maître-ès-Arts (d. 1307) in the full-length figure of him, taken from a missing statue, to be found among the Gaignières drawings in the *Bibliothèque nationale*. Over a *tunica* he wears a shorter *supertunica* or *pallium* which has short sleeves. A hood rests on his shoulders.[3]

The next reference we have to academical dress appears in the statutes for the English nation (1251/2). Determining Bachelors of Arts were to wear the cloth *cappa* with an absolutely plain hood of the same material. A hood was always to be worn with the *cappa*, but it was not to be worn on the head, for it is expressly stated that they must go bareheaded. As admitted bachelors, however, they were to lecture in a *pallium* with a *cappa rotunda* over it, in other words the same full dress as masters except that they had no head-dress. The masters

---

[1] C. Meiners, art. 'Kurze Geschichte der Trachten' in *Göttingische akademische Annalen*, i (1804), 206.

[2] H. Denifle and E. Chatelain, *Chartularium Universitatis Parisiensis*, i, no. 20, p. 79; C. E. Du Boulay, *Historia Universitatis Parisiensis*, ii. 672 and iii. 82; J. B. L. Crévier, *Histoire de l'Université de Paris*, i. 300–1 and ii. 423.

[3] Paris, Bibl. Nat. Dépt. des Estampes Oa 10, J. Gaignières, *Recueil des portraits* fo. 83.

wore a *mitra* (skull-cap) which served to distinguish them from others.[1] The same dress for admitted Bachelors of Arts is again mentioned in 1280 and in 1341.[2]

Although as early as this there does not seem to have been any definite dress for undergraduates,[3] certain colleges ordered a special uniform dress for all their members, such as appears in the foundation statutes of the Sorbonne College (1274). All members of this college were to wear an entirely plain closed *supertunica*.[4] Such a dress with a hood falling back on the shoulders appears on a thirteenth-century Paris seal,[5] now lost.

As to head-dress, by 1272 the *pileus* was worn by Masters of Medicine,[6] and by incepting Bachelors of Medicine.[7]

The Fourteenth Century

In 1336 (not 1334 as is usually given) Pope Benedict XII, who as Jacques Fournier had been educated at Paris, allowed all regents in the Faculty of Canon Law to wear red 'shoulder pieces'.[8] In 1377 we find further mention of the red *cappa* (i.e. 'shoulder piece') furred with miniver worn by Doctors of Canon Law,[9] and again in 1386[10] and in 1388.[11] During this period the head-dress of Doctors of Canon Law had become a doubled scarlet *pileus*, called *birettum* to distinguish it from the lower *pileus*.[12]

The colour red seems soon after the enactment of the pope in 1336 to have spread to other parts of the dress of Doctors of Canon Law, for in an illumination in a manuscript of the *Psalterium cum Canticis* of about 1340[13] are to be seen at the

---

[1] H. Denifle and E. Chatelain, i, no. 201, p. 228, and i, no. 202, p. 230.

[2] H. Denifle and E. Chatelain, i, no. 501, p. 586; C. E. Du Boulay, iv. 273.

[3] V. de Viriville, *Histoire de l'Instruction publique*, p. 176.

[4] H. Denifle and E. Chatelain, i, no. 448, p. 506.

[5] V. de Viriville, p. 129.   [6] C. E. Du Boulay, iii. 402.

[7] H. Denifle and E. Chatelain, i, no. 444, p. 502.

[8] In the chartularies they are termed *cappa*, but with the meaning which the word sometimes has in early times of 'cape', H. Denifle and E. Chatelain, op. cit. ii, no. 1002, pp. 464–5; G. Péries, *La Faculté de droit dans l'ancienne Université de Paris* pp. 47 and 248; E. Dubarle, *Histoire de l'Université de Paris*, i. 143; J. B. L. Crévier, ii. 325.   [9] H. Denifle and E. Chatelain, iii, no. 1414, p. 233.

[10] H. Denifle and E. Chatelain, iii, no. 1531, p. 434.

[11] H. Denifle and E. Chatelain, iii, no. 1546, p. 473.

[12] H. Denifle and E. Chatelain, iii, no. 1708, §§ 20 and 24, p. 653.

[13] Cambridge, Sidney Sussex Coll. Libr. MS. James 76, fo. 56 (see Ps. lii (liii), Dixit insipiens').

bottom of the border six figures of seated doctors on benches
reading books, the third, fourth, and fifth wearing blue or pink
robes over red *supertunicas*, the group, if we may trust the artist,
consisting probably of Doctors of Canon Law and of Civil Law,
those in the pink robes being perhaps those of Both Laws.

Regents in the Faculty of Medicine were in 1350 instructed
to wear a *cappa rotunda* of good cloth of a violet-brown colour.[1]
According to an illuminated manuscript, a Life of Raymond
Lull, their head-dress about 1320 was a white coif, with a
chin-strap.[2]

The dress of regents in the Faculty of Theology would appear
to have been simpler if we are to form any judgement of it from
the figure of Aristotle dressed as such a regent in a miniature
in a manuscript of the year 1372; for he wears a skull-cap with
an 'apex', a plain *supertunica*, and a furred hood hanging down
the back with two fur 'labels' on the chest[3] (Pl. 3).

It was during this century that the dress of Masters of Arts
of Paris was regulated. In 1339 the Masters of the Four Nations
of France met together and decided that for the future masters
who took part in academical acts and ceremonies should wear
a *cappa* and a furred 'shoulder piece' (*épitoge*) and *not* merely
a tabard.[4] This regulation was repeated in 1363.[5] The dis-
placed stone effigy of Jean Perdrier (d. 1376), who was a Master
of Arts, shows him wearing over a *subtunica* a closed *supertunica*,
moderately full, with small 'bell' sleeves reaching only just
below the elbows. He has a close hood falling on the upper part
of the shoulders, but no 'shoulder piece'.[6]

In the statutes of the Navarre College (1315) Bachelors of
Arts were ordered to wear, before they had 'determined',
tabards of a brown-black colour, but when they had 'determined', a blue *cappa rotunda*.[7] This dress for full bachelors is
more clearly mentioned in 1341 when their costume is de-

---

[1] A. Franklin, *La Vie privée d'autrefois*, xi. 42.

[2] Karlsruhe, Badische Landesbibliothek, Cod. St. Peter MS. 92, fo. 11ᵛ.

[3] C. Gaspar and F. Lyna, *Bibliothèque Royale de Belgique—Principaux Manuscrits à Peintures*, i, pl. lxxviii, text pp. 354 ff. (Aristote, Éthiques, trad. de Nicole Oresme), MS. 9505–9, fo. 2ᵛ (3rd compartment).

[4] M. Félibien and G. A. Lobineau, *Histoire de la ville de Paris*, tom. i, pp. 593–4.

[5] J. B. L. Crévier, ii. 423.

[6] B. de Montfaucon, *Les Monumens de la Monarchie françoise*, iii, pl. xvii, p. 68, fig. 5; J. Malliot and P. Martin, *Recherches sur les costumes*, iii, pl. l.

[7] J. Launoy, *Regii Navarraei Gymnasii Parisiensis Historia*, i. 32.

PLATE 3

Regent Master of Theology of Paris lecturing, 1372

scribed as a *pallium* (loose *supertunica*) or *cappa rotunda* of brown-black, blue (*parsicus*) black, or full black cloth. The hood was long and full, and furred with miniver or similar fur.[1]

The first reference to the dress of students appears during this century. In 1346 students of Ave Maria College were ordered to wear the *subtunica* for ordinary occasions and for feasts a *supertunica* as well.[2]

The Fifteenth Century

By the beginning of this century if not before the dress of the rector consisted of a scarlet closed pleated and girded *supertunica* with a close hood and a 'shoulder piece' of the same colour.[3] The proctors had the same dress,[4] but it was purple.[5] The dress of the proctor of the Picardy nation about 1477 consisted of a tall rigid hat of the *mortier* type, a close miniver hood falling on the neck, a cassock, and over this a closed gown with large bell-shaped sleeves, the gown being shorter than the cassock.[6]

It was during this century that the *chaperon* or *chausse* (also called in the particular square form used by men of law, *cornette*),[7] abandoned as a lay fashion, became associated in certain instances with the dress of the universities and men of law.[8] In Paris by 1498 it had become an indispensable part of the dress of regents,[9] and of all Licentiates of Law.[10] Other lay influences which affected the academical dress of the time were the head-dress and the use of fur and embroidery on garments. The *mortier*, originally associated with the head-dress of kings, princes, and knights, by 1449 began to be worn by persons of academical dignity, while the fashion for large hats and bonnets which appeared as a general fashion about the same time also came to have a profound effect on academical head-gear.[11] The

[1] C. E. Du Boulay, iv. 274.
[2] A. L. Gabriel, *Student Life in Ave Maria College*, pp. 227 and 357–8.
[3] C. E. Du Boulay, *Remarques sur la dignité. . . . du recteur de l'Université de Paris*, p. 24; V. de Viriville, p. 177, ill.
[4] V. de Viriville, p. 179; C. E. Du Boulay, *Remarques*, pp. 24–26.
[5] H. Rashdall, *Universities*, iii. 389, n. 3.
[6] V. de Viriville, p. 126.
[7] J. B. Thiers, *Histoire des Perruques*, p. 89.
[8] A. de Caumont, *Cours d'antiquités monumentales*, vi, pt. 6, pp. 382–3, n.
[9] G. Péries, p. 48.   [10] C. Loyseau, *Traité des ordres*, p. 6.
[11] D. Diderot and J. le R. D'Alembert, *Encyclopédie*, ii. 324 a–b, s.v. Bonnet.

use of three rows of fur on the *chaperon* of doctors was, like the *mortier*, originally a sign of royalty.[1]

Masters of Theology were in 1452, according to the reforms of Cardinal d'Estouteville, ordered to wear an unspecified ankle-length, closed dress without a girdle, and were to have a short 'shoulder piece' with a hood.[2] In 1436 they had been allowed the *birettum*.[3] They wore a round violet *pileus* in 1478;[4] and this last form of head-dress is again mentioned in 1485.[5] The colour of the robe, which was perhaps a *cappa manicata*,[6] was sombre, such colours as grey, dull blue, dark green, and emerald-black being much used at this time.[7]

Doctors of Canon Law were also ordered in 1452 to wear a sombre dress, a *cappa* and a 'shoulder piece',[8] but whether or not this means that they had to give up their scarlet, they certainly wore it not long afterwards, and at the time of the second marriage of Francis I in the following century they wore their *chapes rouges* as a matter of course.[9]

A Doctor of Both Laws, who appears in an illumination in a late fifteenth-century French *Book of Hours*, wears a grey *mortier*, a closed pink gown with full hanging sleeves, and a large white 'bib' or 'label' without a division in it.[10] By 1491 doctors of this degree were wearing a red *birettum*.[11]

A doctor of the Faculty of Medicine of the early fifteenth century, in a miniature in a French translation by Jean Corbechon of *De Proprietatibus Rerum*, wears a violet skull-cap, a violet *supertunica*, and over this a scarlet *cappa manicata* lined with miniver. In addition he wears a 'shoulder piece' with a small hood attached, both lined with miniver[12] (Pl. 4a). In the middle

---

[1] B. de Montfaucon, iii, pl. lvii, figs. 4 and 8, p. 276 (portraits of Charles, duc de Bourbon, and Louis III, King of Sicily); and cf. J. Quicherat, *Histoire du costume en France*, p. 324.   [2] C. E. Du Boulay, *Histoire*, v. 564.
[3] H. Denifle and E. Chatelain, iv, no. 2489, p. 591.
[4] J. Launoy, i. 195.   [5] J. B. L. Crévier, iv. 419.
[6] Cf. R. Goulet, *Compendium on the Magnificence of the University of Paris*, pp. 38 and 78.
[7] J. Quicherat, p. 323.   [8] C. E. Du Boulay, *Histoire*, v. 567.
[9] G. Péries, p. 48.
[10] B.M. MS. Add. 25695, fo. 165.   [11] J. Launoy, i. 199.
[12] Cambridge, Fitzwilliam Museum, MS. 251 (Bartholomaeus Anglicus, *De Proprietatibus Rerum*), miniature No. 9, fo. 106, lib. vii. Another example of this dress with the addition of a 'bib', the same as that worn by the Doctor of Both Laws mentioned above, is given in R. Bruck, *Die Malereien in den Handschriften des Königreichs Sachsen*, pl. no. 113, p. 299 (Galen, at Dresden).

of the century, according to the contemporary treatise, *The Commendation of the Clerk*, the red *cappa* was the particular mark of the medical man,[1] but by the latter part of the century the faculty colour for medicine appears to have been regarded as green if we are to judge from another illumination in the *Book of Hours* referred to above.[2]

In the Estouteville statutes (1452) Bachelors of Theology and Bachelors of Canon Law were apparently expected to use the same modest dress as Doctors of Canon Law.[3]

Masters of Arts were at the same time forbidden to use short garments and lay 'bourrelet' caps.[4] At this time they wore a black *cappa rotunda* of the best material, lined with fur.[5] Their proper head-dress was before about 1460 a tall rigid *pileus* 'after the fashion of a Turkish fez',[6] but by the end of the century they had exchanged this for a round bonnet (*birettum*), and were distinguished by having a *chaperon* on the left shoulder.[7] In 1447 the particular insignia of all regent masters were the *birettum* and gloves.[8]

Bachelors of Arts remained with the same dress they had had in the previous century, and no definite dress seems to have been prescribed for students as such, nor was it for a long time to come. We learn only that students of the law faculty of noble birth had no right to any particular dress differing from that of other students.[9] If they needed fur for warmth students were permitted the use of otter-fur.[10]

The Sixteenth Century

It was about the middle of the sixteenth century that the rector gave up his scarlet dress, for in the reign of Henri III

[1] L. Thorndike, *University Records in the Middle Ages*, p. 214.

[2] B.M. MS. Add. 25695, fo. 15ᵛ. There is a good German example which is worth comparing with this. It appears in an illumination in a fifteenth-century manuscript of the first part of Ludolphus of Saxony's *Vita Christi*. In it is a Doctor of Medicine wearing a green robe, a miniver 'shoulder piece', and a red *mortier*. B.M. MS. Add. 25885, fo. 72.

[3] C. E. Du Boulay, *Histoire*, v. 567.

[4] C. E. Du Boulay, *Histoire*, v. 576.

[5] L. Thorndike, p. 213.   [6] J. Quicherat, p. 322.

[7] A. de Caumont, vi, pt. 6, pp. 382–3; J. B. Thiers, op. cit., p. 88.

[8] C. E. Du Boulay, *Histoire*, v. 542.

[9] G. Péries, pp. 23–24; cf. for the different dresses allowed them at Montpellier, M. Fournier, *Universités françaises: Les statuts et privilèges*, ii. 50 and 156.

[10] G. Péries, p. 48.

(1575–89) he wore a soft violet bonnet, a white ruff, a pleated tight violet *supertunica* worn closed, and a full 'shoulder piece' of white fur on a violet foundation. Some of the white fur lining of a hood fell in front. With this dress was worn a gold belt and a gold purse hanging down from it on the right side.[1]

Proctors then wore scarlet robes and had their miniver 'shoulder piece' until the latter part of the sixteenth century when the 'shoulder piece' was given up and a fur flap collar was substituted for it.[2]

Masters of Theology were in 1517 described as wearing if seculars a full grey-brown *cappa*, if regulars the habit of their Order.[3] Their head-dress was a bell-shaped black silk *pileus*.[4] In 1587 on the reform of the Faculty of Theology the *cappa* was again insisted on and cloaks were particularly condemned.[5]

In the miniature of Christ with the Doctors in an illuminated manuscript, 'Le Chappelet de Jhesus et de la Vierge Marie', of early in this century, the second of the three doctors appears dressed as a Doctor of Both Laws.[6] He wears a scarlet robe, closed, with tight sleeves. If we notice the opening in the breast of the robe we shall realize that this is the same type of *supertunica* such as may be seen in the later dress of English judges. The head-dress of this doctor is a blue-grey Ulysses cap, this part of his dress representing the Canon Law half of his double degree.

By 1540 the dress of this degree had changed in that the tight sleeves had become 'bell' sleeves, while the head-dress varied between a low *pileus* and a *mortier*. This is to be seen in a cartoon satirizing the court of King Francis I.[7] However, in the stone effigy of Pierre Rabuf (Professor of Law, 1487–1557) at the Collège d'Autun, Paris, his hands pass through the slit on the breast of what is the *cappa clausa* in its original character, and the dress is decorated with miniver.[8]

[1] G. Ferrario, *Le Costume*, v, pt. 2 (Europe), pl. 42; C. E. Du Boulay, *Dignité*, pp. 24–25.
[2] C. E. Du Boulay, *Dignité*, p. 25.
[3] R. Goulet, p. 38.
[4] E. E. Viollet-le-Duc, *Dictionnaire Raisonné du Mobilier français*, iv. 280–2 and fig. 41.
[5] C. E. Du Boulay, *Histoire*, vi. 791–2 and 794–5.
[6] B.M. MS. Add. 25693, fo. 15.
[7] B. de Montfaucon, iv, pl. xxxv, pp. 319–20.
[8] G. Péries, p. 168.

A Doctor of Medicine, in an illumination in 'Le Chappelet' referred to above, wears a light green, tight-sleeved robe with an opening in the breast, a pale orange 'shoulder piece', and a mid-blue 'turban' bonnet.[1] By the latter part of the century there had been a revolution in fashion, and such doctors wore a black *bonnet carré*, a white ruff, a red 'shoulder piece' trimmed with miniver with a 'roller' hood close round the neck, a scarlet sleeveless *pallium* or *tabard* edged at the bottom with miniver and reaching only to the knee, and under this a closed black *tunica*, with glove sleeves.[2]

In 1517 at the *Signita*, that is the ceremony taking place the day before the granting of the degree, the *Paranymphus* or legate of the chancellor, who was the chief state officer responsible for the granting of degrees, appeared in a scarlet *cappa* and a velvet cap.[3]

Bachelors of Theology wore *cappas* in 1517,[4] and this dress was still enforced in 1587.[5] Bachelors of the other faculties wore the same, and later in the century a black *chaperon* (*chausse*) is mentioned as being worn by them on formal occasions.[6] Bachelors of Theology at public disputations were ordered in 1561 to wear *calottes* (skull-caps).[7]

Masters of Arts wore about 1520 a round bonnet, a closed gown with a 'shoulder piece', a hood close round the neck, and a *chaperon* like a sash running over the right shoulder and under the left arm.[8] By 1593 their hood, which was attached to the 'shoulder piece', had become much enlarged, and they still wore the round bonnet,[9] which E. Pasquier writing in 1596 says were the special features of a master's dress,[10] but in 1598 they were told to wear the square cap (*pileus quadratus; bonnet carré*) instead of the round one.[11]

---

[1] B.M. MS. Add. 25693, fo. 15.

[2] C. Piton, *Costume civil en France*, p. 150 (bottom right a drawing of 1581 by the antiquary Gaignières); G. Ferrario, v, pt. 2 (Europe), pl. 42, no. 8; E. D. Glasson, art. 'Les Origines du costume de la magistrature', in *Nouvelle Revue historique de droit français et étranger* (1884), pp. 117–18.

[3] R. Goulet, p. 89.   [4] R. Goulet, p. 78.

[5] C. E. Du Boulay, *Histoire*, vi. 791–2 and 794–5.

[6] C. Jourdain, *Histoire de l'Université de Paris*, i. 43.

[7] J. B. Thiers, p. 121.

[8] V. de Viriville, p. 136.   [9] E. Dubarle, ii, 144.

[10] D. Diderot and J. le R. D'Alembert, iii. 178a.

[11] N. F. Robinson, art. 'The *Pileus Quadratus*' in *Transactions of St. Paul's Ecclesiological Society* (1901), v, pt. 1, p. 9.

In 1600 all regents were ordered to wear the square but not rigid bonnet, the *bonnet carré*.[1] As early as 1554 they had been collectively ordered to wear a full sleeved robe and 'shoulder piece',[2] but seem usually to have preferred the dress of their particular degree, and the enactment became a dead letter.

By this time we have reached the stage when besides the *mortier*, latterly confined to the legal profession, three types of head-dress had developed. There was the round bonnet, the square but not rigid bonnet (*bonnet carré*), and the stiff biretta, worn only by ecclesiastics (Pl. 2 c), a dress which arose in the later sixteenth century before which time they had worn the round bonnet.[3] The *bonnet carré* became rigid in the early years of the seventeenth century.[4] The ecclesiastical biretta was in the course of the seventeenth century given ridges, such as the academical *bonnet carré* never had.[5]

The Seventeenth and Eighteenth Centuries

The rector. There is a fine water-colour made by the German traveller Friedrich Rhetinger of Ingolstadt in 1605 of the Rector of the University of Paris wearing a black *bonnet carré*, a large miniver 'shoulder piece' reaching right over his chest and almost to his elbows, a closed violet robe with tight sleeves, and a violet girdle and violet purse[6] (Pl. 4b). In 1668 the particular features of the rectorial dress are described as being a very large violet 'shoulder piece' lined and edged with miniver, and a great violet purse at the girdle. At this date the rector seems to have worn a *bonnet carré* and continued to do so in the eighteenth century. The 'shoulder piece' had since the sixteenth century been worn without hood and liripipe.[7]

Throughout the eighteenth century the rectorial dress consisted of the violet robe with the miniver and violet 'shoulder piece', a silk violet belt decorated with gold tassels, a violet

[1] C. Jourdain, i. 32; D. Diderot and J. le R. D'Alembert, op. cit. xvi. 420[b], s.v. Toque; N. F. Robinson, art. cit., op. cit. v, pt. 1, p. 9.

[2] A. Franklin, x. 45.

[3] E. Pasquier, *Les Recherches de la France*, pp. 382D—383B; illustrations of these kinds of head-dress are given in J. B. Thiers, p. 107, and the three appear in a tail-piece in C. Du Molinet, *Figures des different habits des Chanoines*, p. 23.

[4] J. B. Thiers, p. 110; C. Du Molinet, pp. 22–23; J. Quicherat, p. 366.

[5] J. B. Thiers, pp. 110–11; G. Burius, *Onomasticon Etymologicum*, p. 34, s.v. Birettum.   [6] Oxford, Bodl. Libr. MS. Douce 244, fo. 31.

[7] C. E. Du Boulay, *Dignité*, pp. 24–26.

PLATE 4

b. Rector of the University of Paris, 1605

a. Doctor of Medicine, Paris, early fifteenth century

PLATE 5

N. Edelinck's 'L'Assemblée de la Faculté de Théologie', 1717

stole (*baudrier*), really a form of *chaperon* which passed from left to right across the chest, and a violet velvet purse (*escarcelle*) decorated with gold tassels and buttons. The *bonnet carré* changed in colour in the course of the century, for in 1719 it was black, but in 1779 violet.[1]

The proctors of the four nations composing the Faculty of Arts. Throughout this period proctors wore red robes, open and faced and lined with miniver, with miniver flap collars, such as they had done since the latter sixteenth century.[2]

Deans and other administrative officers. Deans and other officials wore the same dress as the proctors.[3] The Dean of the Faculty of Medicine had formerly worn as distinct from the other deans, a light blue purse edged with miniver.[4]

The Faculty of Theology. Doctors on important occasions wore until the eighteenth century a violet bonnet, and during nearly the whole of both centuries a violet gown and a violet *chaperon* dressed with miniver.[5] For ordinary occasions all the above-mentioned dress was black. The gown worn in either case was open, and either bell-sleeved, the sleeves being edged with black braid, or else narrow-sleeved and had buttons by which the sleeves could be held close to the arms. It had a flap-collar and broad black cloth facings down the front. A *chaperon* consisting of a doubled straight section of black silk edged and lined with miniver was worn with the undress.[6] By 1779 the use of violet seems to have been abandoned and only black was used.[7]

By 1717, the date of N. Edelinck's engraving, 'L'Assemblée de la Faculté de Théologie' in the Louvre,[8] Doctors of Theology were wearing a *bonnet carré* instead of a round bonnet[9] (Pl. 5).

---

[1] P. T. N. Hurtaut and –. Magny, *Dictionnaire historique de la ville de Paris*, iv. 160 s.v. Procession, and iv. 742, s.v. Université; A. Franklin, x. 250.

[2] C. E. Du Boulay, *Dignité*, p. 25; D. Diderot and J. le R. D'Alembert, xiv. 309a, s.v. Robe.

[3] P. T. N. Hurtaut and –. Magny, iv. 159–60, s.v. Procession; D. Diderot and J. le R. D'Alembert, xiv. 309a, s.v. Robe.

[4] G. Ferrario, v, pt. 2 (Europe), pl. 42, no. 8.

[5] P. T. N. Hurtaut and –. Magny, iv. 160; A. Franklin, x. 250.

[6] D. Diderot and J. le R. D'Alembert, op. cit. xiv. 309a, s.v. Robe; P. T. N. Hurtaut and –. Magny, iv. 160; A. Franklin, x. 250; P. Pic, *Guy Patin*, pl. opp. p. 142 (Portrait of Antoine Arnauld, D.Th. of the Sorbonne); C. Perrault, *Les Hommes illustres qui ont paru en France*, i, ill. p. 15 (same portrait).

[7] P. T. N. Hurtaut and –. Magny, iv. 160.

[8] Reproduced in J. Bonnerot, *L'Université de Paris du moyen âge à nos jours*, p. 36.

[9] D. Diderot and J. le R. D'Alembert, ii. 324 a–b, s.v. Bonnet.

They continued throughout the century to wear a cassock underneath their gown even when outside.[1] There is a story of Voltaire's adopting the disguise in his favourite *Café de Procope* of a Doctor of the Sorbonne (i.e. of Theology), on which occasion he wore a cassock, a gown, black stockings, cincture, bands, and a large unpowdered wig.[2]

Bachelors of Theology wore throughout the period a black cassock, with a long black gown lined and dressed with white fur, and a black silk bonnet lined with miniver.[3]

The Faculty of Law. The dress of full professors (*antécesseurs*) at their investiture consisted of a purple robe (*chlamys sive toga*), a scarlet 'shoulder piece' edged with wool, a girdle of black watered silk fastened on the left side, and a black *bonnet carré*,[4] in virtue of their being professors, not doctors. But after this ceremony they always wore for formal occasions a full and long open red-scarlet robe of wool with full bell-sleeves, lined with black silk, a scarlet 'shoulder piece' dressed with miniver, and a scarlet *bonnet carré*.[5] For informal occasions they wore an open black gown lined with red and a red *chaperon*.[6]

Those Doctors of Law who were assistant professors (*agrégés*) only wore the full scarlet dress of the *antécesseurs* if they deputized for them, but whenever (and this was usually the case) they took second place to the *antécesseurs*, they wore an open black bell-sleeved gown and a red *chaperon*.[7]

During the eighteenth century the *agrégés* became more and more discontented that the *antécesseurs*, even if they were *Licenciés* only, should wear the scarlet robe, while they (the *agrégés*), who were generally doctors and had undisputed right to scarlet, should have to wear black, except when they acted as deputies of the *antécesseurs*. When it was pointed out that the *antécesseurs* wore scarlet in virtue of their being professors, the

---

[1] P. Lacroix, *The Eighteenth Century*, p. 243, fig. 141.

[2] T. Carlyle, *Miscellaneous Essays*, ii (1888 edn.), p. 141.

[3] P. T. N. Hurtaut and –. Magny, iv. 159; D. Diderot and J. le R. D'Alembert, ii. 7b; A. Franklin, x. 249.   [4] G. Péries, pp. 248 and 318, n. 2.

[5] P. T. N. Hurtaut and –. Magny, ii. 674 and iv. 159; A. Franklin, x. 249–50; D. Diderot and J. le R. D'Alembert, ii. 324 a–b, s.v. Bonnet and v. 5b, s.v. Docteur en Droit; G. Péries, p. 248. For a literary allusion to this dress see Boileau's Eighth Satire, ll. 171–2. This satire was composed in 1667.

[6] G. Péries, p. 248.

[7] G. Péries, p. 248; D. Diderot and J. le R. D'Alembert, v. 8a, s.v. Docteur en droit.

agrégés replied by wearing the scarlet robe and scarlet and miniver 'shoulder piece' on all occasions that the *antécesseurs* wore them.[1] In 1766 affairs came to a head, the *antécesseurs* accusing the *agrégés* of always wearing scarlet robes when they did, but when the parties appealed to the Paris Parliament that body decided in favour of the latter, and they were allowed to wear the scarlet robe on the same occasions as the *antécesseurs*.[2]

Other Licentiates of Law on special occasions wore as full dress an open scarlet robe with a scarlet 'shoulder piece' trimmed with miniver, but the robe was not as full as that of doctors.[3] Ordinarily their dress consisted of an open black gown and a red *chaperon* decorated with miniver.[4]

Bachelors of Law wore open black gowns and black *chausses* trimmed with miniver.[5]

The *bonnet carré*, red for those who had the right to the red robe on formal occasions, black otherwise, was worn by all, and the black cassock and white bands.[6] All gowns were bell-sleeved.[7]

The Faculty of Medicine. The dress of Regent Doctors of Medicine remained the same during this period. For full dress it consisted of an open scarlet robe with wide bell-sleeves and a scarlet and miniver 'shoulder piece' completely covering the shoulders, a black cassock with many small buttons running vertically down the front, white bands, and a scarlet *bonnet carré*.[8] A cincture round the cassock was worn until about the middle of the seventeenth century.[9]

The undress garments of Regent Doctors of Medicine were the black gown of the same shape as the scarlet one, a scarlet *chaperon*, a black cassock, and a black *bonnet carré*.[10]

Bachelors of Medicine wore a black bell-sleeved gown and a black *chaperon* trimmed with miniver.[11]

---

[1] G. Péries, p. 318, n. 2.   [2] G. Péries, p. 256.
[3] D. Diderot and J. le R. D'Alembert, v. 8a.
[4] G. Péries, p. 318, n. 2.
[5] P. T. N. Hurtaut and –. Magny, iv. 159.
[6] D. Diderot and J. le R. D'Alembert, ii. 324 a–b, s.v. Bonnet.
[7] Cf. A. Franklin, x. 249.   [8] G. Patin, *Lettres choisies*, frontispiece.
[9] G. Patin, pl. opp. p. 22.   [10] G. Patin, *Nouvelles lettres*, i. 167.
[11] A. Franklin, x. 249. In their professional as opposed to their academical capacity, doctors in the seventeenth century wore high pointed bonnets in shape like candle-extinguishers which appeared ludicrous on top of large wigs, and did not fail to amuse Molière (A. Franklin, xi. 146) who makes play of them in *Le Médecin malgré lui* (1666). The head-dress was derived from the *mortier*.

The Faculty of Arts. The dress of a Master of Arts at the Collège de Clermont in 1644 consisted of a violet cassock, a black sleeveless gown, and a black *chaperon*.[1] By 1719 the dress of Masters of Arts throughout the university had come to be a black bell-sleeved open gown with a plain black *chaperon* (*chausse*) and a black *bonnet carré*.[2] In 1766 on appealing to the Paris Parliament, regent masters obtained the right to wear as full dress the scarlet robe and scarlet and miniver 'shoulder piece' like that of other regents.[3] Bachelors of Arts probably wore the same dress as Bachelors of Law and Medicine. No particular mention is made of them.

Undergraduates. It was not until the beginning of the seventeenth century that a definite dress for undergraduates came into being. Throughout this century they wore an open sleeveless gown with a flap collar of black stuff, and a round bonnet.[4] They had worn this bonnet since 1600.[5] In the eighteenth century they continued to wear the same gown, but gave up the round bonnet, and wore instead a rigid variety of *toque*,[6] a flat bonnet. They wore bands in common with all other members of the university.[7]

Séminaristes were theological students at a college associated with the university run by the Church. They wore a short cassock reaching some way below the knees with numerous small buttons down the front, bands, and round felt hats.[8]

But during the eighteenth century more and more members of the University of Paris were leaving off their academical dress except on formal occasions, and were wearing lay dress which was far from being 'modest and fitting'.[9] Academical dress vanished in 1792 when the university ceased to function. By a law of the National Convention of 15 September 1793 all the universities of France were abolished.

[1] P. Lacroix, *XVIIe Siècle: Institutions, usages et costumes*, pl. p. 470.
[2] P. T. N. Hurtaut and –. Magny, ii. 790, s.v. Examinateurs; A. Franklin, x. 248. [3] P. T. N. Hurtaut and –. Magny, iv. 159.
[4] F. Hottenroth, *Handbuch*, p. 762, and fig. 217, no. 4.
[5] C. Jourdain, i. 32; D. Diderot and J. le R. D'Alembert, xvi. 420b, s.v. Toque; N. F. Robinson, art. cit., pt. i, p. 9.
[6] D. Diderot and J. le R. D'Alembert, xvi, 420b, s.v. Toque; G. Dupont Ferrier, *Du Collège de Clermont au Lycée Louis-le-Grand*, p. 430; R. Somerset Ward, *Robespierre*, pp. 29–30.
[7] P. T. N. Hurtaut and –. Magny, iv. 159–60; A. Franklin, x. 248, and xi. 145.
[8] P. Lacroix, *XVIIe Siècle*, p. 358, fig. 156. [9] J. B. L. Crévier, vii. 73.

II. TOULOUSE (1229)

In the 'Grands statuts de l'Université et des Facultés de droit et de decret' (1314), Doctors and Masters of Law are forbidden to lecture or to take part in any public act unless wearing a *cappa manicata* or *cappa rotunda*. Licentiates and Bachelors of Law are likewise at their own lectures or when taking part in disputations or other acts bound to wear either of the two forms of *cappa* above mentioned unless with some reasonable excuse, having obtained leave of the rector. Masters of Arts were to wear a black *cappa clausa* or *cappa rotunda* for lecturing. Doctors of Law only wore the *pileus*; the rest were bareheaded.[1] Students were to use on formal occasions a closed *tunica*, but on informal occasions they might wear open ones with hoods, or other more comfortable dress, but they might never wear sleeveless dress, nor might they have mittens, boots, and caps.[2]

In 1407[3] the ordinary dress of students was regularized. They were to wear ankle-length costume of sufficient fullness, and their shoes were to be plain.

Nothing more is heard of dress until 1572 when it was forbidden to all members of the university to wear in churches, at the palace, and in courts of justice any dress whatever of a red, yellow, green, or blue colour.[4]

III. MONTPELLIER (1289)

Already a School of Medicine, Montpellier did not become a *studium generale* until so created by Pope Nicholas IV in 1289,[5] and after this fifty years passed before any enactments regarding dress appeared.

In 1339 Regent Doctors of Law and Bachelors of Law were required to wear the *cappa clausa* if in orders, but if laymen they might have the choice of wearing at all times the *cappa rotunda*, the *cappa manicata*, or a long *tabard*, which dress was always to be worn, even when walking in the town. Laymen Regent Doctors of Law (*doctores decretorum*) were to lecture in red *cappas*. No miniver was to be worn in the dress except by the rector, regent

---

[1] M. Fournier, i. 484–5 (Order no. 545, ¶ x, Year 1314).
[2] M. Fournier, i. 484–5 (Order no. 545, ¶ xl, § 3, Year 1314).
[3] M. Fournier, i. 727, §§ 2–7.
[4] R. Gadave, *Les Documents sur l'histoire de l'Université de Toulouse*, p. 179, § 500.
[5] E. Dubarle, i. 122.

doctors, those of noble blood, and those clergy who were of cathedral or ecclesiastical collegiate bodies, and even in these cases they were allowed miniver only on their hoods. At the same time students were ordered to wear a long and sufficiently full costume of the *supertunica* variety, and this dress was to be plain and without a hood.[1] By 1391 it had become necessary to forbid the wearing of any but cheap fur or lamb's wool by any but the rector, doctors, nobles, and licentiates. Regents in orders were still forced to wear a *cappa clausa*, or at least some form of *cappa*, but laymen regents might wear simply a cloak and at any rate nothing more formal than a tabard.[2]

From a title of 1462—all but the title is wanting—it is learnt that a *pileus* was bestowed on licentiates.[3] After this there is no more information about dress for more than a century.

In 1628 all professors were ordered to lecture in a gown (*toga*) and a *bonnet carré*.[4]

Until the seventeenth century the newly created Doctor of Laws, dressed in his doctoral robe and bonnet, was conducted to his house on horseback to the music of fiddles and hautboys.[5] As late as 1711 a Professor of Medicine is described as wearing at a ceremony white boots with gilt spurs.[6] This was a survival of the medieval idea of the doctor being a nobleman in the realm of learning.

At a visit of some members of the royal family to the Faculty of Medicine in 1701, the Professors of Medicine wore red damask robes with a doubled miniver *chaperon* (*chausse*), while *agrégés* wore the same *chaperon*, but a black damask robe. At a

---

[1] M. Fournier, ii. 50 (Order no. 947, ¶ iv); F. K. von Savigny, *Histoire du droit romain au moyen âge*, tom. iv, p. 494; A. Germain, art. 'L'École de Droit de Montpellier' in *Académie des Sciences et Lettres de Montpellier* (*Sect. des Lettres*, vi), p. 257ᵇ.

[2] M. Fournier, ii. 156–7 (Order no. 1040, Year 1391).

[3] M. Fournier, ii. 237 (Order no. 1163).

[4] A. Germain, art. 'La Faculté des Arts et l'Ancien Collège de Montpellier' in *Académie des Sciences et Lettres de Montpellier* (*Sect. des Lettres*, vii), p. 220, § iii; see the water-colour and pen and ink drawing dated 1579 of Laurence Joubert, M.D. and Chancellor of the University (d. 1582), in the Hope Collection in the Ashmolean, Oxford, for a good illustration of the *bonnet carré*.

[5] A. Germain, art. 'L'École de Droit de Montpellier' in *Académie des Sciences et Lettres de Montpellier* (*Sect. des Lettres*, vi), p. 245. This dress, an open bell-sleeved robe with facings, and a cassock, is to be seen in the print of François Gibieuf, M.D. (d. 1634), in the Hope Collection.

[6] A. Germain, art. 'Notice sur le cérémonial de l'Université de Médecine de Montpellier' in *Académie des Sciences et Lettres de Montpellier* (*Sect. des Lettres*, vi), p. 433.

funeral in 1711 all professors wore a plain black gown and no *chaperon*.[1] This plain black gown was the undress gown for all, the red damask being the full dress of *antécesseurs* and the black damask of *agrégés*. A black gown called at the present day the 'Robe de Rabelais' is said to be still preserved and to have belonged to the satirist. In the seventeenth century it is certain that his actual bonnet and gown were used at Montpellier on certain occasions.[2]

At the funeral of a Professor of French Law at Montpellier in 1738 the body of the dead was dressed in a red robe, a black cassock, a miniver-furred *chaperon*, white bands, a full wig, a *bonnet carré* with a tuft of red and green,[3] gloves, a sword, and boots with gilt spurs.[4] Those who attended wore the plain black gown and the *bonnet carré*.[5]

Bachelors and undergraduates at this time wore plain black gowns and round bonnet.[6]

In 1755 at a ceremony of the Faculty of Medicine, the professors wore the black gown only, bands, and an ordinary hat, except for M. Lamure, the professor who presided, who alone wore the *bonnet carré*.[7]

As late as January 1791 academical dress was still used at Montpellier.[8]

IV. AVIGNON (1303)

Not until 1503 were the statutes of the University of Avignon published, and in them is some mention of dress. No one but doctors were to wear the *birretum rotundum*.[9] Apparently of late years licentiates and even bachelors had presumed to wear this important part of the doctoral *insignia*. Licentiates and bachelors were not allowed a biretta at all. They had apparently been

---

[1] A. Germain, art. 'Le Cérémonial', pp. 421 and 433-4.
[2] D. J. Cunningham, *The Evolution of the Graduation Ceremony*, p. 31.
[3] Cf. B.M. MS. Ar. 484, fos. 61 and 105 (a German *Justiniani Digestum* with miniatures of 1399) for these two-coloured tufts used in the Middle Ages by Doctors of Both Laws, red representing Civil and green Canon Law.
[4] A. Germain, art. 'L'École de Droit', p. 244.
[5] Ibid., loc. cit., and cf. A. Germain, art. 'Le Cérémonial', pp. 433-4.
[6] A. Germain, art. 'L'École de Droit, p. 244.
[7] A. Germain, art. 'Le Cérémonial', p. 427.
[8] A. Germain, art. cit., p. 416.
[9] Cf. M. Fournier, ii. 703.

in the habit of wearing hoods lined with silk or rich furs, for they
are forbidden such decoration.[1]

The doctoral *birretum* was made of two pieces and was scarlet.
Doctors wore also gloves, which together with the *birretum* were
presented to them on their creation. Those below the rank of
doctor, such as Masters of Arts and licentiates of the various
faculties, were presented with gloves but naturally not the
birretum. Strangely enough the so strictly guarded doctoral
head-dress was worn by those licentiates and bachelors, four
in all, who actively took part in the ceremony of a doctor's
creation.[2]

V. ORLÉANS (1312)

An order of 1336 informs us that the doctoral dress shall be
made of good cloth, and that doctors are to wear a miniver-
furred *mantellum*.[3] In 1363 a *supertunica* dressed with miniver
might be used instead of the *mantellum*, and a miniver hood
was to be used with it.[4]

In 1365 students of two or more years' standing were to wear
the *cappa manicata*, but those of less standing were to continue
as before to use the short *tabard*. Senior students were only
allowed the *tabard* when riding.[5]

Not a word more is heard about dress until in a royal edict of
1679 it is ordered that the old ceremonial should be revived.
Processions should again take place, the rector should use his
red robe, the *Docteur-régents* (*antécesseurs*) should also use their
red robes, and *agrégés* a black gown and a red *chaperon* (*chausse*).[6]

VI. PERPIGNAN (1349)

In 1426 students in the Faculty of Arts were ordered to wear
a dress neither too long nor too short but keeping the mean.

The *pilei* of Masters of Medicine and Masters of Arts were to
be the same, that is of blood-red wool.[7]

---

[1] M. Fournier, ii. 527 (Order no. 1421, § 36).
[2] M. Fournier, ii. 528 (Order no. 1421, § 38).
[3] M. Fournier, i. 100 (Order no. 117).
[4] M. Fournier, i. 120 (Order no. 161).
[5] M. Fournier, i. 122 (Order no. 167).
[6] J. Loiseleur, art. 'L'Université d'Orléans' in *Mém. de la Soc. d'Agriculture
d'Orléans*, t. xxv, no. 3, p. 208.
[7] M. Fournier, ii. 703 (Order no. 1505).

VII. ANGERS (1364)

Certainly as early as about 1396 the rector has as his ceremonial dress a red robe furred with ermine, and wore as head-
dress a very large and long hood of the same colour and similarly furred.[1]

In the reformed statutes (1398) the full dress of Regent
Doctors of Canon and of Civil Law is ordered to be the *cappa*
and 'shoulder piece', or other suitable becoming dress,[2] and
in a new title[3] added to these statutes in 1410, bachelors of all
faculties were told to wear a *cappa* both going to and returning
from their lectures.

In 1431 it was found necessary to legislate against the wearing of miniver on their hoods by bachelors and licentiates.
They were to wear black lamb's wool according to the original
statutes of the university. A hood lined with miniver was really
only for the rector's wear, but by this time doctors and masters
were allowed this fur.[4]

In 1484 Bachelors of Medicine taking part in any public
scholastic act were to use the *cappa cathegorica* (i.e. a large
round-shaped *cappa* closed in front, having a large hood attached
to it), but candidates for the Licence of Medicine taking part
in the Act of Licence were to wear a short straight *tabard* unfurred, not reaching farther than the knees, and a hood.[5]

In 1494 regents in the Faculty of Arts lecturing or attending
any scholastic act are simply ordered to wear a decent habit,
but they must have a hood or 'shoulder piece'.[6]

VIII. AIX (1409)

In the fifteenth-century seal of the University of Aix the rector
wears a long closed robe with fairly full sleeves and a large
round *pileus* like a tam-o'-shanter.[7]

Among the voluminous statutes of this university (1420–40)
are a few references to dress. Doctors were to wear a gold

[1] L. de Lens, *Université d'Angers*, i. 49.
[2] M. Fournier, i. 324 (Order no. 434, ¶ xxxviii, § 17).
[3] Ibid. ¶ cxxxvii, § 15.
[4] M. Fournier, i. 390 (Order no. 470).
[5] C. Port, *Statuts des Quatre Facultés de l'Université d'Angers, 1464–94*, p. 33, § 33.
[6] C. Port, p. 49, § 21.
[7] R. Gandilhon, *Sigillographie des Universités de France*, p. 43 and ill. pl. i, no. 2.

cincture.[1] Masters of Theology and doctors of the other faculties wore a *pileus* of the colour of their faculty; for Theology, white; for Canon Law, green; for Civil Law, red; for Medicine, violet; and for Both Laws, red and green.

At the same time it was enjoined that candidates for the doctorate should obtain *pilei* and gloves of good quality before the ceremony of creation.[2]

IX. DÔLE (1424)

In the statutes of about 1424 the rector was ordered to wear a pleated (*rigatus*, i.e. *rugatus*) *cappa* with a cloth hood decorated with miniver.[3] At this university noblemen-students were admitted as a privileged class as at Montpellier. They were allowed special seats in university assemblies on festal occasions and were also allowed servants; but they were given no latitude as regards dress, which had to be of cloth and conformable with their standing as scholars.[4]

No one beneath the degree of doctor was allowed to wear the *birretum rotundum*.[5]

At the same time students were ordered to wear the *cappa manicata*, or at any rate a seemly dress, which was to reach *ad cavillam pedis*, to the heel, or at least to the top of the boots. Apparently this dress might be lined with fur, for students were warned that no fur must be seen at the edges of it. They were not to wear girdles unless very plain, nor were they to have convex-shaped wallets (*gibosserius*), purses, or large knives hanging from their girdles. Their dress was to be conformable to their standing and faculty, and they were to wear hoods in a modest manner and not twisted up round their heads.[6]

X. POITIERS (1431)

In 1438 Licentiates and Bachelors of Law were ordered to attend the schools in a long and ankle-length dress without a

---

[1] M. Fournier, iii. 23 (Order no. 1582, § 110).
[2] M. Fournier, iii. 24 (Order no. 1582, § 116).
[3] M. Fournier, iii. 107 (Order no. 1616, §xxiii); H. Beaune and J. d'Arbaumont, *Les Universités de Franche-Compté*, p. xlix, n. 2.
[4] M. Fournier, loc. cit., § xxxviii.
[5] M. Fournier, iii. 112 (Order no. 1616, § xlii).
[6] M. Fournier, iii. 114–15 (Order no. 1616, § xlix).

PLATE 6

Rector and Doctor of the University of Bourges, 1624

girdle.[1] No more information about the dress of this not very important university is to be found.

XI. CAEN (1432)

In 1439, by the statutes of King Henry VI of England, it was ordered that the dress of a Licentiate of Medicine who was to be created master was to be of good new cloth of a violet-brown colour with a close-fitting *pileus* of the same colour. This dress was to be worn by these masters, as all other Masters of Medicine, on all academical occasions.[2] The new master was to present a *pileus* and gloves to all already existing Masters of Medicine.[3] At the same time it was desired that all doctors, masters, and bachelors of the various faculties should use the *cappa clausa*, or some other decent and pleated form of *cappa* at all academical acts as at Paris.[4]

In 1457 the dress of the rector was ordered to consist of a cloth *tunica*, a pleated *cappa* (*capa rigata*, i.e. *rugata*), and a cloth hood lined with miniver.[5]

The statutes of the Faculty of Medicine (1478) contain a clause directing Doctors of Medicine to wear a violet *cappa* and a round bonnet of the same colour.[6]

XII. BORDEAUX (1441)

In 1443 doctors and masters of all faculties of the University of Bordeaux were ordered to wear a *cappa* when lecturing,[7] and at the same time students were ordered to wear ankle-length dress of such colour as befitted their station.[8]

The next mention of dress is in 1558 when regent doctors and stipendiary doctors (*agrégés*) were ordered to wear long robes to accord with their standing.[9]

---

[1] M. Fournier, iii. 303 (Order no. 1723, § vi).

[2] M. Fournier, iii. 168. (Order no. 1652, ¶ III, § 18).

[3] M. Fournier, iii. 168 (Order no. 1652, ¶ III, § 19); M. Fournier, iii. 398–9 (Order no. 1842, § xxviii).

[4] A. de Bourmont, art. 'La Fondation de l'Université de Caen' in *Bulletin de la Société des Antiquaires de Normandie*, t. xii, pp. 500 and 504–5.

[5] M. Fournier, iii. 209 (Order no. 1680, § 7); A. de Bourmont, art. cit., t. xii, p. 581.

[6] A. de Bourmont, art. cit., t. xii, p. 421.

[7] M. Fournier, iii. 342–3 (Order no. 1771, § 49).

[8] M. Fournier, loc. cit., § 54; H. Barckhausen, *Statuts et règlements de l'ancienne Université de Bordeaux*, p. 14.   [9] H. Barckhausen, p. 56.

In 1793, when the affairs of the university were wound up, an inventory was made of goods in the university's possession. Only two articles of dress are mentioned, and they no doubt formed the rector's official dress. They were an old crimson satin robe dressed with ermine, and a new gold-braided *chaperon* with tassels on it. The latter had been made in 1784.[1]

XIII. NANTES (1460)

In 1462 it was ordered that the rector's dress was to be, at scholastic acts of a solemn nature and in congregation, a *capa aperta* (probably open at the side from shoulder to hem as was sometimes the medieval practice) lined and trimmed with miniver; but in the schools at the hearing of lectures and at other less formal acts he was to use the *caputium* (i.e. the 'shoulder piece' with a hood attached) lined and trimmed with miniver in winter, but in summer lined with silk (*sandat*, i.e. 'sendal').[2]

In the same statutes of this year it was ordered that in processions and at ordinary lectures regent doctors and masters should wear a *cappa* with a furred hood or a silk one according to the season. The *cappa* itself was similarly to be worn either lined with fur or with silk.[3]

At the same time Masters and Bachelors of Theology were ordered at all acts to wear a *cappa clausa* and a hood of a becoming colour, the shape of these garments and the quality of fur used in them being suitable to their dignity. At the ceremony of licentiates becoming Masters of Theology they were to give a *birretum* (here called *birra*) to the already existing masters present.[4]

In the law faculty all nobles, licentiates, bachelors, holders of benefices, and the rest of the scholars were to appear in the schools and at all public acts of the university in a fitting ordinary dress, and over this ankle-length academical dress with a hood.[5] Regent Doctors of Law were to wear a hooded dress, furred in winter, and lined with silk in summer;[6] while

---

[1] H. Barckhausen, p. 146.   [2] M. Fournier, iii. 46 (Order no. 1595, § 8).
[3] M. Fournier, iii. 49 (Order no. 1595, § 29).
[4] M. Fournier, loc. cit., § 18.
[5] M. Fournier, iii. 64 (Order no. 1595, § 3).
[6] M. Fournier, iii. 69 (Order no. 1595, § 28).

Licentiates of Law on full ceremonial occasions at least were to use a black *cappa* and a hood, the hood only being lined and trimmed with miniver. The dress of Bachelors of Law was to be the same, except that probably the fur of the hood was to be of less expensive fur than miniver.

Students of the law faculty were to wear ankle-length dress, probably of black cloth, with a plain cloth hood. They were not to have any form of head-dress.

Proctors were to be distinguished by their 'shoulder pieces'.[1]

XIV. BOURGES (1465)

From what we read of the presentations to be made by newly created Doctors of Law who were noblemen or of other dignity, the dress of Regent Doctors of Law during the period 1470–80 consisted of a scarlet mantle with a miniver-furred hood, a scarlet *tunica*, and a scarlet *birretum duplex*. Masters of Laws (i.e. including Canon Law), Regents of the Faculties of Theology and Medicine, and the Dean of Arts also wore the scarlet *birretum duplex*.[2] In an album (Pl. 6) once owned by a member of the university are two figures in miniature dated 1624. The left-hand figure is a rector of the university, and wears a biretta, an open scarlet robe with moderately hanging sleeves, the facings in front and the cuffs of the sleeves being of black velvet, and on his left shoulder rests a scarlet *chaperon* edged with fur. The figure on the right is a doctor in undress. Over a black silk cassock he wears a black sleeveless cloak with a flap-collar. His black hat is of everyday fashion.[3]

XV. PONT-À-MOUSSON (1572), afterwards NANCY (1769)

The rector, from the time of the foundation of the university, wore a *cappa* or some kind of closed robe, and an *épitoge* ('shoulder piece'), both garments of a violet colour edged with red.[4]

All graduates wore a gown, either black or near-black, and a *bonnet carré*, but there is no mention of there having been a particular dress for students, and students of theology, about

---

[1] M. Fournier, loc. cit., §§ 29–31.
[2] M. Fournier, iii. 431–2 (Order no. 1862, § 14).
[3] B.M. Eg. MS. 1264, fo. 150ᵛ.
[4] E. Martin, *L'Université de Pont-à-Mousson*, p. 272.

whose dress we have information, must have been, according to the practice at all universities, already graduates of the Faculty of Philosophy (Arts).

Bachelors of Philosophy wore the gown and *bonnet carré* alone, Masters of Arts wore with the gown a black *chaperon* edged with violet, and on their black *bonnet carré* was a violet tump.[1] Professors (Doctors) of Philosophy wore under a cloak a cassock fastened at the waist, and above the cloak was a 'shoulder piece', but there is no information about the colour.[2] This dress is well illustrated in a sixteenth-century woodcut depicting four figures, one being the rector.[3]

Students of Theology, Bachelors of Theology, and licentiates of the same faculty wore a black gown, a black *bonnet carré*, and a *chaperon* (*chausse*) edged with white silk, but the size of the *chaperon* indicated the status, the largest indicating the licentiate. Doctors of Theology wore the same dress as licentiates except that they had a white tump on their *bonnet carré*.

Full professors of the Faculty of Law wore a black gown, over it a short knee-length *tunica* of scarlet satin, a scarlet satin *chaperon*, and a black *bonnet carré* with a red and violet tump. In 1693 they found it necessary to add to the *chaperon* a border of white fur to distinguish them from the mayor of the town. The dean of the Faculty of Law was dressed the same as the professors but the bottom of his *bonnet* was bordered with ermine.

The dress of the full professors of the Faculty of Medicine consisted of the black gown, above it a purple cloth cloak, and over both an ermine-furred 'shoulder piece'. On their *bonnet carré* they had a white and violet silk tump.[4]

The eighteenth-century seal of the Faculty of Medicine of the University of Nancy is the most useful of all French university seals for evidence of academical dress, for it is large and clear. Saints Cosmas and Damian are depicted as full Professors of Medicine (*Docteurs antécesseurs*) and wear full closed gowns with miniver-faced sleeves, miniver 'shoulder pieces', bands, and *bonnets carrés*. Below them kneels a *Docteur agrégé* wearing a long closed gown with tight sleeves, bands, and a *toque*.[5]

---

[1] E. Martin, p. 271.
[2] E. Martin, p. 272.
[3] V. de Viriville, p. 125.
[4] E. Martin, p. 272.
[5] R. Gandilhon, pp. 77–78 and pl. xi, no. 84.

XVI. PAU (1726)

The statutes of 1725 ordered full professors (*Docteurs antecésseurs*) to wear a black gown with a red *chaperon* bordered with ermine and a *bonnet carré* for ordinary academical occasions, and a red robe with the same *chaperon* for outstanding ceremonies.[1] *Docteurs agrégés* were to use on ordinary occasions a black gown with a black *chaperon* bordered with ermine, and a *bonnet carré*, and on the occasions when the professors wore the red robe, a black gown, and an ermine-bordered red *chaperon*.[2]

In 1777 the rector was ordered to wear a *bonnet carré* with a red silk tump if an ecclesiastic, but if a layman a hat with a gold and red silk hat-band with red silk tassels hanging off it. Rectors, whether ecclesiastics or laymen, wore a 'shoulder piece' (*épitoge*) of crimson satin bordered with ermine over presumably an open robe, and a cassock, but an ecclesiastic had the distinction of wearing a red cincture with tassels of gold and red silk on the ends of it.[3]

The prestige of a Professor of Law at Pau is indicated by the fact that for his funeral the dead professor's body was dressed in the red robe and was adorned with sword, boots, and spurs.[4] There is no mention of any other faculty besides that of Law.

XVII. OTHER UNIVERSITIES

The records of the other French universities are defective except for Gray and Valence, whose documents are fairly complete. None of them contain any reference to academical costume.

---

[1] J. Maisonnier, *Le Faculté de Droit de l'Université de Pau*, p. 331 (Stat. § ix).
[2] J. Maissonier, p. 333 (Stat. § xvii).
[3] J. Maisonnier, p. 95.
[4] J. Maisonnier, p. 299, as at Montpellier.

3

GREAT BRITAIN AND IRELAND

I. OXFORD

(a) The Chancellor

THE first example which we possess of a chancellor is the main figure on the chancellor's first seal, an impression of which is attached to a deed of 1238.[1] The figure, which appears as half-length with the face in profile, wears a *pileus* and a loose *supertunica*.[2]

In the early fourteenth-century stained glass in Merton College Chapel given by Henry de Mannesfield (or Mamesfield), the donor's portrait is depicted twenty-four times. He was a Master of Theology and is described as *Magister*, but the dress he wears, a wide-sleeved *supertunica* and an amess (almuce), is not the costume of that degree. As he was chancellor it seems likely that he wears the dress of that office. In addition he has a *pileus*.[3] The *supertunica* and *pileus* vary in colour in nearly every miniature portrait, but this is simply according to the artist's fancy.

A remarkable miniature of 1375 in *Registrum A* in the university archives shows a chancellor kneeling before Edward III and receiving a charter from him.[4] The kneeling figure is bareheaded and tonsured, and is clad in a scarlet *supertunica* with great hanging sleeves,[5] which are lined with grey fur and edged with it. Over this can be seen what is almost certainly an amess, worn no doubt in virtue of the chancellor's ecclesiastical standing.[6]

---

[1] At Magdalen.

[2] E. T. Beaumont, *Academical Habit illustrated by Ancient Memorial Brasses*, p. 63.

[3] L. B. Saint and H. Arnold, *Stained Glass*, pp. 157–8.

[4] Registrum A, fo. 13.

[5] J. E. Sandys (art. 'Ancient University Ceremonies' in *Fasciculus Ioanni Willis Clark dicatus*, p. 238) wrongly states that it is sleeveless.

[6] N. F. Robinson, art. 'The Black Chimere of Anglican Prelates', in *Transactions of St. Paul's Ecclesiological Society*, iv (1898), 182, n. 2.

From the chancellor's fourth seal of 1429 it can be seen that the chancellor's costume has not changed. A long loose *super-tunica* with large sleeves and an amess again appear, and in addition there is a head-dress, a *pileus* with a small brim.[1]

There are no more examples of the chancellor's dress until it had been completely changed to a robe such as was worn by great officers of the Crown. Before this time there is the portrait of Sir Christopher Hatton painted at the time of his appointment to this office in 1588, but its value as evidence is very small owing to the darkening of the picture, and we are left in doubt as to whether or not he is wearing a distinctive dress or, as seems more likely, merely the dress of his degree, which was Master of Arts.[2]

The chancellor's gold-brocaded black robe of the winged-sleeved variety, the same as that of lord chancellors of England, except that the Oxford robe has a gold rosette on each sleeve and in the middle of the train,[3] was a development of a late Elizabethan fashion. A good example of this dress is to be found in one of James Roberts's water-colours of 1792, in which we see worn over ordinary dress a black brocaded robe with panel sleeves. It is braided with gold lace on the facings, the hem, on the sides, and on the sleeves.[4] The head-dress was a round black velvet cap.[5]

(b) The Vice-Chancellor

At no time did the vice-chancellor have any special dress. He wore the dress of his degree which was usually Doctor of Divinity. Thus on the occasion of Queen Elizabeth's departure after her visit to Oxford in 1566 the vice-chancellor and three other doctors, who rode before her, wore their full-dress scarlet.[6] In 1588 it was decreed that all Bachelors of Civil Law on their presentation should give the vice-chancellor gloves,[7]

---

[1] E. T. Beaumont, loc. cit.
[2] E. St. J. Brooks, *Life of Sir Christopher Hatton*, pl. opp. p. 234.
[3] L. H. D. Buxton and S. Gibson, *Oxford University Ceremonies*, p. 43.
[4] Oxf. Bodl. Libr. MS. Top. Oxon. d. 58, 8–9.
[5] Cf. T. Uwins's plate (1815). W. Combe and T. Uwins, *History of the University of Oxford*, ii. 17–18.
[6] Oxf. Bodl. Libr. MS. Twyne 17, fos. 157ᵛ and 159.
[7] A. Clark, *Register of the University of Oxford* (O.H.S., 1887), ii, pt. 1, p. 115.

and as late as the third quarter of the seventeenth century they wore them.[1]

(c) Proctors and Collectors

There are no early records of proctors' dress, nor is there any illustrative material in which they are depicted.

It is not until the first half of the seventeenth century that the dress which they still wear is mentioned.

This costume, consisting of a black bell-sleeved gown with black velvet facings, a rudimentary tippet on the shoulder, reminiscent of the fifteenth-century liripipe, and a large miniver hood, is representative of the late medieval dress of Masters of Arts. When a lay fashion of Tudor times altered the character of the masters' dress, proctors continued to use the old form. As late as the seventeenth century, however, the wide-sleeved gown was worn with a miniver hood by masters as a formal dress on special occasions such as at the time of Charles I's visit to Oxford in 1636.[2] The white furred hood in imitation of the original miniver, always worn by Masters of Arts before the introduction of silk in 1432 as an alternative for summer wear, was technically allowed to masters as full dress even as late as the statutes of 1770.[3] Proctors continued to wear this dress—the velvet facings were a Jacobean addition—as the spokesmen of Masters of Arts.[4]

As with all other Oxford dresses of modern times the seal of the Laudian statutes is set upon them. During the Civil War and Commonwealth period when the use of academical dress was to a large extent discontinued, and the wearing of hoods especially became more and more curtailed, proctors continually wore theirs.[5]

The dress of proctors and pro-proctors was at this date laid down for proctors as a bell-sleeved gown with black velvet laid on the sleeves and facings down the front, and for pro-proctors

[1] Oxf. Bodl. Libr. MS. Wood 276b, xix, 2.
[2] Oxf. Bodl. Libr. MS. Twyne 17, fo. 187.
[3] G. R. M. Ward, *Oxford University Statutes*, ii. 11.
[4] J. Wells, *Degree Ceremony*, p. 59. As late as 1873 a Master of Arts gown faced with velvet was worn by the senior of the two fellows of New College who went to Winchester to conduct the examination for scholarships, but its use on this occasion was thereafter discontinued (A. Clark, *The Life and Times of Anthony à Wood* (O.H.S.), iii. 226–7, n.).
[5] J. Walker, *Oxoniana*, iv. 210–11.

the ordinary Master of Arts gown with black velvet on the facings down the front only. A good example of the first of these gowns of the year 1675 is to be seen in one of Loggan's figures.[1] From this we see that as yet the tippet was much larger than it subsequently became. In No. 18 the miniver hood is shown, very full and completely covering the shoulders. Proctors still wore gloves which were presented to them by the Oxford City companies, but by the end of the century they had ceased to have any academical significance.[2] A square cap was worn with this dress.

In 1792 in a water-colour showing a proctor back-view he wears a square cap with a tassel, a full black gown with bell-sleeves, the upper part faced with black velvet, a 'bridge' yoke like those on masters' gowns, and from the lower left side of this yoke hangs a small pyramidal tippet from two buttons. The full miniver hood has all the fur showing.[3]

In 1792 the pro-proctor wore the black square cap with a tassel, and an ordinary master's gown faced on both sides down the front with black velvet, down the outside edge of which facings ran a thin line of alternating orange and yellow thread, which was simply the selvage of the velvet, and appeared also on proctors' gowns in the same place.[4] Pro-proctors wore with this gown a master's hood, although it is not shown in this Roberts water-colour, and on the gown was a tippet fastened to the lower left side of the yoke. After the expiry of their office proctors wore a tippet on their ordinary master's gown; not so pro-proctors.[5]

Collectors were representatives of Bachelors of Arts as proctors were of masters. Their gowns were exactly the same as those of bachelors with long and pointed sleeves, except that they had a broad piece of black velvet on the sleeves reaching half-way up them.[6] This proves that their dress was originally what we should call a full Bachelor of Arts dress and not a full Master of Arts dress of the old type, for at the time of Loggan's plates

---

[1] D. Loggan, *Oxonia Illustrata*, no. 17.
[2] L. H. D. Buxton and S. Gibson, op. cit., p. 35; cf. W. Dugdale, *Origines juridiciales*, p. 137.
[3] Oxf. Bodl. Libr. MS. Top. Oxon. d. 58, 38–39.
[4] Oxf. Bodl. Libr. MS. Top. Oxon. d. 58, 41–42.
[5] J. Woodforde, *Diary*, i. 171 (year 1775).
[6] D. Loggan, no. 10.

(1675) their sleeves were more pendulous than those of proctors, though afterwards owing to a misunderstanding of their origin the two gowns became identical. In Loggan's time they had no tippet, but the authorities of the eighteenth century, careless of tradition in many ways, allowed them to assume one and shorten the sleeves to the proctors' size, as is to be seen in the official engravings executed to illustrate the statutes of 1770 which contained clauses about academical dress (Pl. 11A)[1]. There is a pencil drawing by T. Uwins (1813–14) of the collector's gown, showing the yoke and the velvet on the sleeves which ends a little way below the shoulders. The pyramidal tippet is large, and an enlarged illustration of it is inset in the same leaf.[2] Their hood had always been the same as that of a Bachelor of Arts.

In 1656 collectors had lost for the time being their special dress, being forced to wear simply the ordinary Bachelor of Arts gown.[3] In 1822 the office, the holder of which was responsible for gathering together the Bachelors of Arts for public acts in the schools, for arranging their disputations in the schools and for collecting the proctors' fees, was abolished.[4]

In a letter of 1721 from William Bishop of Gray's Inn to Arthur Charlett, Master of University College, it is mentioned as being maintained by a certain Dr. Crowder, a contemporary, that deans of colleges should wear a proctor's hood when in Congregation, and Henry Gandy, the then Dean of Oriel, on the persuasion of Crowder wore the hood on these occasions. The outcome of this move for the revival of the wearing of proctorial dress by deans was that Dr. Haughton, the vice-chancellor in this year, explained that certainly deans used to wear such miniver hoods, but that as they were so expensive they were dispensed from wearing them. In 1721, however, it was still the custom for Bodley's librarian to wear a proctor's gown on public days.[5]

(d) Doctors of Divinity (originally called Masters of Theology)

The earliest reference to the costume of Masters of Theology in the *Statuta Antiqua* of Oxford belongs to a date previous to

---

[1] Oxf. Bodl. Libr. MS. Top. Oxon. c. 16, 9; G. V. Cox, *Recollections*, pp. 228 and 241–2.   [2] Oxf. Bodl. Libr. MS. Top. Oxon. d. 130, leaf 18.
[3] Oxf. Univ. Archives, Registrum T (1647–59), fo. 282; Oxf. Bodl. Libr. MS. Wood, F 27, fo. 73.
[4] G. V. Cox, pp. 228 and 241–2.   [5] J. Walker, iii. 162–3.

PLATE 7

Members of New College, Oxford, in a group with the Warden, *c.* 1463

PLATE 8

Philip Bisse in Oxford D.D. Convocation dress, 1612

1350 when they were ordered to have the *cappa clausa* for formal and the *pallium*, a sleeveless dress[1] worn over a full sleeved *roba*,[2] for informal occasions, furred with lamb's-wool but never with miniver.[3] At the same period the head-dress of Masters of Theology is described as the *pileus*,[4] that is, the *pileus rotundus*.[5] In this early statute monks (*religiosi*) are naturally excluded from the use of this pileus.[6] Later, at any rate by the mid-fifteenth century, the date of the Chaundler New College group (Pl. 7), a 'stalk' apex was added in order that by means of it the close-fitting *pileus* might be pulled off the head.[7] With the *cappa* a hood and 'shoulder piece' were worn. By the beginning of the fifteenth century Masters of Theology of sufficient ecclesiastical dignity had these outer garments lined with miniver, as can be seen from the inventory of the goods of Walter Skirlaw, Bishop of Durham (d. 1406), in which two of his hoods, one of miniver and one of ermine, are described.[8]

There are some good fifteenth-century examples of the dress of Masters of Theology. Consisting of a *cappa clausa* with its one large opening in front, a hood and its 'shoulder piece', a *sub-tunica* (cassock), and a 'stalk'-apexed *pileus*, it appears in the brass of Thomas Hylle, S.T.P. (1468) in the chapel of New College, Oxford.[9] This *pileus* was black for Masters of Theology as a good fifteenth-century example in the east light of the north window of Newington Church, Oxon., shows.[10]

In the painted glass in the main lights of the fifth window at Clavering, Essex, the subject of which is St. Catherine disputing with the philosophers, the latter are given the *cappa clausa* and are no doubt intended to be Masters of Theology.[11]

[1] First mentioned in a general way at Oxford in 1322 (S. Gibson, *Statuta Antiqua Universitatis Oxoniensis*, p. 126).
[2] E. C. Clarke, art. 'English Academic Costume' in *Archaeological Journal*, l (1893), 101.
[3] S. Gibson, pp. 51–52; E. C. Clarke, art. cit. l. 205; F. E. Brightman, Preface to R. T. Günther's art. 'Description of the Chapel Brasses' in *Magdalen College Register*, N.S. viii (1915), p. v.   [4] S. Gibson, p. 37.
[5] E. C. Clarke, art. 'College Caps and Doctors' Hats', in *Archaeological Journal*, lxi (1904), 33–34.   [6] S. Gibson, loc. cit.
[7] E. C. Clarke, art. cit. in op. cit., l. p. 144.
[8] *Testamenta Eboracensia*, iv (Surtees Soc. liii (1868), 322).
[9] E. T. Beaumont, *Ancient Memorial Brasses*, pp. 106 and 108; F. H. Crossley, *English Church Monuments*, p. 231.
[10] Illustrated in *Oxford Archaeological Society*, no. 84 (1938), pl. 3, no. 2.
[11] F. C. Eeles, art. 'The Clavering Glass' in *Transactions of the Essex Archaeological*

On the other hand, in the miniatures illustrating a manuscript of a collection of English theological orations of about 1475 the Masters of Theology here depicted[1] appear in undress, which consists of a *supertunica* with moderately hanging sleeves, a 'shoulder piece' with a hood close round the neck, and a black *pileus* sometimes with an apex and sometimes without one. The colouring varies in the different miniatures.[2]

As was the case with all academical costume, in the sixteenth century the dress of this degree changed considerably. During this period the full festal scarlet dress appeared, as well as the Convocation 'habit' and the undress, all of which gradually came to be opened up down the front, and took on approximately the same shape as was afterwards maintained.

Henry VIII's *Act for the Reformation of Excess of Apparel* (1533), which, while forcing all people of private standing to adopt a more sober dress, allowed those of position to use such a colour as scarlet, no doubt gave a stimulus to its use on the festal robe which Doctors of Divinity and other doctors were beginning to wear. This robe, which originated in a lay fashion—we find such a one worn by courtiers of the day with official posts such as Sir Thomas More—was similar to those of mayors and aldermen. It seems likely that it was introduced into the universities at this time, although there are no details about its use until the reign of Elizabeth, by which time its was well established.

In the later fifteenth century, when Masters of Theology gave up wearing the *cappa clausa* with one slit, they used the *cappa* with two slits as their formal dress. This was what came to be known in the course of the sixteenth century as the 'Convocation habit', and was worn over the *supertunica*, which gradually developed into the *roba* (gown). In the inventory which was made about 1508 of the goods of the late Warden of Canterbury College, who was of this degree, we read of 'a coote of cloyth in grayn made when he was doctor, also hys doctors abett of the same cloyth', which seems to indicate that such a dress was

---

Society, xvi (1922), pt. 2, N.S., p. 83, and fig. 1, opp. p. 77; J. D. Le Couteur, *English Mediaeval Painted Glass*, pp. 115–16, fig. 32.

[1] B.M. MS. Harl. 2887, fos. 56, 56ᵛ, and 58.

[2] For this see above, (a) Chancellor. Even if this is simply the result of the artist's whim, it was the cut of the dress rather than the colour which was as yet only important. The undress for this degree was the same at Cambridge at the same period.

already in being, the 'abett' being the *cappa* with two slits and the 'coote' being the *supertunica* (*roba*).[1]

The *supertunica* itself during the same period changed into a full-sleeved gown, but in the latter part of the century the gown of Doctors of Divinity, Bachelors of Divinity, and Masters of Arts, as a result of lay fashion, was given glove-sleeves.[2] When worn under the 'habit' these sleeves were pulled through its arm-holes and hung down at the sides. For Convocation dress a hood was worn with 'habit' and gown. Earlier in the century this was scarlet and lined with miniver, as is to be seen from the inventory of goods left by John West, D.D. (d. 1543),[3] but later black silk replaced the miniver. The 'habit' was by this time scarlet.[4]

In 1566, at the time of Queen Elizabeth's visit to Oxford, doctors, though described as wearing 'habits' and hoods when she arrived, wore their festal dress when they rode with her to see her on her way at the time of her departure.[5] On the occasion of Charles II's visit to Oxford in 1663, the full dress of Doctors of Divinity is described as a full-sleeved scarlet robe, faced with velvet, which means black velvet,[6] but sometimes the hoods belonging to Convocation dress were wrongly worn with the full dress robe, as at the time of the visit of Charles I in 1636.[7]

A good example of the Convocation dress at the beginning of the seventeenth century is to be seen in the portrait (1612) of Philip Bisse (1540–1613) (Pl. 8), Archdeacon of Taunton and founder of Wadham College Library.[8] He wears the scarlet habit, open some way down the front, the opening becoming of a sharp V-shape towards the waist, the hood fastened low in front, while the gown appears underneath the habit with very short glove sleeves appearing through the arm-holes.

Until the end of the fifteenth century the *pileus rotundus*

---

[1] The inventory is given in W. A. Pantin, *Canterbury College*, i (Inventories) (O.H.S., N.S. vi. (1947)), 84.
[2] A. Clark, *Wood*, i. 68–69.
[3] *Somerset Mediaeval Wills, 1531–58* (Somerset Record Soc. xxi, 1905), p. 76.
[4] E. C. Clarke, art. cit., l. 138.
[5] Oxf. Bodl. Libr. MS. Twyne, 17, fos. 157ᵛ, 159, and 173ᵛ.
[6] A. Clark, *Wood*, i. 494.
[7] Oxf. Bodl. Libr. MS. Twyne, 17, fo. 187.
[8] Mrs. R. L. Poole, *Oxford Portraits* (O.H.S.), iii, frontispiece (Wadham College, no. 8).

continued to be the head-dress of Doctors of Divinity as of other doctors, but by the beginning of the sixteenth century it had lost its 'stalk' apex and had begun to assume a cusped shape, doubtless arising from the necessity of a convenient grip, now that there was no longer a 'stalk', when putting it on and off.[1] By 1520 the academical *pileus* had become rigid and square at the University of Paris, and this fashion rapidly spread to the other universities of Europe.[2]

Unlike the *pileus quadratus* of the Continent the *pileus* of Oxford and Cambridge developed in a particular way un-parelleled elsewhere. Instead of taking either the form of a biretta or of a small square bonnet, it became a very large flat, shallow, square cap, loose and flagging at the corners. Under it a skull-cap was usually worn, and during the first part of the seventeenth century the upper cap and the skull-cap were joined to form one article.[3] As early as 1600 a board was introduced to prevent the side-pieces falling over the face, so long had they become.[4] A tump appears on top of the cap by the beginning of Charles II's reign. It is very large in Samuel Cooper's miniature (about 1663) of Gilbert Sheldon, Archbishop of Canterbury in the collection of the Duke of Portland. The square top was still wide in 1663, according to the engraving of Bishop Sanderson of this date,[5] but by 1674, the year of G. Edwards's costume plates of Oxford, it had become much smaller.[6]

In the Laudian statutes of 1636 we find that the scarlet Convocation habit might either be entirely closed, or have an opening down the front which was buttoned up after it had been put on. This latter form had been introduced in the early seventeenth century in order to facilitate the drawing on of it.[7]

---

[1] E. C. Clarke, art. cit. lxi. 36.

[2] J. Launoy, *De vera causa de secessu Brunonis*, p. 121; N. F. Robinson, art. 'The *Pileus Quadratus*' in *Transactions of St. Paul's Ecclesiological Society*, v, pt. I (1901), p. 2.

[3] E. C. Clarke, art. cit. lxi. 36, 38, and 42. See for a good example of this the portrait of James Warner, Bishop of Rochester, painted in 1637, at Magdalen (Mrs. R. L. Poole, op. cit. ii, pl. xxvii, no. 1, opp. p. 210).

[4] H. Norris, *Costume and Fashion*, iii, bk. II, p. 733. For heraldic representations of the square cap in England see W. Berry, *Encyclopaedia Heraldica*, iii, pl. xxix, no. 32.

[5] Oxf. Bodl. Libr. MS. Top. Oxon. c. 16, § 74.

[6] Oxf. Bodl. Libr. MS. Wood 276B, xix, 7 (*Artium Baccalaureus*).

[7] G. R. M. Ward, i. 153, n.

In the eighteenth century only this form was used, according to all the illustrations. It was laid down by Laud that the hood of a Doctor of Divinity was to be scarlet lined with black silk, and the 'habit' is to be 'turned up' (that is, faced) with it. A square cap was to be used.[1] The three costumes of this degree are shown in Loggan's plate of 1675, Nos. 26, 27, 28. The dress in each case is very full and cumbrous, the heavy dress of a slow-moving age, and the plane of the square board of the cap is tilted forward very much. In 1679 the inventory of Michael Roberts, D.D., gives the value of 'two habits (i.e. Convocation habits), two hoods, and a gown scarlet' (i.e. festal robe) as £5 the lot.[2]

To the original tump on the square cap a tassel was unofficially added during the 1730's.[3] It was given official approval in the statutes of 1770.[4]

In the statutes of the university published in 1770 Doctors of Divinity were ordered to wear, in common with other doctors, their Convocation dress on all Sundays within term, at St. Mary's in the morning, and in Lent and on Easter Sunday in the afternoon at St. Peter's-in-the-East:[5] a modification of the times and places at which this dress was to be worn from those mentioned in the Laudian statutes.[6] C. Grignion's engravings of 1770 (Pl. 11 A) which were made after drawings of academical dress by two amateur artists, Huddesford, Keeper of the Ashmolean, and Taylor for the registry to be kept there for reference, show the three Doctor of Divinity dresses as being somewhat less full than the Loggan plates.[7] It is worth noticing that the square board of the cap is larger than in Loggan, but it is still inclined forward.

In James Roberts's water-colours of 1792, the Doctor of Divinity in full dress[8] wears bands, carries his black square tasselled cap, and wears a broad black scarf as long as his dress. His scarlet robe with black velvet bell sleeves is as now, but it is

---

[1] G. R. M. Ward, i. 70–71 (*Laudian Statutes*, cap. 5).
[2] Oxf. Univ. Archives, Hypomnemata Antiquaria, B. 18—Inventories R–S, s.v. Roberts.
[3] A. D. Godley, *Oxford in the Eighteenth Century*, p. 167.
[4] G. R. M. Ward, ii, 9–10.
[5] G. R. M. Ward, ii. 11.
[6] Cf. G. R. M. Ward, i. 153.
[7] Oxf. Bodl. Libr. MS. Top. Oxon. c. 16. 19, 20, 21.
[8] 11–12.

noticeable that his broad black cincture is drawn over the scarlet robe and holds it closed. The Convocation dress consists of bands, a square cap, a long broad scarf, a full scarlet hood lined with black fastencd high in front, and the scarlet habit which is so long that it sweeps the ground, so that all that can be seen of the master's gown is the gloved and key-shaped ended sleeves appearing on each side. As can be seen from a plate of the Doctor of Divinity in chapel dress (that is surplice and hood) from the back view, the shape of the hood is very full and rounded with a square liripipe (Frontispiece). The ordinary dress was cap, hood, and master's gown, with cassock, cincture, and scarf.[1]

The scarf associated academically with Oxford and Cambridge Doctors of Divinity[2] does not appear to have any connexion with the stole ($\sigma\tauo\lambda\acute{\eta}$; *orarium*), though they (and particularly the black stole when compared to the scarf) superficially appear to be like one another. The origin of the scarf is to be found in the long piece of stuff to which the roundlet was attached, and which was later detached and hung round the neck, being held in place by means of a loop on the back of the collar of the gown. The stole was a vestment, the scarf simply a symbol of dignity and learning. This can be the more readily realized if it is remembered that until about the middle of the nineteenth century the mayor of Christchurch, Hants, wore a broad scarlet silk scarf with a narrow border of black velvet over his gown to distinguish him from the councillors.[3] In 1522 in Bishop Smyth's statutes for Brasenose it is called a 'tippet',[4] which implies that it was not regarded as anything particularly ecclesiastical.[5]

A good example of the scarf worn with his black gown by a Doctor of Divinity is the engraving of John Wythines on his brass (1615) at Battle, Sussex. In the *Spectator*[6] is a satirical

---

[1] Oxf. Bodl. Libr. MS. Top. Oxon. d. 58, 14–15; 17–18.

[2] M. E. C. Walcott, *Constitutions and Canons*, p. 82, n.

[3] H. Druitt, *Manual of Costume*, p. 109, n. 2.

[4] *Brasenose College Quatercentenary Monographs* (O.H.S.), ii, pt. 1, Monograph IX, p. 36.

[5] It certainly was not a debased form of amess, for the use of the amess was forbidden in 1559, and the scarf survived, being used by royal and collegiate chaplains as well as by Doctors of Divinity.

[6] No. 609, 20 Oct. 1714.

account written in 1714 of the wearing of the scarf by young clergymen who wanted to pass for Doctors of Divinity.

(e) Doctors of Canon Law

The full dress of the degree of Doctor of Canon Law was also the *cappa clausa*.[1] According to an enactment of before 1350, at lectures they might use a *pallium* instead of a *cappa clausa*, both of which were to be black, and they might have them furred with lamb's-wool, but never with miniver. They were never to use a *cappa manicata*.[2] Their head-dress in the fourteenth century was for all solemn occasions the *pileus rotundus*.[3]

A large hood furred or lined 'extending beyond the points of the shoulders' was allowed to them in the sumptuary laws of Henry IV (1403) in common with Masters of Theology and other regents, the lord chancellor, and high law officers.[4] An example of the *cappa clausa* with one slit worn by a fifteenth-century Doctor of Canon Law appears in a brass of William Hautryve (1441) in the chapel of New College, Oxford.[5]

In Chaundler's New College drawing of about 1463 (Pl. 7) the Masters of Theology and Doctors of Canon Law to the immediate right and left of the warden, two on each side, all wear the same dress, which consists of *cappa clausa* with one slit, 'shoulder piece', and *pileus*.[6]

Indeed, the dress of this degree had the same character as and followed the same development as that of the degree of Master of Theology. It did not survive the Reformation.

(f) Doctors of Civil Law

According to an illumination in the Holkham Bible (*c.* 1330), the head-dress of a Doctor of Civil Law was a red *pileus rotundus* with a blue button on top.[7] In one of the earliest clauses in the Oxford statutes concerning a distinctly academical dress (prior to 1350) doctors of this degree were ordered to wear a *pileus*.[8]

---

[1] E. C. Clarke, art. cit. I. 205; F. E. Brightman, Preface, p. v.
[2] S. Gibson, pp. 51–52 and 56–57.
[3] S. Gibson, p. 37.
[4] J. Strutt, *Dresses and Habits*, ii. 224.
[5] H. Druitt, pl. opp. p. 129.
[6] M. R. James, *The Chaundler Manuscripts*, pp. 21–22 and pls.
[7] W. O. Hassall, *The Holkham Bible Picture Book*, p. 106, pl. of fo. 19.
[8] S. Gibson, p. 37.

At the same time they were told to use a *cappa manicata*, a long garment closed in front but having long sleeves, through which the arms passed. The sleeved tabard, a garment with shorter sleeves, was soon allowed to them as a more convenient alternative.[1] Under this, as is the case with all other degrees, were worn an ordinary loose over-tunic, the *supertunica* (*roba*), and under that the *subtunica* (cassock).[2]

A fine example of the dress of a Doctor of Civil Law of about 1408 is to be seen in a miniature in a manuscript, *De Regimine Principum*,[3] in which a doctor of this degree among the courtiers of Henry IV wears a long red trailing *cappa clausa* with two side slits, a mid-blue 'shoulder piece' lined with white fur, a pointed *pileus*, and white gloves. During the fifteenth century the use of the *cappa manicata* for this degree was still maintained on occasion. It was sometimes red and sometimes blue, as in the fifth window of the main lights in Clavering Church, Essex;[4] but they wear the *cappa* with two slits in the Chaundler drawing of about 1463 (Pl. 7). They stand with the Doctors of Medicine behind the clerical doctors.[5]

The *cappa clausa* with two slits appears in a particular character in the brass of John Lowthe, a Doctor of Civil Law (d. 1427), at New College, for attached to the back of the dress on each shoulder are two hollow pendants or liripipes, the open ends being dressed with fur, and as long as the main costume. These liripipes were merely an extravagance and do not seem to have had any significance.[6] They were looked upon critically by the authorities, and in the visitation of Magdalen College by Bishop Foxe's commissary in 1507 the wearing of liripipes beyond the precincts of the college was deemed unsuitable.[7] No more is heard of this fashion. By 1529, the date of the brass of Bryan Roos, D.C.L., in Childrey Church, Berks., the *supertunica*, the outer garment when the *cappa* was not used, has become a true gown, a full-sleeved *roba*.[8]

---

[1] E. C. Clarke, art. cit. l. 139 and 206; F. E. Brightman, Preface, p. vi.
[2] F. E. Brightman, Preface, p. v.
[3] Oxf. Bodl. Libr. MS. Digby 233, fo. 1.
[4] F. C. Eeles, art. cit., p. 83 and fig. 1, opp. p. 77.
[5] M. R. James, loc. cit.
[6] H. Druitt, pp. 131-2. There was also a temporary fashion for liripipes at Cambridge. See also E. C. Clarke, art. cit. l. 188.
[7] W. M. Macray, *Register of the Members of Magdalen College, Oxford*, n.s.i, §§ 44-45, p. 55.   [8] E. C. Clarke, art. cit. l. 101.

Hoods, which were worn in conjunction with the 'shoulder piece', might be lined with rich fur or silk according to the enactment of Congregation of 1432,[1] and it is doubtless one of these silk hoods which an Oxford Doctor of Civil Law, William Poteman, Archdeacon of the East Riding (d. 1493), leaves in his will, describing it as a 'doubled' (i.e. doubled back to show the lining) silk hood, to Robert Both, late Dean of York.[2]

The changes in the dress for this degree at the end of the Middle Ages followed the same development as that of Masters of Theology in that in this case the *cappa manicata* being entirely left off, a modified form of the *cappa* with two slits became the outward garment for solemn occasions. The *roba* was used alone for informal ones, while the full-dress robe for the most outstanding ones made its appearance about the middle of the sixteenth century.

In the sixteenth century Doctors of Civil Law and other secular doctors began to wear two articles of dress directly derived from lay fashion. The first was the round velvet bonnet, the head-dress of dignity of the time of Henry VIII, which Doctors of Civil Law, Medicine, and Music wore with festal dress, although for undress they followed the Elizabethan statutes in wearing the *pileus quadratus*.[3]

The second was a black gown with a flap collar and winged sleeves, such as was worn by wealthy citizens, often decorated on the sleeves and the skirt with straight lines of black braid with usually three buttons to a line.[4] Such a gown came at this period to be used for undress by all graduates except those of the Faculties of Divinity and Arts. A good example of the winged-sleeved gown worn by a Doctor of Civil Law is to be found in the brass of Hugh Lloyd (1601) at New College.[5] In another brass (1605) also at New College, that of Hugh Barker, D.C.L., is to be found the first example of black tassels added to the buttons in the rows of braid,[6] but long after that there is proof that this winged-sleeved, flap-collared gown was worn

---

[1] S. Gibson, pp. 239–40.

[2] *Testamenta Eboracensia*, iv (Surtees Soc. liii (1868), 82).

[3] S. Gibson, pp. 525 and 540.

[4] See the full-length effigy of Sir Eubule Thelwall (1630) in Jesus College Chapel, Oxford, where it is worn not as the gown of a degree, but as a dress of dignity.

[5] H. Druitt, p. 132.

[6] Mrs. R. L. Poole, i (New Coll., no. 29).

absolutely plain by some Doctors of Civil Law, as in the case of John Favour (d. 1623) whose monumental effigy is in Halifax parish church, Yorks.[1]

In Loggan's plate of 1675 the three forms of dress are given. No. 25 is the festal dress described in 1663 on Charles II's visit to Oxford as a wide-sleeved scarlet cloth 'gown' faced with scarlet taffeta,[2] but without the taffeta on the sleeves, which are hitched up with a cord and buttons; No. 24, the Convocation dress, perhaps better illustrated in Edwards, consists of hood, 'habit', and black winged-sleeved gown; No. 23, the undress, consisted of the black gown. In these plates the round bonnet is worn only with festal dress, but in Robert Sayer's *Oxonia Illustrata* (1700), a reissue of Loggan brought up to date as to contemporary fashion, but very inferior in quality and accuracy it is worn with the undress.[3]

The undress gown as it appeared in 1710 is clearly seen in the portrait in Bodley's Library of Edmund Halley, D.C.L., the astronomer.[4] It is of black silk and decorated on sleeves and skirt with cord-braid and black tufts. Another painting in oil, in the Bodleian Law Library, second room, provides an excellent example of the festal robe in the first half of the eighteenth century. In his portrait Richard Rawlinson, D.C.L. (d. 1755), wears a scarlet cloth robe with salmon-coloured silk on the facings in front and half-way up the bell-sleeves, which are no longer held up by means of a cord because they have been reduced in size. Laud had in 1636 ordered that the silk used on the facings and hoods of Doctors of Civil Law and Doctors of Medicine should be of a colour 'intermediate' to scarlet. Hence the subsequent use of salmon-pink as the colour of these faculties.[5]

In Grignion's plates of 1770 the festal dress is shown. The bonnet is small and toque-like, while the robe has a narrow cord just below the throat, probably to keep the dress steady and the garment from riding up.[6] Among the water-colours of Roberts (1792) the full dress appears again (Frontispiece), consisting of

---

[1] J. Horsfall Turner, *Coats of Arms of Yorkshire*, i. 161.
[2] A. Clark, *Wood*, i. 494.
[3] Oxf. Bodl. Libr. MS. Top. Oxon. a. 36, fos. 77–78.
[4] Mrs. R. L. Poole, i, pl. xvi, no. 3, opp. p. 101.
[5] G. R. M. Ward, i. 70–71, cap. 5.
[6] Oxf. Bodl. Libr. MS. Top. Oxon. c. 16. 18.

PLATE 9

Stained glass window of an Oxford Doctor of Medicine, 1440

the small black velvet toque-bonnet, and the scarlet bell-sleeved robe, the lower part of the sleeves faced with salmon-pink silk[1] (Frontispiece). The other dresses are not given, but Thomas Uwins (1815) gives the three kinds of costume which show what they must have been like in the later eighteenth century. First, there is the festal dress consisting of a scarlet cloth robe, with sleeves and facings of pink silk, and a round black velvet bonnet; secondly, the convocation dress, which consists of the 'habit' and the hood of scarlet cloth, the habit with an opening down the front and faced with pink silk, the scarlet cloth hood being lined with pink silk, and the black gown, whose sleeves appear through the openings of the 'habit'; and the black silk gimp gown.[2] It is to be noticed that gimp has taken the place of tufts, and that the round velvet bonnet is worn instead of the square cap with the Convocation dress.

(g) Doctors of Medicine

In common with other doctors, Doctors of Medicine, had as head-dress before 1350 the *pileus rotundus*.[3] They originally wore the *cappa manicata*, but soon wore in its place except on the most formal occasions a *cappa clausa* with two slits. For undress they wore a sleeveless tabard like a *pallium*,[4] which later became shorter, with or without sleeves.[5] In 1432, again in common with other doctors, they were allowed to use silk in their hoods in summer.[6] In the Chaundler drawing of about 1463 (Pl. 7), they wear, as do the Doctors of Civil Law, who appear with them behind the Masters of Theology and Doctors of Canon Law, a *cappa clausa* with two slits, 'shoulder piece', hood, and *pileus*,[7] but in a stained glass window of about 1440 in Minster Lovell Church, Oxon., a Doctor of Medicine, holding the symbols of his profession, a bottle and staff, wears a crimson *cappa manicata* lined with miniver, and a black *pileus* (Pl. 9).

The *Act for the Reformation of Excess in Apparel* of 1533 allowed them, as other doctors, the use at all times of 'sarcenet' (silk) in the lining of their gowns, as well as satin or velvet for facings, and they were privileged enough to be able to use such colours

---

[1] Oxf. Bodl. Libr. MS. Top. Oxon. d. 58, 20–21.
[2] W. Combe and T. Uwins, ii. 16 and plates.
[3] S. Gibson, p. 37.
[4] F. E. Brightman, Preface, p. vi.   [5] E. C. Clarke, art. cit. l. 206.
[6] S. Gibson, pp. 239–40.   [7] Cf. M. R. James, pp. 21–22.

as scarlet, murrey, and violet,[1] proof that even yet uniformity of colour in academical dress was not assured.

There are only three undoubted examples in brasses of Doctors of Medicine wearing academical dress, and these are all Post-Reformation. They are those of Walter Bailey (1592) at New College, Richard Radcliff (1599) at St. Peter's-in-the-East, Oxford, and Anthony Aylworth (1619) at New College.[2] All wear the undress false-sleeved gown, and Aylworth also wears a hood, deep and V-shaped in front.

A fine water-colour copy, in the possession of the Royal College of Physicians, of the oil portrait formerly in the hall of the Barbers' Company, shows Sir Charles Scarburgh (1616–94), who attended Charles II in his last illness, giving an anatomy lecture. The picture was executed in 1651. Scarburgh wears a Doctor of Medicine's Convocation dress, consisting of a very high bonnet, a very large white fur hood with only a thin line of pink silk showing, a scarlet 'habit', closed in front except for a little furred slit on the chest, and a black winged sleeved gown under it.[3] The height of their bonnets seems to have been a particular feature of their dress until the end of the seventeenth century, and it appears in the portrait of Richard Hale, D.M. (1670–1728), worn with the festal robe.[4] Otherwise the dress is the same as that of Doctors of Civil Law.[5]

In the diary of Dr. Claver Morris, he mentions that in 1691, on taking this degree, he paid £2. 13s. for having velvet and tufts added to his Bachelor of Medicine gown,[6] which means that the doctor's undress gown differed from it in having extra decoration.[7]

In R. Sayer's plates (1700),[8] in those of Grignion (1770)[9]

---

[1] *Statutes of the Realm*, iii. 430–2: 24° Hen. VIII, c. 13.

[2] H. Druitt, p. 133.

[3] The picture is reproduced in R. Crawfurd, *The Last Days of Charles II*, opp. p. 52.

[4] Mrs. R. L. Poole, i, opp. p. 96, pl. xiv, no. 1 (Bodleian, no. 229).

[5] See Loggan's plate (1675). The only difference between the dress of the two degrees is that in No. 23 the Doctor of Medicine wears the round bonnet with the undress gown instead of the square cap.

[6] E. Hobhouse (ed.), *Diary of a West Country Physician*, p. 148.

[7] Cf. a plate by Edwards (1674) in Oxf. Bodl. Libr. MS. Wood 276B, xix, 4. This is still the case today, for the undress gowns of doctors of all 'lay' faculties have an extra decoration of gimp under the arms. Those of bachelors of the 'lay' faculties do not have this.   [8] Oxf. Bodl. Libr. MS. Top. Oxon. a. 36.

[9] Oxf. Bodl. Libr. MS. Top. Oxon. c. 16, 17.

(Pl. 11 B), and in the water-colours of 1792[1] the festal dress of Doctors of Medicine is exactly the same as that of Doctors of Civil Law, as were their other dresses.[2]

(h) Doctors of Music

This degree until recent times has had a surreptitious existence. It appeared at the beginning of the sixteenth century, but was never considered of much importance and was granted after the manner of a diploma to proficient musicians. At Oxford no actual regulations as to the dress of the musical degrees were ever formulated, but it seems probable that originally, as was the case at Cambridge,[3] Doctors of Music made use of the dress of those of Medicine,[4] on the rare occasions when they did appear at academical functions, as can be seen from the fact that until the nineteenth century Bachelors of Music wore blue hoods like those of Bachelors of Civil Law and Medicine.

There are no brasses or other illustrations to aid us in the earlier period, but it seems likely that the elaborate dress of Doctors of Music was adopted in late Elizabethan or early Jacobean times, at any rate before the statutes of 1636 when Laud ordered inceptors in Music at the Vesperies and Act to wear sleeved gowns with 'white wavy damask capes' and round black caps, all of silk,[5] which shows that they were to wear a hood with the festal robe.

The development of the dress was the same as that of other secular doctors, and thus by the beginning of the seventeenth century Doctors of Music wore the black tufted winged sleeved gown and the square cap for undress, and the round velvet bonnet with their full dress. Their position in the academical hierarchy was uncertain, for the degree did not carry with it membership of Convocation, since it was open to all who had passed Responsions. In fact doctors of this degree were generally regarded as infrequent visitors to functions such as Encaenia, loosely attached to the university.

---

[1] Oxf. Bodl. Libr. MS. Top. Oxon. d. 58, 23–24.
[2] W. Combe and T. Uwins, ii. 16.
[3] Cambridge Grace Books, Δ, p. 28.
[4] C. A. H. Franklyn, art. 'Dress of the Clergy' in Parson and Parish, no. 16, p. 33.
[5] G. R. M. Ward, i. 70–71, cap. 5.

They naturally had no Convocation 'habit',[1] but until recently, as Laud had ordered, wore their hood with their festal dress. Their position in the seventeenth century was so far depressed that they had no place in the procession in honour of Charles II's visit to Oxford in 1663.[2]

John Evelyn in his diary describes the Encaenia of 10 July 1669 at which the Professor of Mathematics introduced a Doctor of Music who was received with the ceremony of cap, ring, and kiss. The robe of the new doctor, he noticed, was of white damask,[3] that is, with no cherry silk on the sleeves, and its shape was the same as that of the festal robes of other doctors as is to be seen in the costume plate of Loggan (1675) where the Doctor of Music (No. 12) wears hood, festal robe, and round bonnet.

The shape of the hood changed during the seventeenth century, for in a print of him Orlando Gibbons (D.Mus. 1623) wears his tucked down in front and fastened underneath his closed robe, but William Child (D.Mus. 1663) wears his hood squarely and not tucked into the robe as in the former example. The hood had again been altered in shape by the early eighteenth century, for William Croft (D.Mus. 1713) wears in his print of that year a smaller one than Gibbons and Child, which unlike theirs is high at the throat and not square on the shoulders.[4]

In Grignion's plates of 1770 the festal dress consists of a small round bonnet, the festal robe, and a very large hood with a square-shaped liripipe;[5] while in 1792 (Frontispiece) it comprises a white damasked robe lined with cherry-red silk, with white damask bell-sleeves, over that a full hood of white damask silk lined with cherry-red silk, the hood having a long square liripipe, and a small black velvet bonnet.[6] Other good examples are Sir Joshua Reynolds's portrait of Charles Burney (D.Mus. 1769) in Bartolozzi's engraving, and J. Russell's portrait of

[1] L. H. D. Buxton and S. Gibson, p. 39.
[2] A. Clark, *Wood*, i. 494. As late as 1857 they were not allowed at Encaenia to sit with the other doctors and, worse still, could not even sit with members of Convocation (*Notes and Queries*, 2nd ser. iii. 115–17, 275–7).
[3] *Diary of John Evelyn*, ed. E. S. de Beer, iii. 533; J. E. Sandys, art. cit., p. 232.
[4] Oxf. Bodl. Libr. MS. Top. Oxon. c. 16, §§ 98, 99 and 101.
[5] Oxf. Bodl. Libr. MS. Top. Oxon. c. 16, 10.
[6] Oxf. Bodl. Libr. MS. Top. Oxon. d. 58, 26–27.

T. S. Dupuis (D.Mus. 1790). Cherry-coloured facings and sleeves are not found until the 1815 plates of T. Uwins.[1]

(i) Masters of Surgery

The degree of Master of Surgery, formerly very rare, was until recent times considered as invariably associated with the degree of Doctor of Medicine, so that it was never mentioned on its own account, and is never considered in statutes, nor does it appear in costume plates.[2]

(j) Masters of Arts

In the fourteenth century the *pileus* was forbidden to Masters of Arts,[3] and it was found necessary as early as before 1350 to prevent them from assuming other articles of dress proper to doctors.[4] It was not until 1529 that we hear of a *pileus* being allowed to a candidate supplicating for this degree,[5] but they had a kind of knitted skull-cap as a protection against cold by the middle of the fifteenth century, for a *caleptra* (hure; coif) is mentioned in the will of John Shyrburn, M.A., fellow of Lincoln College, in 1452.[6] Their other dress consisted of what was originally the *cappa manicata*, but they soon gave this up as inconvenient, and took to a variety of *cappa clausa*, a shorter dress closed in front with side slits and without sleeves, the sleeves of the *supertunica*, later to become the *roba* or *toga*, passing through the arm-holes. This was their dress of dignity, and was ordered as late as 1480–8 to be worn in Congregation by regent masters in statutes in which it is referred to as the *cappa nigra*.[7] The earliest example of this costume on brasses appears in that

---

[1] W. Combe and T. Uwins, loc. cit.

[2] Masters of Surgery once claimed, at the period during the nineteenth century when the degree became a separate entity, to wear the scarlet dress of Doctors of Medicine, but it was considered that if they did not hold the doctor's degree they had no right to it. They came to have as their dress in the nineteenth century the black silk laced gown, and wore a plain blue hood of the same shape as that of Masters of Arts. From the fact that the hood was of navy blue it can be seen that it was derived from the old Civil Law faculty colour of blue, which in the fifteenth century Bachelors of Medicine assumed in common with Bachelors of Law as the colour of their hood (L. H. D. Buxton and S. Gibson, pp. 38–39).

[3] E. C. Clarke, art. cit. lxi. 33.

[4] S. Gibson, pp. 28 and 40.

[5] E. C. Clarke, art. cit. l. 148.

[6] H. E. Salter, *Registrum Cancellarii* (O.H.S.), i. 293.

[7] S. Gibson, p. 292.

of John Kyllingworth (1445) at Merton College, Oxford.[1] With this was worn a *subtunica* (cassock), a 'shoulder piece' edged with fur only at the lower edge, and a hood.[2]

During the mid-fifteenth century the *cappa clausa* with two slits was worn less and less by masters except on the most formal occasions, and otherwise the *roba* was used alone. This can be well seen in the Chaundler manuscript (Pl. 7) in which the Masters of Arts stand facing the warden with their backs to the onlooker. The sleeved *robas* which they wear reach to their feet and have short bell sleeves which come only to the elbow. With this dress is worn a 'shoulder piece' and a hood with a long, square-ended liripipe, and they still have no head-dress;[3] but in the brass of Walter Wake, M.A. (1451), in New College Chapel, Oxford, the bell sleeves are much fuller and the 'shoulder piece' is completely lined with fur.[4]

It was from the *roba* which was increasingly worn as the outer garment that the Master of Arts gown of later times developed, gaining towards the end of the sixteenth century its rudimentary glove or bag sleeves, at first very short and which hung down below the elbow. As late, however, as 1636, according to the Laudian statutes, the old full-sleeved gown was still to be worn by all inceptors in Arts,[5] as is to be seen in the fine oil-painting attributed to J. de Critz, of the poet Richard Lovelace at Worcester College, Oxford. Lovelace was created M.A. in 1636. At the time of Charles I's visit to Oxford in the same year all masters were ordered to wear this type of gown,[6] and probably the Lovelace portrait was painted on this occasion. With this gown he wears a fairly soft square cap with a tump. Good examples of the glove-sleeved gown in the course of its earlier development in which the sleeves reach only half-way down the length of the dress are to be found in the monumental effigy of an unknown clergyman (1615) at Steeple Langford, Wilts., and in another to another unknown clergyman (about 1630)

[1] E. C. Clarke, art. cit. l. 199.
[2] H. Druitt, p. 135.
[3] M. R. James, loc. cit.
[4] M. Stephenson, *List of Monumental Brasses*, p. 414 (New Coll. ix).
[5] G. R. M. Ward, i. 70–71, caps. 4–5.
[6] Oxf. Bodl. Libr. MS. Twyne 17, fo. 187. Not only, according to the Laudian Codex, was the wide-sleeved Master of Arts gown to be worn on formal occasions, but also during the year of 'necessary regency', that is the academical year after taking the degree.

PLATE 10

a. An Oxford Master of Arts

b. An Oxford Bachelor of Arts

c. An Oxford Commoner

d. An Oxford Servitor, 1695

a–c from G. Edwards, *Omnium Ordinum Habitumque Academicorum Exemplaria*, 1674

at Bishopstone near Salisbury. In both cases the gown is peaked at the shoulders, a passing fashion.[1]

Square caps without any stiffening in them so that the corners flagged had made their appearance some years before the Reformation.[2] Masters took to them, and in 1565 the use by them of the *pileus quadratus* was given official sanction.[3]

They had been allowed silk in their hoods in 1432 in common with doctors.[4] By 1592 they had come to be worn with the lining displayed[5] and were generally preferred to the furred ones. On special occasions even as late as 1636 the old 'shoulder piece' as a kind of cape (*mantellum*) was still worn by all inceptors.[6] This did not survive the Civil War, and was after all a revival of an obsolete medieval dress which appealed to Laud; but miniver was still officially allowed in masters' hoods as late as the statutes of 1770.[7] Hoods during the early seventeenth century were very broad in front as is to be seen in the monumental effigy in St. John's College Chapel, Oxford, to Ralph Huchenson (1606).

By 1674 the sleeves of the gown had reached the length of the hem and had a key-shaped ending which was copied from the similarly shaped liripipe of the hood (Pl. 10a).[8] The gown, which in 1701 cost £4,[9] was very full and long, and the hood large but not as full and rounded as those of doctors. As can be seen in figure No. 14 of Loggan's costume plate it was worn in such a way that only the crimson lining showed. In the plates of both Edwards and Loggan the square cap has a large tump, and the plane of the square board is inclined very much forward. It remained so inclined until the last quarter of the eighteenth century.

In the oil-painting by Hogarth, *The Western Family* (about 1735), the clergyman wears a master's gown which is less full than shown in Loggan's plates and is the same as it is now,[10]

---

[1] K. A. Esdaile and S. Sitwell, *English Church Monuments*, pls. 57 and 59, opp. p. 61.

[2] J. Walker, i. 20.   [3] S. Gibson, p. 386.

[4] S. Gibson, pp. 239–40.

[5] A. Clark, *Register of the University of Oxford*, ii. 231.

[6] G. R. M. Ward, i. 70–71, cap. 4.

[7] G. R. M. Ward, ii. 11.

[8] Oxf. Bodl. Libr. MS. Wood 276B, xix, 8.

[9] Oxf. Bodl. Libr. MS. Rawl. Letts. 108, fo. 279.

[10] S. Sitwell, *Conversation Pieces*, pl. 14; R. B. Becket, *Hogarth*, pl. 94.

otherwise the dress continued the same throughout the earlier eighteenth century, except that a tassel was added to the tump on the cap unofficially in the 1730's.[1] The cassock had been left off under the gown by lay masters in the previous century.

The statutes of 1770 were generally a reiteration of the Laudian *Codex*,[2] but in the engravings which Grignion made (Pl. 11) in order to illustrate the academical dress mentioned in 1770[3] there is a notable change in the Master of Arts hood. It has become narrow and deep, as have those of all non-doctors except Bachelors of Divinity. In the Roberts water-colours of 1792 the crimson hood and the gown of the master are the same as before.[4] The neck-band of the hood was of the same colour as the lining of the hood of the various degrees, at any rate until 1815.[5]

(k) Bachelors of Divinity

In the fourteenth century Bachelors of Divinity had no head-dress.[6] The best early example of the dress is to be seen in the bracket brass in Merton College Chapel representing both John Bloxham and John Wytton. Bloxham is described as a Bachelor of Divinity who died in 1387, but the brass was not executed until 1420. He wears a *supertunica* and a *cappa clausa* with two side slits such as Masters of Arts at this time wore, a white fur hood, and a 'shoulder piece', and he is bare-headed.[7]

In 1426 Bachelors of Divinity in common with Bachelors of Canon Law were allowed hoods of black cloth furred inside with budge, or of black cloth lined with black silk,[8] an enactment which distinguishes between a summer and winter dress, and precedes by six years the comprehensive statute (1432) already referred to.[9]

[1] A. D. Godley, loc. cit.　　　　　　　　　　[2] G. R. M. Ward, pp. 9ff.
[3] Oxf. Bodl. Libr. MS. Top. Oxon. c. 16, 12, § 32.
[4] The change from the key-shaped end to the sleeves to the lunated end did not take place until after 1840, for in that year, according to N. Whittock's *Costumes of Oxford*, key-shaped ended sleeves were still worn.
[5] W. Combe and T. Uwins, loc. cit.
[6] E. C. Clarke, arts. cit. l. 147–8 and lxi. 33.
[7] Oxf. Bodl. Libr. MS. Top. Oxon. a. 36, fo. 13 (water-colour of 1792); M. Stephenson, p. 413 (Merton iii).
[8] W. A. Pantin, *English Black Monks*, ii (Camden Soc. xlvii (1933)), p. 177 (§ 172, 7).
[9] The summer variety of this hood is still worn by Bachelors of Divinity.

Collector

Doctor of Divinity in full dress

Doctor of Divinity in
Convocation dress

Doctor of Divinity in
undress

HUDDESFORD AND TAYLOR'S PLATES TO ILLUSTRATE
THE OXFORD STATUTES OF 1770

Doctor in Medicina.

Festal dress of Doctor of Medicine

Artium Magister.

Master of Arts

Baccalaureus in Theologia.

Bachelor of Divinity

Legum Baccalaureus caputio indutus.

Bachelor of Civil Law

According to the Chaundler drawing (Pl. 7) the Bachelors of Divinity behind the doctors to the warden's left wear the *cappa clausa* with two slits.[1]

By the early sixteenth century they, like the Masters of Arts, had left off the upper dress, so that the by now full-sleeved *supertunica* appeared as the outer garment (*roba*), as is to be seen in the brass of John Spence, B.D. (1517), at Ewelme, Oxon.[2] During this century they took to a head-dress which developed in the same way as those of Doctors of Divinity, Masters of Arts, and others, finally becoming the *pileus quadratus*, a head-gear regulated by Elizabethan enactments and confirmed as their official head-covering in 1617 and 1620.[3]

The 'shoulder piece', which had long been abandoned, appears again in the Laudian *Codex* (1636) in the form of a cape, to be worn on certain occasions,[4] but the 'civil hood' mentioned in the inventory of Edward Cooper, B.D. (1640) was an ordinary lay cape to put round the shoulders in cold weather and had nothing to do with an academical hood.[5]

The development in the latter sixteenth century and early seventeenth century of the Bachelor of Divinity's gown was similar to that of the Master of Arts, and in Loggan's costume plate (figure No. 19) the two are exactly the same. With this is worn a full black hood and a square cap with a tump.

During the eighteenth century, when the hoods of all other non-doctors became narrower and deeper, that of the Bachelor of Divinity preserved the full shape. In Grignion's plates (1770) (Pl. 11 B) the dress of the Bachelor of Divinity consists of a square black tasselled cap, a gown exactly the same as that of masters, and a cassock with a sash.[6] The hood is not shown in this example, but in the water-colour by Roberts of 1792 the very large hood is made entirely of black silk, there being no difference in material between the outside and the lining,[7] but this is an eighteenth-century innovation.

[1] Cf. M. R. James, loc. cit.; E. C. Clarke, art. cit. l. 101, 202, and 207–8; E. T. Beaumont, *Academical Habit*, p. 27.

[2] H. Druitt, p. 135.

[3] S. Gibson, pp. 525 and 540.

[4] G. R. M. Ward, i. 70–71, cap. 4.

[5] Oxf. Univ. Archives, Hypomnemata Antiquaria, B. 11–Inventories BR–C, s.v. Cooper (Cole misunderstood this and suggested 'sable' for 'civil').

[6] Oxf. Bodl. Libr. MS. Top. Oxon. c. 16, 16.

[7] Oxf. Bodl. Libr. MS. Top. Oxon. d. 58, 29–30.

(*l*) Bachelors of Canon Law

Bachelors of Canon Law originally had no head-dress.[1] At first they wore the sleeveless tabard (*pallium*) over a *supertunica*,[2] but by the middle of the fifteenth century they were wearing a sleeved tabard and a 'shoulder piece' with a 'roller' hood close to the neck, as can be seen in the Chaundler drawing.[3] In 1426, as has already been noticed, in common with Bachelors of Divinity they had been allowed hoods of black cloth lined with budge fur or black cloth lined with black silk.[4] In the Chaundler drawing (Pl. 7) the group of Bachelors of Canon Law stands among the Masters of Arts, but a little below them from the warden. None has any head-dress.[5]

By the end of this century at any rate, like those of other degrees Bachelors of Canon Law had taken to wearing the *roba* (*supertunica; toga*) alone as their outer dress, for in 1507 the *toga talaris* is mentioned as their costume on the occasion of their being allowed a *typet* or *cornetum* as an alternative.[6] This may mean a robe-like garment and not merely a liripipe, in fact a *roba* whose particular features were that it had liripipes attached to it, as is to be seen in the brass of John Lowthe, D.C.L. (d. 1427). If this is so then the tendency to adopt lay fashions in academical dress was officially recognized as early as this.

The last example of the dress of this degree, which certainly did not survive Mary Tudor, appears in the painted alabaster figure in St. Aldate's Church, Oxford, of John Noble, B.Can.L. (d. 1522), who was Principal of Broadgates Hall. He wears over a *roba*, a full 'shoulder piece' which covers the shoulders and arms as far as the elbows. The hood is detached from the 'shoulder piece' in a deep V-shape. Hood and 'shoulder piece' are red.[7]

(*m*) Bachelors of Civil Law

The outer dress of this degree was in the fifteenth century the sleeved tabard, as can be seen in the Chaundler drawing,[8] a

---

[1] E. C. Clarke, art. cit. l. 33.   [2] F. E. Brightman, Preface, p. vi.
[3] M. R. James, loc. cit.
[4] W. A. Pantin, *Black Monks*, loc. cit.
[5] M. R. James, loc. cit.; E. C. Clarke, art. cit. l. 207–8. See also the brass of Richard Wyard, B.Can.L., New Coll. Oxf. (1478) (M. Stephenson, p. 415 (New Coll. xiv)).
[6] G. Clinch, *English Costume*, pp. 250–2.
[7] T. and G. Hollis, *Monumental Effigies*, pl. St. Aldate's Ch. Oxf. effigy; Mrs. R. L. Poole, op. cit. iii (Pembroke, no. 1).   [8] M. R. James, loc. cit.

dress that they wore in common with bachelors of other faculties except Divinity, who wore the *cappa clausa* with two slits at this time. They also had a 'shoulder piece', a liripiped hood, and a *roba* (*supertunica*) which was worn underneath the tabard. The best examples of Bachelors of Civil Law on brasses are those of John Mottesfont (1420) at Lydd, Kent,[1] and David Lloyd (1510) in the chapel of All Souls College, Oxford.[2] The colour of the dress of this degree, as was the case with all medieval academical dress at an early period, greatly varied, and might be of such as russet, tawny, or blue, but the dress of bachelors was restricted as to the fur with which it was edged, for it might only be of cheap kinds or of wool.[3] In 1490 they and all other bachelors were ordered to have their hoods lined with fur throughout.[4] They had no head-dress in the Middle Ages, and like other bachelors they did not enjoy the privilege granted to doctors and masters in 1432 of wearing silk in their hoods,[5] except Bachelors of Divinity who had been allowed silk six years before. In 1533 by Act of Parliament all bachelors were allowed a choice of a variety of inferior furs.[6]

By the beginning of the sixteenth century Bachelors of Civil Law seem to have left off their tabard, and their *roba*, which had been worn underneath the tabard as a *supertunica*, became their outer garment, full sleeved, and so remained until in Elizabethan times it was replaced by the winged-sleeved lay gown. It was at this latter period also that they came to have an official head-dress, the square cap, which they wore in common with other graduates.

Their gown had reached its present shape in 1631, as the brass of Jeremy Keyt (1631) in Woodstock Church, Oxon., shows. There is a good illustration of it in Loggan's costume plate, No. 11. Here are to be seen the black tufts in rows joined together by pieces of braid, and these are laid on the upper part of the sleeves, and on the skirt of the gown in three places, that is the sides and the back. It was long after this date that gimp took the place of tufts and cord braiding. It was probably introduced from France, for gimp appears on ordinary dress

---

[1] H. Druitt, p. 139.   [2] M. Stephenson, p. 410.
[3] A. Clark, *Wood*, i. 69.   [4] S. Gibson, p. 297.
[5] S. Gibson, pp. 239–40.
[6] C. Wordsworth, *Social Life at the English Universities*, pp. 489–90.

in a French print of 1694 which depicts an interior with courtiers at Versailles. It is laid on the skirt of the coat of one of the men in three places, in shape square at three sides and with a pointed top,[1] exactly as later it was placed on the Oxford winged-sleeved gowns.

The tufts are still to be seen in Overton's print, *Habitus Academici in Universitate Oxoniensi*, of 1730,[2] but in Reynolds's portrait of Sir Robert Chambers (1765) the sleeves of the Bachelor of Civil Law gown are decorated with gimp in place of tufts and cord-braid.[3] It will be noticed that a closed seam runs through the middle of the upper part of the sleeve from elbow to shoulder, and that the gimp is laid close to this and not generally over the whole sleeve as was the case later. The gown is silk, which probably was less usual a century before.

In the Grignion plates of 1770 (Pl. 11 B) the Bachelor of Civil Law wears a square cap with a tassel, a long deep hood, a silk gown with the false sleeves key-shaped at the ends, with gimp of square pattern on the sleeves, in three places on the skirt, and on the flap collar.[4]

Roberts took the Grignion figures as a basis for his water-colours of 1792. In his water-colour of this degree the dress consists of a black and tasselled square cap, a long and deep lavender-blue hood with white fur along the top edge, and a black silk gown with winged sleeves, decorated with black gimp on the upper and the middle of the lower parts of the sleeves and in three places on the skirt. The design of the gimp on the skirt is square at three sides and pointed at the top, but on the lower part of the sleeves it is round. Gimp appears on the collar.[5]

(n) Bachelors of Medicine

Evidence for the dress of Bachelors of Medicine in the Middle Ages does not exist in any form. All that can be said is that in common with other bachelors they wore the sleeved tabard, the *roba*, the small close hood, and the 'shoulder piece', and had

---

[1] P. Lacroix, *XVIIe Siècle*, p. 208, fig. 70.

[2] Oxf. Bodl. Libr. G.A. Oxon., a. 72, leaf 3.

[3] R. Ingpen, *The Life of Samuel Johnson by James Boswell*, ii. 929.

[4] Oxf. Bodl. Libr. MS. Top. Oxon. c. 16, 11. These changes in the undress gown were the same for D.C.L., D.M., D.Mus., B.C.L., B.M., and B.Mus.

[5] Oxf. Bodl. Libr. MS. Top. Oxon. d. 58, 32–33.

no head-dress.[1] All subsequent enactments which involved the dress of bachelors collectively naturally applied equally to them.

In the seventeenth century their dress was exactly the same as that of Bachelors of Civil Law as Loggan's engravings show. In fact, not until 1815 was there any difference in the dress of the two degrees, in which year Bachelors of Medicine are said to have a hood, not of 'dark blue' lined with fur like that of Bachelors of Civil Law, but one of lilac silk lined with fur.[2]

(o) Bachelors of Music

The degree of Bachelor of Music was the lowliest in the university, for whereas Bachelors of Arts might be considered as potential members of Convocation, Bachelors of Music who held no Arts degree would never be. The degree is first mentioned in 1502.[3]

There were no actual regulations for the dress of this degree, but the dress of Bachelors of Civil Law and Medicine seems to have been adopted for it during the seventeenth century. The gown of Bachelors of Music was, however, never as richly decorated as those of the two above-mentioned bachelors, though of the same winged-sleeved, flap-collared shape; and thus in Loggan's costume plate (No. 7) it has no tufts, but only rows of cord-braiding with three buttons to a row. A square cap with a tump was worn in the seventeenth century. Their hood was less full than those of other degrees.

In the plate of the Bachelor of Music by Grignion (1770) (Pl. 11 c) a black silk gown is worn with gimp of a rounded pattern on the collar, on the upper half of the winged sleeves, and at the sides and in the middle of the skirt. The whole decoration is much lighter than that found on the Bachelor of Civil Law and Bachelor of Medicine gowns.[4] This lightness of decoration can again be noticed in Roberts's water-colours of 1792. The hood, which is long and deep, is of powdered blue silk and edged at the top with white fur.[5] There has always been

---

[1] E. T. Beaumont, *Academical Habit*, p. 27.
[2] W. Combe and T. Uwins, loc. cit.
[3] C. F. Abdy Williams, *Historical Account of Degrees in Music*, p. 154.
[4] Oxf. Bodl. Libr. MS. Top. Oxon. c. 16, 6.
[5] Oxf. Bodl. Libr. MS. Top. Oxon. d. 58, 35–36.

confusion about this hood's colour, resulting from the lack of legislation about it.[1]

(p) Bachelors of Arts

At a date prior to 1350 Bachelors of Arts were refused any form of head-dress, and in another university statute of about 1425 there is mention of their being refused the use of a *birretum* or even a skull-cap (*tena*).[2] In 1379 their accepted outer dress was a sleeveless tabard, according to a reference in the statutes of New College,[3] but later they wore sleeved tabards lined with fur, the sleeves at first reaching only to the elbow and later to a point behind, over a full, but tight-sleeved *roba* (*supertunica*), together with a close hood and a 'shoulder piece'. Such is the dress worn by Geoffrey Hargreve, B.A., 1447, at New College.[4] Later the sleeves began to grow pointed,[5] and by about 1463, the date of the Chaundler drawing (Pl. 7), the sleeves had become fuller still, as can be seen from studying the young-looking group of Bachelors of Arts who are standing in the middle.[6] A good example of the dress in its final stage, consisting of the tabard with full and pointed sleeves, with tight sleeved *roba* and hood and 'shoulder piece', is to be found in the brass of John Palmer (1479) at New College.[7] This tabard, which is shorter than the *roba*, is lined with fur, and its sleeves reach to the wrist in front and fall far behind to a point.[8]

By the beginning of the sixteenth century, as is the case with all other outer academical dress, the tabard was generally laid aside and the *roba*, now opened down the front, became the outer garment. It has been suggested[9] that the tabard and *roba* (or *toga*) were fused into one dress during the fifteenth century, but it seems more likely that when the tabard was left off, the *roba*'s sleeves from being tight to the hand under the sleeved

[1] The violet colour used in recent times (L. H. D. Buxton and S. Gibson, p. 40) seems to be an uncertain compromise, no doubt reminiscent of the cherry of the Doctor of Music.
[2] S. Gibson, pp. 229-30.
[3] *Statutes of the Colleges of Oxford for the Royal Commission*, i. 45–46 (R. 23).
[4] J. G. and L. A. B. Waller, *Monumental Brasses*, no. 44.
[5] F. E. Brightman, Preface, loc. cit.
[6] M. R. James, loc. cit.
[7] H. Druitt, p. 141; E. T. Beaumont, *Academical Habit*, p. 29.
[8] H. Haines, p. lxxxiv.
[9] G. Clinch, pp. 250–1 and 253.

tabard, now became large and hanging. This process of development seems the more likely when it is considered that about 1510 the sleeves of surplices had become wide-sleeved after being tight-sleeved in the previous century.[1]

It was thus by the early sixteenth century that the wide-sleeved gown had come into being. It had during the Tudor period, as was the case with masters' gowns, a 'standing collar', that is an upright one such as is mentioned in the Ecclesiastical Canon No. 74 of the Church of England of the year 1604, in opposition to the flap collar of the lay type of gown; but in the course of the seventeenth century this collar was cut away for greater comfort and for the better fitting of the dress underneath.[2]

After the Reformation the privilege of a head-dress was extended to Bachelors of Arts, and in 1565 in common with other graduates they were ordered to wear a square cap.[3] In the Laudian statutes of 1636 they were to wear loose-sleeved gowns and square caps, and at special services miniver hoods, instead of the ordinary budge-furred ones, with the lining showing. They were also to wear 'capes' (i.e. the remnant of the old 'shoulder piece') and their hood was to be square in shape.[4]

During the Protectorate there was an influx into Oxford of Cambridge men who were eager to fill the empty sister university. Among them the Bachelors of Arts seem to have been conspicuous, and the Oxford bachelors began to copy their gowns which had large hanging sleeves, larger than their own.[5] This was checked by Vice-Chancellor Fell's statute concerning academical dress of 1666.[6] In the memorandum addressed to tailors it is said: 'Bachelours of Arts . . . to weare wide-sleeved gowns, the sleeves not reaching beyond the fingers' ends nor above an ell in compass.' They were to 'hang at length', which means fairly close to the arms. They were thus reduced to a reasonable size.

In the large plate of Edwards (1674) (Pl. 10b) and in figure

---

[1] M. H. Bloxam (*Gothic Architecture*, pp. 47 and 74) gives examples of this change in 1510.

[2] M. E. C. Walcott, p. 104; H. Druitt, p. 112, n. 3; L. H. D. Buxton and S. Gibson, p. 39.   [3] S. Gibson, p. 386.

[4] G. R. M. Ward, i. 152–3, cap. iii.

[5] A. Clark, *Wood*, i. 149.   [6] A. Clark, *Wood*, ii. 84–85, § 7.

No. 8 in Loggan's costume plate (1675) the large gown with full bell sleeves but with no cuff strings (a cord with a loop and button later introduced to hold back the sleeve from the arm) appears. A square cap with a tump is worn, and a large black hood with a white fur lining. A determining bachelor wore the hood with the fur fully displayed,[1] but when the degree had been taken the fur was not displayed. The first reference to the use of cuff strings appears in a letter of 1684, in which is a description of the material used in making a Bachelor of Arts gown at a cost of £3. 14s. 11d. The material consists of hair prunella, serge, a neck-loop, calico, buckram, tape (for the cuff strings), galloon, and wax-light.[2]

In 1770 the square cap's tassel was given official sanction,[3] and at the same time, besides the miniver hood, which Laud had allowed to all graduates on special occasions, but which for a long time had never been used, certainly not by Bachelors of Arts, two other bachelor's hoods were mentioned. One was the ordinary Bachelor of Arts hood bordered with a fringe of fur to be worn at the act and always afterwards, and the other was the displayed hood for determining bachelors with a piece of white wool and lamb's-skin ('wool fells') fastened to the upper edge of it.[4] Both are illustrated in Grignion's plates (Pl. 11c).[5]

The determiner's hood is full and deep, showing the ordinary fur halfway down its length, while the darker wool appears on the topmost edge. This upper piece of wool is described by a contemporary as 'a little piece of lambskin with the wool on it'.[6] The gown had no cuff strings when worn by a determining bachelor, but they were used after the degree had been taken, and were worn fastened to hold the sleeve some way up the arm.[7]

In Roberts's water-colour collection (1792) the Bachelor of Arts wears the tasselled square cap. His gown is full, and the

---

[1] D. Loggan, op. cit., No. 9. Determining bachelors were those performing the last exercises for their degree.

[2] J. R. Magrath, *The Flemings in Oxford* (O.H.S.), ii. 123.

[3] G. R. M. Ward, ii. 9–10.

[4] G. R. M. Ward, ii. 11.

[5] Oxf. Bodl. Libr. MS. Top. Oxon. c. 16, 8 and 7.

[6] V. Knox, *Essays Moral and Literary*, i. 335.

[7] Oxf. Bodl. Libr. MS. Top. Oxon. c. 16, 7 and 8.

PLATE IIC

Bachelor of Music

Bachelor of Arts with ordinary hood

'Determining' Bachelor of Arts

Student of Civil Law

Nobilis.

Nobleman

Baronettus.

Baronet

Commensalis

Commoner

Serviens seu Battellarius.

Servitor or Battelar

cuff strings are used to fasten the sleeves up at the elbows, while his deep hood of black stuff is trimmed with rabbit fur at the top edge.[1] It should be noticed that only the determiner's hood was *lined* with fur. The other was merely trimmed with fur after the seventeenth century.

(q) Undergraduates

1. *Students of Civil Law, or civilians.* According to Vice-Chancellor Fell (1666) Students of Civil Law were 'persons studying the law being above four years standing in the University and being entered into the law-book'.[2] It was possible by becoming a civilian to avoid reading for a Bachelor of Arts degree, and so it was an immediate step into a higher faculty, that of Law.[3]

The civilian had a special dress, the form of which in Pre-Reformation times is to be seen in the brass of Thomas Baker (1510) at All Souls, Oxford. He wears a cloak of the pattern familiar to us from the *armelausa* of judges, but as if to show that he is a legal tyro, it is the left side that is open, while the right is closed, the opposite of theirs. There are buttons on the shoulder of the cloak on the open side. Under it he wears an open tabard with furred bell-sleeves, and under the tabard a *supertunica* with a girdle. A hood rests on his shoulders.[4] Nothing more is heard of their dress until after the middle of the seventeenth century.

In Fell's order of 1666 their costume is described as a half-sleeved gown without any decoration such as buttons on the sleeve, and a square cap.[5] In Edwards's plate of 1674[6] the gown is of black silk with a plain flap collar and plain *glove* sleeves like those of a master at that time, straight at the ends, but in Loggan's plate (figure No. 6) of 1675 the tops of these sleeves are decorated with formal square pleats. In both examples there is a large tump on the square cap.

According to the statutes of 1770 civilians were allowed to

[1] Oxf. Bodl. Libr. MS. Top. Oxon. d. 58, 47–49.
[2] A. Clark, *Wood*, ii. 84–85.
[3] This special status was not abolished until 1853 (*Notes and Queries*, 2nd ser. vi. 258[a]).
[4] H. Druitt, p. 141; E. T. Beaumont, *Ancient Memorial Brasses*, p. 110; M. Stephenson, p. 410 (All Souls, iii). I cannot agree with Stephenson, who believes that Baker is wearing ordinary civil dress with a scholar's gown.
[5] A. Clark, *Wood*, ii. 85.
[6] Oxf. Bodl. Libr. MS. Wood 276B, xix, 10.

have a tassel on their square cap,[1] and in Grignion's plate of this year (Pl. 11c) the gown is silk, very full, with a flap collar and plain false winged sleeves with some vertical braid; a gown in fact the same as that of the Bachelor of Civil Law but without the gimp.[2] This gown is the same in Roberts's water-colour of 1792, and the hood is long and deep, entirely of lavender-coloured silk and without any fur, the same in fact as that of the Bachelor of Civil Law without the fur edging.[3] A hood was worn in virtue of the wearer's belonging, even though a *studiosus*, to a senior faculty. The flap collar was removed from the gown before 1815.[4]

In the later seventeenth century many undergraduates wore this dress who had no right to it.[5] The reason for their adopting it was that they might pass for gentlemen-commoners.[6]

2. *Noblemen and gentlemen-commoners*. No doubt, as was the case in most other universities, noblemen undergraduates were allowed special privileges probably including those concerning dress, but the *Statuta Antiqua* contain no mention of a special dress for noblemen until 1490. In that year noblemen were allowed, in contradistinction to other undergraduates, to have their hoods and liripipes hanging free and not stitched down, as those of lesser birth were to wear them.[7] Probably gentlemen-commoners did not exist as a recognized body of favoured undergraduates in early times.

The Reformation no doubt caused a relaxation of discipline, for the authorities soon began to show indulgence to com-moners (those not on foundations) as regards dress, particu-larly when outside their colleges.[8] As the century advanced the universities became more fashionable and so money and social position began to have an effect on the academical world as never before. Undergraduates of social standing, whether titled or not, were openly recognized in a decree of Convocation of 1576, which allowed a special latitude in dress to peers' and

[1] G. R. M. Ward, ii. 9 ff.
[2] Oxf. Bodl. Libr. MS. Top. Oxon. c. 16, 5.
[3] Oxf. Bodl. Libr. MS. Top. Oxon. d. 58, 65–66.
[4] W. Combe and T. Uwins, ii. 17.
[5] A. Clark, *Wood*, iii. 300. The printed proclamation denouncing this practice is to be found in Bodl. MS. Wood 276A, No. ccclxxxviii, 3, Year 1689.
[6] Cf. the early nineteenth-century conversation about this in H. Coombs and A. N. Bax, *Journal of a Somerset Rector*, p. 88.
[7] S. Gibson, p. 297.   [8] S. Gibson, p. 386.

knights' sons and to the heirs of esquires,[1] while in the same year when graduates and scholars were allowed to wear ordinary hats of lay fashion while outside the university precincts but always black ones, *generosi* were granted a free choice of colour.[2] In the decrees of 1617 and 1620 when they were all ordered to wear round caps (*pilei rotundi*), the three grades of undergraduates not on foundations, noblemen, gentlemen-commoners, and commoners, are officially approved.[3]

In the Laudian statutes a stricter discipline is to be seen and only sons of peers were allowed bright colours in their dress. This refers only to sons of peers who were members of the House of Lords as distinct from those who had only a courtesy peerage, and the sons of Scottish and Irish peers, whose dress was to be black or at least dark.[4]

During the residence of Charles I's court at Oxford the observance of the Laudian statutes broke down—for instance we find gentlemen-commoners imitating court fashions, wearing velvet facings on their gowns[5]—but Fell in 1666 as vice-chancellor laid down definite rules for undergraduate dress in the tradition of Laud. In his *Orders to Tailors* he described the dress for these privileged undergraduates:

The gent.-commoner's gown to be half-sleeved, and, if they please, to have buttons not exceeding 4 doz. nor the rate of 5/– the doz. nor the bigness in the public patterns. A baronet's or knight's gown, the same as the former, only distinguished (if they please) with gold and silver buttons. Noblemen to wear (if they please) coloured gowns, of the same form with the former.[6]

The gowns of these first two orders were black.

In figure No. 5 of Loggan's plate (1675) the gentleman-commoner wears a winged-sleeved gown with a flap collar, the shoulders of the gown and the sides of the skirt being richly decorated with button and cord braiding. The cap is round and black, though gentlemen-commoners had been for some time covetous of the square cap and in 1675 were wearing it by permission of the vice-chancellor.[7] They had already in 1669

---

[1] S. Gibson, p. 404.   [2] S. Gibson, loc. cit.
[3] S. Gibson, pp. 525 and 540.
[4] C. E. Mallet, *History of the University of Oxford*, ii. 333.
[5] A. Clark, *Wood*, i. 149.
[6] A. Clark, *Wood*, ii. 84–85.
[7] A. Clark, *Wood*, ii. 300.

sought to distinguish themselves from lesser undergraduates by wearing silk bonnets,[1] for although as gentlemen they were allowed a band round the bonnet to distinguish them from servitors, this could not clearly be seen because it was black; but square caps, they felt, would produce even better the necessary distinction. In 1686 this practice of wearing a square cap was well established;[2] but was forbidden and finally suppressed in 1689.[3] Another abuse, which was never effectively controlled, was the wearing by noblemen and gentlemen-commoners of ordinary lay hats about the university.[4]

In Loggan (figure No. 29) the sons of esquires and baronets wear a black winged-sleeved, flap-collared gown, decorated on the sleeves, half-way down the front, and on the skirt at the back and on each side with what in fact was silver braid of the cord and button variety. The sons of noblemen, who are illustrated in Loggan's plate as figure No. 30, wore the same dress, but the braid was gold. The round black silk bonnet worn by these orders had by 1700 come to be made of black velvet.[5]

During the eighteenth century such dress became more and more elaborate. The practice continued for peers and the sons of peers to wear gowns of any colour adorned with gold braid to which gold tufts were soon added, while baronets, their sons, and the sons of knights wore black silk gowns embellished with gold braid, and gentlemen-commoners black silk gowns decorated with black braid.[6] All wore round black velvet bonnets.[7] The wearing of gold tassels on their bonnets by noblemen made its appearance in 1738, but was not as yet countenanced by statute.[8]

The statutes of 1770, however, allowed noblemen, baronets, and gentlemen-commoners to have square black velvet caps instead of round bonnets, with tassels, gold ones for noblemen and black ones for baronets and gentlemen-commoners. Noble-

---

[1] A. Clark, *Wood*, ii. 164.   [2] A. Clark, *Wood*, iii. 181.

[3] Oxf. Bodl. Libr. MS. Wood 276A, no. ccclxxxviii, 4.

[4] Oxf. Bodl. Libr. MS. Wood 276A, no. ccclxxxviii, 4.

[5] Oxf. Bodl. Libr. MS. Top. Oxon. a. 36, leaves 77–78.

[6] Certainly as early as 1721 (*Brasenose College, Quatercentenary Monographs* (O.H.S.), ii, pt. 1, xiii, p. 42).

[7] [J. R. Green], *Oxford during the Last Century*, p. 48.

[8] A. D. Godley, loc. cit., the term 'tuft-hunter' refers to this, or possibly to the gold tufts on the dress gown. The *New English Dictionary* gives a reference to the term in 1755 as being the earliest. This was at Cambridge.

men were still to have coloured gowns for formal occasions, but for undress, in common with baronets, black bell-sleeved gowns with a tippet on the left shoulder like those of proctors, but smaller.[1]

In Grignion's plates of this year, the gentleman-commoner wears the silk winged-sleeved gown decorated on the sleeves and skirt with patches of braid with tassels;[2] but the baronet's undress gown is bell-sleeved and reaches to the ground, and has a tippet fastened by two buttons to the left-hand lower corner of the yoke.[3] The nobleman's undress gown is the same.[4] The full dress of baronet and nobleman was the same in shape, both having winged sleeves and panels, and a flap collar, but whereas that of the first was black, the nobleman's was coloured, purple being particularly favoured. Tippets were not worn on the full dress[5] (Pl. 11 D).

In Roberts's water-colours of 1792[6] the nobleman in full dress[7] wears a square black velvet cap with a gold tassel, and a gown of purple brocade with winged sleeves with false panels. The gown is faced with gold braid, which also runs round the wings, and near the bottom of the false panels is a square patch of gold braid with a pointed top (Frontispiece). His undress is the same as to head-dress, but he has a black silk gown with bell sleeves and a tippet attached to the yoke.[8] The baronet in full dress[9] wears the same as the nobleman in every detail except that the gown is of black brocade, but the gentleman-commoner's full dress consists of a black silk gown with winged sleeves and false panels, with a series of black tassels joined by rows of braid on the upper arm and at the bottom of the false panelled sleeves. He wears a square black velvet cap with a black tassel.[10] In undress[11] his gown is different, for though it has the same sleeves, the middle of the wings of the sleeves is decorated with small black 'pebble' pleats formed into a square with a pointed top, of the same shape as the gold decorations on the nobleman's full dress gown.[12]

---

[1] G. R. M Ward, ii, loc. cit.; Oxf. Bodl. Libr. MS. Top. Oxon. c. 16, 22 and 24.　　　　　　　　　　　　　[2] Oxf. Bodl. Libr. MS. Top. Oxon. c. 16, 4.
[3] 22.　　　　　　　　[4] 24.　　　　　　　　　　　[5] 23 and 25.
[6] Oxf. Bodl. Libr. MS. Top. Oxon. d. 58.　　　　　　　　[7] 50–51.
[8] 53–54.　　　　[9] 56–57.　　　　[10] 60–61.　　　　[11] 62–63.
[12] Gimp was introduced in place of tassels on the gentleman-commoner's full dress gown between 1792 and 1815 (W. Combe and T. Uwins, loc. cit.).

3. *Scholars or students*. The original dress of those under-graduates who were on foundations except at New College, was the sleeved tabard.[1] It is worn by scholars in an alchemical manuscript of 1479.[2] They were bare-headed in medieval times but had a plain black cloth hood which is referred to in a statute of 1490,[3] when they were ordered to have the liripipe of their hood stitched to it (*consutum*) and not worked into the same piece (*contextum*). The reason for this was probably that its being stitched down would prevent the liripipe's being thrown round the neck like a scarf or the hood's being worn on the head.[4] The tabard was always worn closed before the sixteenth century but in 1507 scholars of Magdalen had to be warned against wearing tabards not sewn together in front.[5]

Presumably, although there is no evidence on which to base the statement, the development of the scholar's dress thereafter was the same as that of the Bachelor of Arts, so that the outer dress (the tabard) was left off and the *tunica*, worn underneath it, became the outer dress with greatly enlarged sleeves.[6]

Scholars were at length, in 1565, granted a head-dress which was to be the square cap. At the same time they were ordered always to wear their black hood at important academical functions, but might use a little shoulder-cape instead of the hood when walking at free times.[7] In 1576, owing to great opposition to the square cap on account of its supposed Romish character, scholars as well as graduates were allowed as a concession to wear ordinary hats of lay fashion outside the university precincts, as long as they were black. At the same time they were forbidden to wear light-coloured gowns or gowns of rich material or decorated with lace.[8] In 1617 and 1620 the square black cap as the head-dress of scholars was insisted on for all occasions.[9]

A fine example of the scholar's dress in Elizabethan times is to be found in a brass (Pl. 12 a) in Oxford Cathedral of Henry Dow, junior student (i.e. scholar of Christ Church) (1578).

---

[1] E. C. Clarke, art. cit. l. 139–40. It is preserved in the name tabarder for open scholars of Queen's (J. Walker, ii. 49). See below, p. 97, nn. 2 and 3.
[2] Cambridge, St. John's Coll. Libr., MS. James no. 182, G. 14, fo. 96b.
[3] S. Gibson, p. 297.   [4] E. C. Clarke, art. cit. l. 88.
[5] W. M. Macray, *Register*, N.S. i, §§ 44–45, p. 55.
[6] Except at New College, see below.   [7] S. Gibson, pp. 386–7.
[8] S. Gibson, p. 404.   [9] S. Gibson, pp. 525 and 540.

PLATE 12

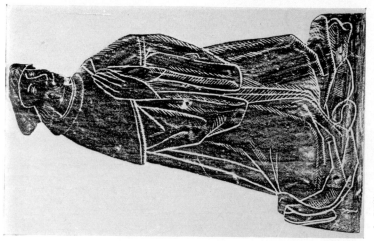

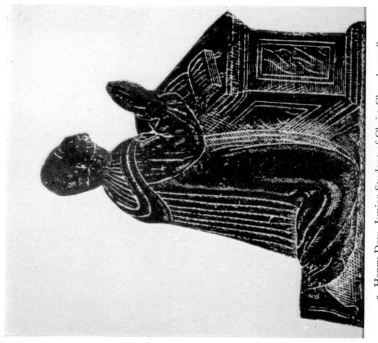

b. William Taylard, a Cambridge D.D., 1530

a. Henry Dow, Junior Student of Christ Church, 1578

He wears a long full gown with a high standing collar and large bell sleeves which hang down below his elbows behind, a ruff, and a small round and unlined hood of black cloth. Another junior student of Christ Church, John Bisshop (1588), whose brass is also in the cathedral, is similarly dressed. Such was the dress which was ordered by Laud in 1636 to be worn with a square cap by all scholars of the university.[1] All scholars thus wore the full-sleeved gown, except the scholars of New College, who clung to the medieval sleeveless serge gown, which Aubrey rightly calls a tabard, together with ruffs, both until the beginning of the Civil War.[2] They had thus kept to the clause in their foundation statutes of 1379 which ordered scholars to wear sleeveless ankle-length tabards.[3] Laud limited the use of their black hood by scholars to the occasions on which they attended the schools.[4]

In 1666 Fell in his *Orders to Tailors*[5] expected 'Foundation Men' (scholars) to wear wide-sleeved gowns, the sleeves 'not reaching beyond the fingers' ends nor above an ell in compass', exactly the same as those of Bachelors of Arts, but with this difference, that whereas the sleeves of bachelors were to hang free, those of scholars were to be held up at the wrists. In figure No. 3 of Loggan's plate, however, though the scholar on the foundation appears in a large bell-sleeved gown, the sleeves hang free and there is no sign of cuff-strings. He wears a black square cap without a tump. In 1682 on his becoming a tabarder at Queen's and so on the foundation, Henry Fleming exchanged his round commoner's cap for a square one, which cost 5s.[6] By 1700, the approximate date of Robert Sayer's *Oxonia Illustrata*,[7] the scholar's square cap had a tump, and in 1770 the use of a tassel was officially recognized,[8] but it seems from an entry in the diary of Dr. Thomas Fry, President of St. John's, that some colleges followed their own rules, and even as late as the latter year only allowed their scholars to wear a tuft or tump as an act of grace.[9]

[1] G. R. M. Ward, i. 152, chap. iii.
[2] Oxf. Bodl. Libr. MS. Top. Gen. c. 25, fo. 201b.
[3] *Statutes of the Colleges of Oxford for the Royal Commission*, i. 45–46, R. 23, *De habitu sociorum et scholarium de collegio.* [4] C. E. Mallet, ii. 324.
[5] A. Clark, *Wood*, ii. 84–85. [6] J. R. Magrath, ii. 83.
[7] Oxf. Bodl. Libr. MS. Top. Oxon. a 36, fos. 77–78.
[8] G. R. M. Ward, ii. 9 ff. [9] MS. Diary of Dr. Thomas Fry, 5 March 1770.

In Grignion's plate of 1770 the scholar wears a full bell-sleeved gown, the sleeves tapering behind to points, hanging loose, and there are cuff-strings hanging from them (Pl. 11);[1] while in the water-colour of Roberts (1792) he wears the square black cloth cap with a black silk tassel, a black cloth gown of the same shape as that of 1770, and a black cloth hood, very narrow and flung loosely over the shoulders.[2] This hood, as has been said above, was only worn in the schools.[3]

4. *Commoners*. Although, as in other European universities, there existed at Oxford an order of undergraduates who were members of the university and paid their own way as opposed to scholars who were in receipt of pecuniary assistance and of assistance in kind and so were 'on the foundation' of their college, there does not appear to be any evidence for a particular dress worn by commoners in medieval times, no doubt because during this period they were not members of colleges, and generally living in hostels in the town, escaped a college discipline.[4]

It is not until Elizabethan times that we have any information about the costume worn by commoners, and then we find that the dress adopted for them and laid down by statute was dress entirely of lay character.

The brass of Edward Chernock, commoner, of Brasenose, who died in 1581 while still an undergraduate, which is to be seen in the church of St. Mary-the-Virgin, Oxford, sufficiently illustrates the lay character of this dress. The gown is winged-sleeved, after the style worn by Bachelors of Civil Law, but not so elaborate.

At some time between this date and 1617 the commoner's gown was altered in that the winged sleeves vanished and the panels became merely strips of stuff fastened to the back of the shoulders of the now sleeveless gown. This is to be seen in the brass of the commoner, John Pendarves of this date at St. Michael's-at-the-North-Gate, Oxford.[5] It is to be noticed that

---

[1] Oxf. Bodl. Libr. MS. Top. Oxon. c. 16, 2.

[2] Oxf. Bodl. Libr. MS. Top. Oxon. d. 58, 71–72.

[3] The sleeves had been shortened by 1828 (N. Whittock, *Topographical and Historical Description of Oxford*, p. 42).

[4] There are records of commoners living in college in the fourteenth and fifteenth centuries. See *Vict. Co. Hist. Oxf.* iii. 63a.

[5] E. T. Beaumont, *Academical Habit*, p. 87 and ill. opp. p. 88.

the little rib of material fastened into the shoulder of the modern commoner's gown resulted from the Jacobean fashion for padded shoulders. This appears in the Pendarves brass.

The head-dress was the round cap, the 'statute cap', which, originally of wool (though afterwards of cloth), the government in 1571 had ordered apprentices to wear.[1] At Oxford as at Cambridge it was adopted as the head-dress of undergraduates not on foundations.[2] These *pilei rotundi* of commoners are mentioned in Oxford statutes of 1617 and 1620.[3] In the Laudian statutes undergraduates not on foundations are to wear long 'square' gowns (i.e. of lay type) and round caps.[4]

In 1666 Vice-Chancellor Fell ordered that the commoner's gown should be such a one as is worn by Pendarves with a square flap collar, decorated on the strips of stuff ('streamers' or 'leading strings' as they came to be called) which hung from the shoulders, with half a dozen buttons, black and of a certain price, laid on the upper part.[5] In Loggan (1675) the commoner (No. 4) wears a gown with these buttons on the upper part of the streamers laid on in rows of three buttons, which are joined together by plain lines of braid, with the addition of tassels. The cap is round. Better illustrations of these caps appear in G. Edwards's plates of 1674 (Pl. 10 c). From these it can be seen that the cap of gentlemen-commoners had a broad band, of commoners a narrow one, while there was no band on the cap of servitors.[6] A commoner's round cap is mentioned as costing between 2s. 6d. and 3s. 6d. in the accounts of Henry Brougham of Queen's and of members of the Fleming family in 1658, 1678, 1682, and 1693.[7]

In 1770 commoners were ordered to wear the square cloth cap with a silk tassel.[8] By this time the buttons had vanished from the tops of the streamers, their place having been taken by a decoration consisting of formal pleating in large squares, which was also placed in a line below the flap collar (Pl. 11 D).[9]

[1] *Statutes of the Realm,* iv. 555 (13 Eliz. c. 19 (1571)).
[2] It is referred to by Shakespeare in *Love's Labour's Lost,* v. ii. 281, where Rosaline says: 'Well, better wits have worn plain statute-caps.'
[3] S. Gibson, pp. 525 and 540.　　　　[4] G. R. M. Ward, i. 153, cap. iii.
[5] A. Clark, *Wood,* ii. 84–85.
[6] Oxf. Bodl. Libr. MS. Wood 276 B, xix, 9, xix, 11, and xix, 12.
[7] J. R. Magrath, p. 120 and n. 1; i. 249; ii. 68; iii. 129.
[8] G. R. M. Ward, ii. 9 ff.
[9] Oxf. Bodl. Libr. MS. Top. Oxon. c. 16, 3.

In 1792 commoners wore the black tasselled square cap, and a black cloth gown with a plain flap-collar. The gown was sleeveless, but had long thick 'streamers', which were decorated on the upper part with pleats in squares, and which were as long as the ankle-length gown.[1]

5. *Battelars and servitors*. These terms do not appear until later times, although servitors had their equivalents during the Middle Ages in all the universities of Europe. Battelars who partly supported themselves but contributed the minimum to their expenses were of a higher order than servitors, who worked their way through the university by waiting on the fellows in hall or doing all kinds of jobs for wealthy undergraduates, in fact taking the place of 'scouts' of whom there were few until the later eighteenth century.[2] In the seventeenth century servitors were referred to as 'gown-men', whereas 'cloak-men' simply meant ordinary servants whom noblemen and gentlemen-commoners sometimes brought with them to college to attend on them when in residence. They then dispensed with the aid of servitors.[3]

In Fell's *Orders to Tailors* (1666) the gowns of battelars and servitors were for the first time described.[4] They were to be the same as those of commoners but without any decoration of buttons on the 'streamers' and collar, and were thus of plain black cloth. The flap collars of the servitors were to be 'round' (that is, with a yoke), but those of battelars were to be 'square', but in Loggan's plate of 1675 their dress which appears in figures 1 and 2 is exactly the same, there being no difference in the collars, which in both cases are square. A plain low round cap is worn by both. There was an excellent drawing of a battelar or servitor by Michael Burghers of about 1695, of which copies of the engraving are at St. Edmund Hall and the Bodleian Library (Pl. 10 *d*).[5]

As time went on it became increasingly difficult to force this humble dress on either of these orders. Of servitors in 1730 Hearne writes: 'Our Servitors now . . . are generally very

[1] Oxf. Bodl. Libr. MS. Top. Oxon. d. 58, 68–69; and see the verses of John Skinner (1792) printed in H. Coomb and A. N. Bax, p. 315.

[2] *Brasenose College, Quatercentenary Monographs* ii, pt. 1, § xiii, p. 45.

[3] R. Magrath, i. 536–7.

[4] A. Clark, *Wood*, ii. 84–85, §§ 2 and 1.

[5] Auct. v. iii. 1 (229).

haughty and scorn to wear their proper habits, their gowns being not what properly belong to Servitors but to Battelars, and their caps (which should be Thrum [i.e. yarn] Caps or Bonnets) being what when I first came to Oxford [i.e. 1695] the Commoners wore.'[1] Hogarth's print *The Lecture* (? 1735) depicts a group of scholars, battelars, and servitors attending an Oxford lecture. The two latter wear round rigid caps with a button on top, very different from the flat bonnets of 1675,[2] and the same as the round cap of a member of a charity school[3].

In 1770 the new statutes gave battelars and servitors the square black cap but without tump or tassel,[4] and in Grignion's plates of the same year the servitor (and this was also the dress of the battelar, the two orders from about this time becoming fused) wears such a square cap and an absolutely plain black cloth gown reaching to the ground, sleeveless but with plain broad 'streamers' fixed behind the shoulders and falling the length of the gown. The gown had a plain flap collar (Pl. 11 D).[5]

(r) Notes

1. *College statutes.* Originally colleges legislated about the particular dress to be worn by their members, and the university as a body left the various foundations to their own devices beyond issuing general rules from time to time. Particularly were Queen's and New College conscious of their individual corporate systems. Thus in the foundation statutes of Queen's (1340) elaborate rules were laid down. Fellows who were Doctors of Divinity and Doctors of Canon Law, at lunch and dinner at particular times of year (*singulis anni temporibus*), in hall were to wear a *pallium* (a large sleeveless outer garment) of a purple colour as a memorial of the blood of Christ, with an opening at the neck (*scissi ad colla*), furred with black budge. The rest of the fellows were to wear a *pallium* of a quieter colour.

[1] T. Hearne, x. 275.
[2] J. Ireland and J. Nichols, *Hogarth's Works*, ii, pl. opp. p. 250.
[3] See the figure in Hogarth's print *First Stage of Cruelty* (1750) (ibid., pl. opp. p. 54).
[4] G. R. M. Ward, ii. 10. In the diary of Dr. Thomas Fry, President of St. John's, under date 6 March 1770, a Bible clerk is refused permission to wear a 'tuft' on his cap. This was reserved for scholars.
[5] Oxf. Bodl. Libr. MS. Top. Oxon. c. 16, 1. The same dress appears in the water-colour of this subject by James Roberts (1792) (Oxf. Bodl. Libr. MS. Top. Oxon. d. 58, 74–75).

As for the other members of the college the provost was to see that their dress conformed in colour.[1]

In the foundation statutes of New College (1379), the warden and members on the foundation were to have their dress cut from the same cloth, made up into the various shapes conformable with their various university degrees, a *cappa* for doctors, a large tabard for masters, and a less full tabard for those of lower degree. A cape or cloak (*mantellum*) was to be worn by inceptors.[2]

A college livery seems to have been used at one time at Merton, for in 1509 violet cloth, presumably for gowns, was to be given by the warden to the eighteen fellows of the college every St. John the Baptist's Day.[3]

In 1555 in the foundation statutes of St. John's it was insisted that the dress, at least of all on the foundation, should be clerkly,[4] but apart from this stipulation the character of the dress was left to the president and vice-president to decide. This seems to have been the last collegiate enactment as regards dress, and thereafter such a question was left to the university. Thus at Jesus (1571), the last of the sixteenth-century foundations, all that is mentioned about the dress of its members is that it is to be conformable with the statutes of the university and according to the discretion of the principal and vice-principal.[5] The university had already taken this matter in hand from 1565 onwards, and the way was prepared for Laud to make his all-embracing rules.

2. *Grand compounders.* One could be a grand compounder for any degree, greatly enlarged fees being paid for the privilege, for instance, £40 instead of £14 for the Master of Arts degree and £30 instead of £7 for that of Bachelor of Arts. Although the practice existed in the sixteenth century it did not become frequent until the seventeenth century. The grand compounder wearing a scarlet Convocation 'habit' (*habitus coccineus*), together

---

[1] *Statutes of the Colleges of Oxford for the Royal Commission*, i. 29.

[2] *Statutes of the Colleges of Oxford for the Royal Commission*, i. 44–45 (R. 22, *De communi annua vestium liberata*) and pp. 45–46 (R. 23, *De habitu sociorum et scholarium de collegio*).

[3] H. E. Salter, *Registrum Annalium Collegii Mertonensis* (O.H.S., 1921), p. 388.

[4] *Statutes of the Colleges of Oxford for the Royal Commission*, iii. 64, cap. 30 (*De vestitu, ornatu*).

[5] *Statutes of the Colleges of Oxford for the Royal Commission*, iii. 62, § 17.

with the gown and hood of his new degree, had his own procession, in which the vice-chancellor, the proctors, and any
members of his college who wished joined, from his college to
the Convocation House, in later times to the Sheldonian, and
back again, while the bells of St. Mary's rang. Before the seventeenth century a trumpet was blown by a *famulus* who walked
before him. He was supposed ever afterwards to wear a scarlet
'habit' with his gown and hood, but usually he obtained a
dispensation which freed him from this necessity.[1]

3. *Boots and shoes of academical significance.* In the Middle Ages
foot-gear of various shapes as befitting various degrees formed
part of academical costume.[2] *Caligae*, which were black or nearly
black boots, are mentioned in the statutes before 1350 as being
worn by regent and non-regent masters.[3] In a statute of before
1477 it is ordered that boots shall be worn by doctors, bachelors,
and inceptors in the Faculties of Theology and Canon Law,
while 'pynsons' (slippers) were to be worn by all other doctors,
masters, bachelors, and inceptors.[4]

In the seventeenth century those who took the degree of
Doctor of Divinity wore boots for the occasion,[5] while Masters
of Arts wore 'shoes and slops'.[6] In 1733 inceptors wore boots
or shoes, according to whether they were taking a divinity or
other degree, though they wore them only for the ceremony,
but after this year nothing more is heard of such a distinction.[7]
In their original form the boots (*caligae*) reached to the middle
of the leg; but the 'pynsons' were like sandals and later like
slippers. The latter appear in Latin under the various terms,
socculi, sandalia, sotularia, crepidae, and *pincernae*.[8]

4. *Gloves.* Gloves were originally regarded as betokening

---

[1] A. Clark, *Register of the University of Oxford*, ii (O.H.S., 1887), pt. 1, pp. 64–65;
A. Clark, *Wood*, iii. 346–7, where is to be found a full account of the ceremony in
1690. Grand-compounding virtually ended in 1821 (J. S. Reynolds, *Evangelicals at
Oxford*, p. 179), but was not formally abolished till 1857 (G. V. Cox, *Recollections*,
p. 236). There were also grand compounders at Cambridge (G. Peacock, *Observations on the Statutes of Cambridge*, app. A, p. xx and n. 3).

[2] H. C. Maxwell Lyte, *History of the University of Oxford*, p. 424.

[3] S. Gibson, pp. 58 and 288.   [4] S. Gibson, pp. 288–9; J. Walker, i. 21.

[5] Oxf. Bodl. Libr. MS. Top. Gen. c. 25, fo. 199 b.

[6] T. Hearne, xi. 229.

[7] T. Hearne, loc. cit. Until the early years of the nineteenth century an annual
formal dispensation from the necessity of inceptors using them was published
(G. V. Cox. p. 414; C. Wordsworth, p. 479).

[8] A. Clark, *Register of the University of Oxford*, ii, pt. 1, p. 87.

dignity or learning.[1] They were to be given to the vice-chancellor and proctors by new Bachelors of Civil Law at the time
of their presentation, according to a statute of 1588.[2] In 1597
incepting Doctors of Theology, Law, and Medicine were to
present gloves through the beadle of whichever faculty each
was a member to the chief officers who took part in the Act,
and to all doctors who attended if suitably dressed, and even to
those who had a reasonable excuse for absence.[3] In the plates
of G. Edwards (1674) the vice-chancellor and the Doctor
of Divinity wear gloves,[4] and there are portraits of Doctors of
Divinity wearing gloves well into the nineteenth century.

5. *The mourning gown.* The mourning gown, exactly the same
as the canonical gown of the Church of England in the seventeenth and eighteenth centuries (e.g. the figure of the cleric
with punch ladle in Hogarth's *Modern Midnight Conversation*
(1735)),[5] was an open full cloth gown with pudding sleeves,[6]
and appeared at Oxford after the Restoration. It was to be
used, as Anthony à Wood correctly used it in 1667,[7] on the
occasion of the death of a personal friend, together with gloves
which had been presented to the mourner. It was to be worn
also at the time of mourning for the death of a monarch.[8]

The wearing of it was much abused, for those who, like
commoners, were dissatisfied with their sleeveless gowns,
seized upon it with avidity, so that they might pass for graduates.
Wood complains of this more than once, as in 1675.[9] After this
the practice became so general an abuse that the authorities
took notice. One of the proctors of 1684 denounced it publicly,[10]
and it was condemned officially in 1689.[11] Even those of standing, such as members of Convocation, took to wearing mourning gowns for no good reason, as is recorded in 1680 and 1693,
with the result that those who appeared in Convocation wearing
such gowns were denied their votes.[12] After 1693 nothing is
heard of the wearing of mourning gowns in the university.

[1] S. W. Beck, *Gloves*, p. 56.   [2] A. Clark, ii, pt. 1, p. 115.
[3] A. Clark, ii, pt. 1, p. 121; S. Gibson, pp. 455–6.
[4] Oxf. Bodl. Libr. MS. Wood 276 B, xix, 2, 3.
[5] J. Ireland and J. Nichols, i, pl. opp. p. 184.
[6] D. Loggan, pl. x, no. 15.   [7] A. Clark, *Wood*, ii. 102.
[8] Ibid. iii. 133.   [9] Ibid. ii. 304.
[10] Ibid. iii. 92.   [11] Oxf. Bodl. Libr., MS. Wood 276 A, no. ccclxxxviii, 1.
[12] A. Clark, *Wood*, ii. 502; and iii. 424.

6. *Bands.* Bands originated in the falling collar of the earlier seventeenth century, but they did not become academically significant until they had been abandoned as an ordinary lay fashion after the Restoration. At the universities they then came to be regarded as an item of academical dress and all of every degree and order wear them in Loggan's plates (1675).[1] They were made of holland (i.e. linen) which was bleached, the two tongues being in the seventeenth century short and broad, but in the eighteenth century longer and narrower, descending parallel and not pointing outwards as they have often come to do in modern times.[2] Cravats were absolutely forbidden at this period, and even Charles II's bastard, the Earl of Southampton, was in 1678 refused the right to wear a cravat instead of bands,[3] but laced bands are worn by Doctors of Medicine in G. Edwards's collection (1674). In 1713, however, William Croft, D.Mus., wears an ordinary cravat probably because not a member of Convocation.[4]

In the new statutes of 1770 all are reminded always to wear bands,[5] and in Roberts's water-colours of 1792 all do so, doctors (except for Doctors of Music) and proctors wearing them with a plain stock, non-doctors and Doctors of Music over a cravat of contemporary fashion.[6] The bands worn with the cravat are very small, but are of the full length when worn with the stock.[7] Until the turn of the century bands were always worn, but by 1807 their use was becoming more and more confined to formal occasions.[8] In later times as a sign of mourning, bands with a double pleat running down the middle of each wing were worn, and still are.

7. *The surplice.* The surplice was in 1603 enjoined upon fellows and scholars on the foundation of their colleges for chapel,[9] and this was repeated in the Laudian statutes. It was very full and long with long pointed sleeves like those of the gown of a Bachelor of Arts.[10] In the later seventeenth century

---

[1] D. Loggan, op. cit., pl. x.

[2] A pair of holland bands (or more correctly 'a band') cost 1s. in 1683 (J. R. Magrath, ii. 122).   [3] J. R. Magrath, i. 245–6.

[4] Oxf. Bodl. Libr. MS. Top. Oxon. c. 16, § 101.

[5] G. R. M. Ward, ii. 12.   [6] Oxf. Bodl. Libr. MS. Top. Oxon. d. 58.

[7] For the difference between the bands of doctors and others see *The Letters of Radcliffe and James, 1755–83* (O.H.S.), p. 72.   [8] J. S. Reynolds, p. 79.

[9] M. E. C. Walcott, p. 37 (Canon 17).

[10] Oxf. Bodl. Libr. MS. Top. Oxon. d. 58, 17–18.

it was opened down the front and fastened with a button at the throat. This was for the convenience of putting it on.[1]

8. *The attempt to abolish academical dress during the Commonwealth.* While on his visit to Oxford in the summer of 1654 John Evelyn noticed that the old ceremonial was still maintained,[2] but in 1658 the most outright republicans and presbyterians were coming to the fore in the university, and as those who would have opposed the abolition of academicals, 'the antediluvian Cavaliers' who had managed to keep their fellowships 'never appeared in Convocation', it looked as though such dress was doomed. One of the proctors of that year, however, Walter Pope, stood out against this, rallied his friends to defeat the attempt in Convocation, and triumphantly succeeded in preserving gowns, hoods, and caps, and the 'distinctions of Degrees'.[3]

[1] L. H. D. Buxton and S. Gibson, p. 37.
[2] *Diary of John Evelyn*, ed. E. S. de Beer, iii. 105.
[3] W. Pope, *The Life of Seth*, pp. 34–35, 40, and 41–42.

4

GREAT BRITAIN AND IRELAND

II. CAMBRIDGE

(a) The Chancellor

DURING the whole of the Middle Ages and beyond them the chancellor had no special official costume, but wore the dress of whatever degree he held, nearly always that of Doctor of Divinity. Even after the Reformation when laymen began to assume this office in place of clerics, their dress as chancellor was markedly similar to the dress which their clerical predecessors wore. The three chancellor's seals which range from the late thirteenth century to 1580 show the chancellor in three stages of the development of the dress of Doctors of Divinity, and until this year the general medieval characteristics of the costume remained.

In the original seal, first used in 1291, the chancellor wears a stiff and apexed *pileus* and a *cappa clausa*,[1] while in the second seal, used from about 1420, the seated chancellor wears a small round *pileus*, a small hood close round the neck, a miniver 'shoulder piece' joined to it, and a full and loose *cappa clausa*.[2] In the third seal, which is still used today and dates from 1580, he wears a *cappa clausa*, a thick and large miniver 'shoulder piece' with all the fur showing, a hood attached to it and lying close round the neck, and a rigid and pointed *pileus* like a top-shell in shape, with flaps over the ears.[3]

A great change appears in another seal also of 1580. In this the chancellor wears the recently altered dress of Doctors of Divinity, showing the great influence of Tudor lay fashion. He appears in a festal robe with pudding-sleeves (i.e. baggy sleeves,

---

[1] W. H. St. J. Hope, *Seals of the University of Cambridge*, pl. ii, fig. 1; A. F. Leach, *The Schools of Medieval England*, pl. opp. p. 156.

[2] W. H. St. J. Hope, pl. ii, fig. 2.

[3] W. H. St. J. Hope, pl. iii; V. de Viriville, *Histoire de l'Instruction Publique*, p. 103.

loose at the elbow and tight at the wrist). The old *cappa* has been reduced to a shortened cape worn over the robe but under a large miniver 'shoulder piece'. This 'shoulder piece' covers the shoulders and the upper part of the arms, and thus almost entirely covers the cape. The head-dress is a *pileus quadratus*.[1]

In the early seventeenth century the chancellor's dress was entirely changed, and he at last had a true dress of office which owed nothing to the costume of a degree. It consisted of a black brocaded winged-sleeved robe with a train, the whole being decorated with gold braid. This dress is depicted in R. Harraden's *Costumes of the University of Cambridge* (1803). Such a dress, hardly academical but rather a dress of dignity, was worn also by such important officials of the realm as the lord chancellor, the lord chamberlain, and the speaker of the House of Commons.

(b) The Vice-Chacellor

As H. Rashdall[2] says, the costume of the Cambridge vice-chancellor was the *cappa clausa* dress of a doctor. The reason for this was the same as that mentioned in regard to the dress of the chancellor. The costume of both chancellor and vice-chancellor differed in no way from one another, as far as one can say owing to a complete lack of records, until the seventeenth century when, as we have seen, the chancellor began to wear his special official dress.

When that occurred the vice-chancellor continued to wear the pudding-sleeved robe with the shortened *cappa* and the large miniver hood which he had used earlier. By the end of the eighteenth century the dress was still much the same as before, for in Harraden's collection it consists of a square black cap,[3] a scarlet cloth robe with pudding-sleeves, and over this a scarlet cape, the shortened *cappa*, which now comes down square over the sleeves of the robe. The robe is edged with miniver, and a huge miniver hood, developed from the original 'shoulder piece', covering the shoulders entirely, is worn over all the other dress. The only significant changes are that both robe and cape are open right down the front as a convenience for putting them on, so that a cassock can be seen underneath, and the cape is now

---

[1] W. H. St. J. Hope, pl. ii, fig. 3.
[2] *Universities of Europe in the Middle Ages*, iii. 392.
[3] Cf. W. H. St. J. Hope, pl. ii, fig. 3.

PLATE 13

Cambridge Vice-Chancellor, 1803

square in front and longer than it had been in the sixteenth century (Pl. 13).

The vice-chancellor had worn a round black bonnet with a gold cord in 1665, according to J. W. Clark's transcript of Bedell Buck's *Book of Ceremonies*,[1] but this practice does not seem to have long survived.

(c) *The Proctors*

In the seal of the late thirteenth century already mentioned the two proctors standing one on each side of the chancellor wear coifs, short hoods falling down a little way behind, and sleeveless tabards open down the sides from the arms.[2] In the fifteenth century seal[3] the two proctors are bare-headed, and their sleeveless tabards, which were plain in the earlier example are pleated.

In the 1580 university seal, which is that at present in use,[4] the two proctors both carry a book of the statutes. Their gowns are full and closed with bell-shaped sleeves, while their fur-lined hoods are very large. The right-hand figure, the senior proctor, wears a large tippet on the left shoulder falling equally before and behind, but the junior proctor is without one. Both wear small turn-down collars.

In the print of Andrew Willet (d. 1621) as a proctor, he is shown wearing a gown with full bell sleeves, open in front and with silk facings, a skull-cap, a ruff, and a very square-shaped miniver hood, fastened far down in front;[5] but in D. Loggan's *Cantabrigia Illustrata* (1690) the proctor (No. 12) wears an ordinary Master of Arts gown and a Regent Master of Arts hood with the white silk lining fully displayed, but with this difference, that there is a large black square of material, a remnant of the medieval *bourrelet-chausse*, hanging behind which, attached to the main hood, lies underneath it and falls below, and is edged all round with white silk. This was the *Ad Clerum* habit, which was the less formal dress for proctors.

The formal one, the 'Congregation habit', consisted of the

---

[1] Cambridge, Univ. Libr. MS. Add. 5107, fo. 31; E. C. Clarke, art. 'College Caps and Doctors' Hats' in *Archaeological Journal*, lxi (1904), 64.

[2] W. H. St. J. Hope, pl. ii, fig. 1.

[3] W. H. St. J. Hope, pl. ii, fig. 2.

[4] W. H. St. J. Hope, pl. iii; V. de Viriville, p. 103.

[5] S. Clark, *Marrow of Ecclesiastical History*, p. 448. Four prints of this in the first state are in the Ashmolean Museum (Hope Collection).

master's gown, a black silk pleated 'shoulder piece' which covered the shoulders, known as the 'ruff', and an ordinary regent master's hood, that is with the white silk lining displayed but with no square of material attached to it.[1] A black square cap with a tuft was usually worn; but they wore in 1665 when presiding at the Act a round bonnet with a gold cord.[2]

In Harraden's plate of 1803 the proctor is shown in his *Ad Clerum* dress, consisting of a black silk master's gown (earlier it had been of cloth), a black square cap of cloth with a black silk tassel, bands, a regent-master's hood with the addition of the square of stuff which lies flat under the hood's liripipe, and a black breeches suit. The two halves of the hood are seen to be folded over one another in front, a shape which was obtained by bringing the two long ends over the shoulder, folding them, and inserting a hook and eye where the edges crossed.[3]

In T. Uwins's illustrations of Cambridge dresses of 1815 we see the proctor in 'Congregation habit' consisting of master's gown, with a cassock and sash, the ordinary regent-master's displayed hood without the square of material, and the 'ruff'. In addition was worn a black stuff tippet falling equally before and behind fastened with a button on the top of the right shoulder. It was exactly the same as that noticed as being worn by the senior proctor on the seal of 1580, but was then worn on the left shoulder.[4] According to H. Gunning, a senior esquire bedell, who in 1828 brought out an edition of Bedell Wall's *Ceremonies observed in the Senate House*, the proctors wore 'ruffs' and displayed hoods at Congregation only,[5] and the *Ad Clerum* dress, that is, the squared hood and no 'ruff' on other occasions.[6]

(d) The Taxor

The original function of the taxor was the taxing of halls of residence. Later his duties approximated to those of the clerks of the market at Oxford.[7] There are no early references of any kind to the dress of this official, but in the seventeenth century,

[1] J. R. Tanner, *Historical Register*, p. 197.
[2] E. C. Clarke, art. cit., lxi, 64.
[3] *Notes and Queries*, 2nd ser. vi. 211.
[4] W. Combe and T. Uwins, *History of the University of Cambridge*, ii. 313 and pl. at end.   [5] H. Gunning, *Ceremonies*, p. 15.
[6] H. Gunning, pp. 28, 41, 61, and 119.
[7] H. Rashdall, iii. 287.

according to Loggan's costume plate (figure No. 11), it still retained a medieval character. Over a master's gown he wore a black silk 'shoulder piece' of the same nature as the 'ruff' of proctors but not pleated, and lined with white silk. This 'shoulder piece' was so long that in front it reached to the waist and behind to the back of the knees. In 1815 taxors wore a 'squared' hood.[1]

(e) Doctors of Divinity

The earliest mention of the dress of this degree is to be found in a university statute of 1414, which in the following year was incorporated in a royal ordinance directed to the university by Henry V. From this we see that it had come to consist of the *cappa clausa* for all but informal occasions when the *pallium* might be used,[2] the *pileus*, though different from that of the lay doctors,[3] and hoods and 'shoulder pieces' lined with a fur of good quality.[4] Examples of this dress showing the *roba* or *supertunica*, the *cappa clausa* over this, the furred hood and 'shoulder piece', and the small apexed *pileus* appear on the brasses of Richard Billingford, D.D., 1442, in St. Benet's Church, Cambridge; of an unknown Doctor of Divinity, about 1490, in St. Mary's-the-Less, Cambridge; and of William Towne, D.D., 1495, in King's College, Cambridge.[5]

In 1533 the *Act for the Reformation of Excess in Apparel* regulated the dress of both the English universities. In common with other doctors, Doctors of Divinity were allowed silk linings to their gown (i.e. the *roba* worn underneath the *cappa*), and black satin linings to their *cappa*. Their outer dress might be of scarlet, murrey, or violet, and they were allowed the use of all kinds of rich fur for facings or linings, the fur or the silk being presumably used according to season.[6] That the favoured colour of the outer dress of Doctors of Divinity at Cambridge was red and the favoured fur miniver in the early sixteenth century is exemplified in the articles mentioned in the inventory of the goods of

---

[1] W. Combe and T. Uwins, ii. 313.

[2] Cambridge, Univ. Libr. MS. Mm. 4.47, § 147, fo. 228 (*De habitubus et insigniis Magistrorum*); J. Heywood, *Collection of Statutes*, p. 159.

[3] Cambridge, Univ. Libr. MS. Mm. 4.47, 148, fos. 229 (23) ff.

[4] Cambridge, Univ. Libr. MS. Dd. 4.35, fos. 75 ff.; *Communications, Cambridge Antiquarian Soc.*, 8vo ser. iv [1854], ¶ iii, p. 87.

[5] H. Druitt, *Manual*, p. 127; E. T. Beaumont, *Academical Habit*, pl. opp. p. 7; H. W. Macklin, *Monumental Brasses*, p. 51.

[6] C. H. Cooper, *Annals*, i. 355; C. Wordsworth, *Social Life*, p. 489.

William Melton, D.D., of Cambridge, in 1496, Chancellor of York, who died in 1528, as 'a gowne of rede scarlet, furred with menyvere and a hood';[1] and there is another example of the same dress in the will of William Elistonn, sub-Dean of York (d. 1548).[2] It was a period of rapid change in academical dress, and this can be particularly well seen in the brass (Pl. 12 b) of the Cambridge Doctor of Divinity, William Taylard, 1530, in All Saints' Church, Huntingdon. He wears a Tudor cap with side pieces, a small hood and a 'shoulder piece', and a closed *roba* with moderately hanging sleeves.[3]

Regents of this degree were ordered to wear a *pileus quadratus* in common with regents of other faculties by command of the parliamentary visitors in 1549,[4] and this order was repeated in 1559.[5]

In 1560 Doctors of Divinity in common with doctors of other faculties and Bachelors of Divinity were allowed to have silk in their hoods when they required a cooler dress, instead of having fur hoods at all seasons. The undress gown for all was to be of the 'priest's' shape (i.e. pudding-sleeved), or of the 'Turkey' variety (i.e. the 'lay' type either with falling collar and false sleeves, or with a yoke and short glove sleeves). The colours of these gowns were to be black or 'London russet', a kind of brown.[6] Here then we have the official recognition of the ordinary undress gown which during the seventeenth century developed into the familiar master's gown, in this case a 'Turkey' gown with a yoke and glove sleeves, and it is worth noticing that at the present day Doctors of Divinity at Cambridge may use a short bell-sleeved gown as an alternative to the master's.[7]

Ten years later Doctors of Divinity were affected as were others by the statute *De Vestitu Scholarium*,[8] which ordered that for all degrees the gown should be ankle-length, that the hood should be constantly worn, that the neck-wear should be of a

---

[1] *Testamenta Eboracensia*, v. 253 [Surtees Soc. lxxix].

[2] *Testamenta Eboracensia*, vi. 198 [Surtees Soc. cvi].

[3] E. R. Suffling, *English Church Brasses*, p. 196, fig. 127.

[4] J. D. Mullinger, *Hist. Univ. of Cambridge*, ii. 392, n. 1.

[5] J. Heywood, p. 241, ¶ 10.

[6] C. H. Cooper, ii. 161–2; B.M. MS. Cole xlii, fos. 290–1, i.e. Add. 5843.

[7] The pudding-sleeved gown was preserved as late as 1803 as the dress of fellows of King's. The mourning gown originated in this.

[8] J. Lamb, *Documents*, pp. 341–2, cap. xlvi; G. Dyer, *Privileges*, i. 195.

priestly character, and that the cap should be square. Those in Orders were to wear a pleated cassock with a collar.[1]

The festal robe for Doctors of Divinity is first directly mentioned in a statute of 1578, which orders that it should be used by all doctors on scarlet days.[2] In 1585 all doctors were allowed full-length facings on their gowns, and the use of silk in their hoods is confirmed,[3] and their hoods might be lined and edged with miniver. In 1588 Lord Burghley, who had been responsible as chancellor for the above enactments of 1578 and 1585, ordered Doctors of Divinity to wear scarlet cloth or black velvet scarves. At the same time he mentioned that the outside of all hoods of whatever degree was to be made of cloth, and pointed out that all graduates must wear the square cap.[4]

In Bedell Buck's book (1665), *Rules for Magna Congregatio or Black Assembly*, the scarlet days and other occasions for festal dress are mentioned.[5] By this time the various other dresses of the Doctor of Divinity had become what they have since been.

What these were can be seen from Loggan's plate in his *Cantabrigia Illustrata* (1690). No. 15 shows the undress consisting of a square black cap with a tuft, a cassock with a sash, and the Master of Arts gown; No. 16 shows the chapel dress, long full surplice with tapering sleeves and full hood; and No. 20 is the Congregation dress. This consists of the same square cap, a scarlet garment open half-way down the front, which was originally placed there to allow for the passage of the arms, the opening being edged with miniver, and over this a miniver-furred hood like a shoulder piece covering the shoulders and reaching half-way down the back.[6] The festal dress (No. 18) consists of an open bell-sleeved robe, the sleeves being folded back at the wrists, a scarf, and a square cap.

From the eighteenth century the Congregation dress was less and less worn by doctors until it came to be used only by professors when presenting candidates for degrees. The cassock

---

[1] Cambridge, Univ. Libr. MS. Mm. 4.51, fo. 243.

[2] C. H. Cooper, ii. 359; G. Dyer, i. 221. See also p. 118, n. 5.

[3] C. H. Cooper, ii. 410–12.

[4] H. Ellis, *Original Letters*, iii. 26, no. ccxxvi ('Ld. Treasurer Burleigh to the University of Cambridge as their Chancellor for the Reformation of Apparel', B.M. MS. Harl. 704, fo. 199).

[5] Cambridge, Univ. Libr. MS. Mm. 1.53, fo. 139; Cambridge, Univ. Libr. MS. Add. 5107, fo. 28.

[6] Cf. the dress of the chancellor and vice-chancellor.

and a broad silk cincture were worn by Doctors of Divinity with all their costumes.

There are two interesting eighteenth-century portraits showing the full dress (or festal) robe. In the portrait of Sir Thomas Gooch, Bart., Bishop of Ely, by an anonymous artist, the scarlet cloth robe is lined with white silk, and the sleeves are not held back by cord and button, as was later the case.[1] Changes are apparent in the second portrait, that of Anthony Shepherd (d. 1796) by L. F. G. van der Puyl, dated 1784. Here the cord and button on the sleeve are to be seen and the robe is lined with scarlet silk (Pl. 15).[2]

By 1803, the year of Harraden's costume book, the colour of the silk lining and the recently introduced facings of the festal robe had come to be salmon-pink, and the full round-shaped scarlet cloth hood, worn only with the chapel dress, was also lined with silk of this colour. The festal robe had by this time come to be used in Congregation instead of the proper Congregation dress. The cord and button had doubtless been introduced in order to keep the hands free of the large sleeves.

A loose plate of the full dress by William Miller (1805) is of much better quality than any in Harraden's collection. It depicts a black square cap with a tassel (the tassel was introduced at Cambridge as at Oxford during the eighteenth century), and the scarlet festal robe lined with cherry-coloured silk, which is incorrect, the long full tapering sleeves being fastened up by means of button and cord. With this is worn a black scarf. The peculiarity of the plate consists in its having in the background a group of Oxford buildings, although this is definitely a Cambridge dress.[3]

T. Uwins's plates (1815) and W. Combe's text give us once more the four dresses of the Doctor of Divinity. First, the festal dress consisted of the open scarlet cloth robe faced with pink silk shot with either pink or violet, the bell sleeves being lined with the same material of the same colour and looped up with a black button and cord. With this was worn cassock, sash, and scarf. The second dress, the Congregation dress, or dress of business, consisted of the scarlet cloth *cappa*, by this time opened

[1] J. W. Goodison, *Catalogue of Cambridge Portraits*, i. 24, and pl. xi, no. 27.
[2] J. W. Goodison, i. 28, and pl. xvi, no. 32.
[3] Oxford, Bodl. Libr. MS. G.A. Oxon. a.72, leaf 21.

right down the front, sleeveless and without holes for the passage for the arms, and so worn like a cloak, fastened at the neck with a bow of scarlet ribbon. It fell to the ground and was edged over three-quarters of the way down the front with white fur. The miniver hood is of the same shape as in 1690, but it is shorter at the back. The third, the undress is not illustrated, but is said to be the pudding-sleeved gown and the cassock, sash, and scarf, although the master's gown was often preferred. The fourth dress was the chapel dress, the same as before described.[1] It should be noticed that the hood worn with the chapel dress was full and rounded, of exactly the same shape as that worn by Oxford doctors.

(f) Doctors of Canon Law

The dress of this degree which existed until the ending of the study of Canon Law at the Reformation,[2] although it was revived for a short time during the reign of Mary Tudor,[3] was, as at Oxford, of the same character as that of the Doctor of Divinity. Thus in 1414 we find that Doctors of Canon Law in common with Masters of Theology and of Arts are to wear the *cappa clausa* for all formal occasions, although at the same time the more comfortable *pallium* is mentioned as also allowable, although less acceptable.[4] Their head-dress was to be the *pileus*.[5] With this was to be worn a hood of the familiar pattern with its 'shoulder piece' lined with the best kind of fur, as runs the royal order of Henry V (1415).[6]

There are no other records of the dress of this degree.

(g) Doctors of Laws (LL.D.)

The dress of Doctors of Laws was in 1414 ordered to be the *cappa manicata* edged with fur certainly, but not lined with it unless the doctors particularly wished it so.[7] They were to wear

---

[1] W. Combe and T. Uwins, ii. 312–13 and pls. at end.
[2] C. H. Cooper, i. 375.
[3] J. Romilly, *Graduati Cantabrigienses*, following p. vi.
[4] Cambridge, Univ. Libr. MS. Mm. 4.47, § 147, fo. 228 (*De Habitubus et insigniis Magistrorum*); J. Heywood, p. 159.
[5] Cambridge, Univ. Libr. MS. Mm. 4.47, § 148, fos. 229 (23) ff.
[6] Cambridge, Univ. Libr. MS. Dd. 4.35, fos. 75 ff.; *Communications, Cambridge Antiquarian Soc.*, 8vo ser. iv (1854), ¶ iii, p. 87.
[7] Cambridge, Univ. Libr. MS. Mm. 4.47, § 147, fo. 228.

this as opposed to the *cappa clausa* of those of Divinity and Canon Law to show their inferiority of position.[1] Their head-dress was the *pileus*.[2] In accordance with the statutes for the *studium* of Cambridge made by Hugh de Balsham, Bishop of Ely, in 1276,[3] incepting Doctors of Laws were to wear a red *cappa manicata*.[4] In the same statute Doctors of Laws are granted the use of the *pallium* as a secondary dress, and when later this *pallium* was dispensed with they were left with the *roba*, which had been worn underneath it, as the outer dress, which developed into the undress gown, which in its turn was discarded for a lay Tudor one. The development was the same as at Oxford. A good example of this secondary dress is to be seen in the brass of Eudo de la Zouch, LL.D., 1414, at St. John's College, Cambridge.

In common with other doctors they were ordered to wear silk linings in their dress according to the Act of Parliament of 1533, and the cloth of their full dress was to be of scarlet, murrey, or violet; they were also allowed a choice of costly furs with which to face or line it.[5] Scarlet was always favoured.[6]

In 1558/9 the square cap was enjoined for them as for others,[7] and in 1576 we hear of insistence upon their wearing the festal robe on suitable occasions.[8] In 1585 they were affected by Burghley's important statutes in that they were to have full-length facings of the same colour as the gown of such stuff as silk. These undress gowns, by this time open, were to be of 'sad color', and as had been enacted in 1560 were to be either false sleeved or of the pudding-sleeved variety.[9] As laymen they took to the first of these shapes.

As to the head-dress, we have seen that the *pileus quadratus* was insisted upon for graduates and for those scholars on foundations in 1559, which followed the enactment of Edward VI's visitors of 1549.[10]

[1] J. Heywood, loc. cit.

[2] Cambridge, Univ. Libr. MS. Mm. 4.47, § 148, fos. 229 (23), ff.

[3] B.M. MS. Harl. 7032, ¶ 146.

[4] Cambridge, Univ. Libr. MS. Mm. 4.47, § 147, fo. 228. This dress is worn by the LL.D. on the extreme right in the illuminated initial of the Confirmatory Charter of Cambridge (1291–2) in the University Archives, Cambridge.

[5] C. H. Cooper, i. 355.   [6] J. R. Tanner, p. 194.

[7] J. Heywood, p. 241, ¶ 10; J. Lamb, p. 290.

[8] C. H. Cooper, ii. 359; G. Dyer, i. 221.

[9] C. H. Cooper, ii. 161–2 and 410–12; B.M. MS. Cole xlii, fo. 29, i.e. B.M. MS. Add. 5843.   [10] J. Heywood, p. 241, ¶ 10; J. D. Mullinger, ii. 392, n. 1.

For full-dress a bonnet with a small brim and a low round pleated top was worn by Doctors of Laws and other lay doctors from the middle of the sixteenth century certainly.[1] A gold cord on these bonnets is mentioned by Bedell Buck in 1665. E. C. Clarke believed that this cord was not a mere decoration but was a symbol of authority.[2] It seems more likely that these gold hat-bands or cords were simply adopted from lay fashion, for late in Elizabeth's reign gold hat-bands were considered a distinguishing feature of the lay dress of noblemen and gentlemen. In Ben Jonson's *Every Man out of his Humour* (1599) a gold cable hat-band is mentioned.[3] Doctors had some pretensions to social standing.

We can see from Loggan (1690) how the dresses of this degree had become stabilized by the later seventeenth century. The undress (No. 14) consists of the black winged-sleeved gown decorated with tassels in rows and with a flap collar much like the Oxford equivalent, and with this is worn surprisingly enough a round bonnet. The Congregation dress (No. 19) is a scarlet dress, closed in front and with holes at the sides for the passage of the arms like the Oxford Convocation habit, with a large hood lined with fur, the flat liripipe of which hangs down almost to the foot of the dress, and a round bonnet; and the festal dress (No. 17) consists of a full scarlet robe with large bell sleeves folded back a little way at the wrists, and a round bonnet. In using the bonnet in the first two instances Burghley's order, to the effect that then the square cap should be worn, was ignored.

After this time the various costumes for the degree changed little. In Uwins's coloured plates of 1815 we see, first, the festal robe of scarlet differing from the festal robe of Doctors of Divinity only in the sleeves being looped up with pink cords and buttons instead of black ones. With this is worn the round black bonnet with a gold cord, and a hood is incorrectly worn over the festal robe. Next, the Congregation dress is shown, which consists of the scarlet cloth *cappa* of the same shape as that of the

---

[1] E. C. Clarke, art. cit., lxi. 33, believed 'in fault of proof to the contrary' that the bonnet appeared at Cambridge in the fifteenth century, but there is no evidence to support him. It was introduced into academical dress from lay fashion.

[2] E. C. Clarke, art. cit., lxi. 64.

[3] J. A. Repton, art. 'Observations on the Fashions of Hats' in *Archaeologia,* xxiv (1832), 184.

Doctor of Divinity. It is faced with miniver and is worn with a scarlet hood lined with miniver of the same shape as worn in 1690. The bonnet is also worn with this dress. The undress, with which a black tasselled square cap is worn, consists of a plain black silk gown (the tufts having vanished) fastened up in front with two pieces of black ribbon to form a bow, the 'strings' of later times.[1] The arms came through a gash, of which the upper part was cut in the shape of an inverted V, from which a seam ran up to the shoulder. The sleeves hung down in square-ended false panels, and the gown had a square flap collar.[2]

(h) Doctors of Medicine

The degree of Doctor of Medicine was instituted after that of Doctor of Laws, the earliest doctorate in a secular faculty, and holders of it wore the same dress as Doctors of Laws.[3] Regents in Medicine are mentioned in 1414, when like legist regents they were ordered to wear the *cappa manicata*, edged with fur or lined with it if they so preferred,[4] but there is at this time no record of inceptors for this degree being ordered to wear a red *cappa* as inceptors in the Faculty of Laws were ordered to do.

From then on in all particulars the history of their costume is that of Doctors of Laws, and so the scarlet festal robe came to them in the sixteenth century, and at the time of Queen Elizabeth's visit to Cambridge in 1564 Doctors of 'Physic' wore this robe with a hood to match lined with miniver.[5] The first evidence that we have of the round bonnet worn by holders of this degree is the 17th century picture of a university procession by Cobbould after Bedell Stokys (1590) in the Registry at Cambridge (Pl. 14).[6]

In Loggan (1690) the dress is the same as that of Doctors of Laws,[7] and consists of the festal robe, the Congregation *cappa* dress, and the undress gown, a bonnet with a gold cord being used in the first two cases and without one in the third.

Late in the eighteenth century, however, while Doctors of Laws continued to wear for undress the plain black silk gown

---

[1] For an account of 'strings' see under § (j), the description of Loggan's illustration of a Master of Arts.   [2] W. Combe and T. Uwins, ii. 312–13.
[3] Cf. *Cambridge Grace Book Δ*, p. 28.
[4] Cambridge, Univ. Libr. MS. Mm. 4.47, § 147, fo. 228.
[5] B.M. MS. Cole xliv, fo. 382, i.e. MS. Add. 5845.
[6] E. C. Clarke, art. cit. lxi. 62.   [7] Nos. 14, 17, and 19.

PLATE 14

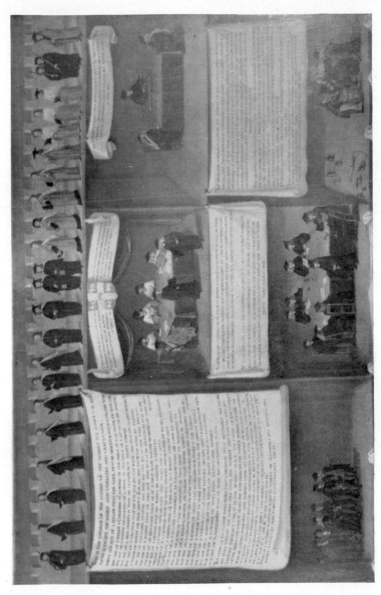

Seventeenth-century picture by Cobbould after the picture by Bedell Stokys (1590) of a Cambridge University Procession and various ceremonies

PLATE 15

Anthony Shepherd, D.D. (d. 1796) by L. F. G. van der Puyl

(without tufts since the previous century), Doctors of Medicine had theirs worked with ornaments of black cross and bead braiding on the upper part of the false sleeve, and with plain braid on the facings and on the flap collar. The engraving of the portrait by J. Page of R. G. Clobury, M.D. (d. 1800),[1] provides a good illustration of this.[2] The change must have come about after 1780, for in John Downman's chalk drawing of Thomas Okes, M.D., of this year, Okes wears a plain silk gown exactly the same as the Doctor of Laws undress gown described above except that no 'strings' can be seen.[3]

(i) Doctors of Music

As was the case at Oxford holders of degrees in Music stood outside university affairs in an ambiguous position. The degree of Doctor of Music was instituted in the early sixteenth century. All that we know of their early dress is the statement in 1545 that an inceptor for the doctorate is to appear in the dress of a Doctor of Medicine,[4] from which we may conclude that by grace and not by right they shared the dress of the Doctors of Laws and of Medicine. This was not the case later in the century, and by 1578 when Burghley ordered the full scarlet festal dress to be worn by doctors on scarlet days,[5] they had perhaps taken to their full dress of white brocade lined with purple silk.[6] In all probability it was as a result of their inferior position as not of necessity being members even of the Black or Non-Regent Assembly, that led to their having a festal dress with no scarlet in it. In 1605 on presentation to this degree by grace, candidates wore the hood and gown of Bachelors of Arts, afterwards assuming the doctoral dress.[7]

In Loggan (No. 13) they wear the round bonnet, the brocaded robe and a hood to match.

In Harraden's plates (1803) this full dress is again shown, and consists of a white satin robe and hood, both lined with crimson silk, and a round black velvet bonnet with a gold cord and tassel. The large tapering sleeves of the robe are caught up

---

[1] Oxford, Ashmolean Museum (Hope Collection).
[2] See also W. Combe and T. Uwins, ii. 312–13.
[3] Cambridge, Fitzw. Mus., no. 1943.   [4] *Cambridge Grace Book Δ*, p. 28.
[5] C. H. Cooper, ii. 359; G. Dyer, i. 221.
[6] Cf. J. R. Tanner, p. 194.
[7] Cambridge, Univ. Libr. MS. Mm. 5.50 (Adam Wall MS. vol. 1), fo. 68.

above the wrist with a crimson cord and button, and the robe, instead of having a yoke as do the other festal robes, has a black velvet flap collar.

Again in Uwins's plate of 1815 the full dress robe is of white damask or satin and the sleeves are lined with crimson satin, while the hood is of white damask lined with crimson satin. The bonnet is the same as in 1803. The undress is described as being the Master of Arts gown, and by grace, though not by right, the non-regent's black hood was worn with it.[1]

(j) Masters of Arts

The history of this dress is in general outline the same as that of the same degree at Oxford.[2]

In 1414 Regent Masters of Arts were ordered to use the *cappa clausa* or *pallium* during lectures and disputations and on all important occasions, but on less formal occasions they were allowed the use of the *cappa manicata*, the much more comfortable substitute.[3] They were not allowed the *pileus*, which was reserved for doctors.[4] At the same time the use of silk on their dress was granted to all masters gremial.[5]

In the following year these enactments were confirmed by the royal order of Henry V when it was added that masters both regent and non-regent were to wear, as showing their dignity, fur of good quality in their hoods.[6]

Until the middle of the fifteenth century the generally worn dress of Masters of Arts consisted of the *supertunica*, the short sleeved *cappa manicata* with pointed ends to the sleeves, a 'shoulder piece' edged with fur only at the bottom edge, and attached to it the fur-lined hood proper, without a head-dress. However, after the middle of this century the *cappa manicata* was

[1] W. Combe and T. Uwins, ii. 312–13.

[2] H. Druitt, p. 135.

[3] Cambridge, Univ. Libr. MS. Mm. 4.47, § 147, fo. 228 (22); J. Heywood, p. 159.

[4] Cambridge, Univ. Libr. MS. Mm. 4.47, § 148, fos. 229 (23) ff.

[5] C. H. Cooper, op. cit. i. 157. Gremials were those who were permanent residents in the university and generally also associated members of it who lived in some college, hall, or hostel, but non-regent masters if resident in the town were also regarded as gremials. This distinction of dress as regards gremials was still observed in the seventeenth century (G. Peacock, *Observations on the Statutes of Cambridge*, app. A, p. xvii, n. 1).

[6] Cambridge, Univ. Libr. MS. Dd. 4.35, fos. 75 ff.; *Communications, Cambridge Antiquarian Soc.*, 8vo ser. iv. ¶ iii, p. 87.

given up by them, and the sleeveless *tabard* (a closed dress shorter than the *supertunica*, which continued to be worn underneath it), with fur-lined slits at the sides for the passage of the arms, took its place as the ordinary outer dress.[1] This dress is seen worn by a Cambridge Master of Arts in the brass of William Blakwey (d. 1521) at Little Wilbraham, Cambs.[2] Early in the sixteenth century the 'shoulder piece' was no longer worn, and the hood, much elongated, was used alone, at any rate by 1545, the date of a brass of a vice-provost in Eton College chapel.

From this time on, as was the case before, the changes in the dress, except hoods, of Cambridge masters followed the same process as at Oxford. The *roba*, developed from the *supertunica*, came into its own during the sixteenth century since the tabard had been left off. By 1589 the *roba* already had very short glove-sleeves.[3]

The head-dress of masters—they do not appear to have been allowed one until the Reformation—was the *pileus quadratus*, which was enjoined upon them in company with other graduates in 1549,[4] in 1559,[5] in 1570,[6] in 1585,[7] and in 1588.[8]

In the Elizabethan statutes we notice that the gown of masters is to be of a black, brown, or other such sombre colour, with a standing collar, the material being wool-cloth, but they might be partly faced with black silk or other material.[9] These statutes, particularly those of 1560, were a reiteration of the Act of Parliament of 1533.[10]

It is in the history of the hoods of Masters of Arts that we find the main differences from those of Oxford, but these differences

---

[1] H. Druitt, pp. 135–6; E. C. Clarke, art. 'English Academic Costume', in *Archaeological Journal*, l (1893), 202.

[2] E. C. Clarke, loc. cit. The long-sleeved gowns of the period 1450–1525 mentioned by Druitt (op. cit., pp. 136 and 137, n. 1) appear to be examples of the priestly gown such as is illustrated in J. S. Cotman, *Sepulchral Brasses of Norfolk and Suffolk*, ii, pl. xcviii).

[3] Brass of Edward Leeds, Master of Clare College, 1589, in Croxton Church, Cambs. See also for another example a brass of 1619 illustrated in J. S. Cotman, op. cit., ii, pl. xliii, brass of Henry Mason (1619), Eyke Church, Suffolk.

[4] J. D. Mullinger, ii. 392, n. 1.   [5] J. Heywood, p. 241, ¶ 10.

[6] J. Lamb, p. 341.   [7] E. T. Beaumont, *Academical Habit*, p. 57.

[8] E. C. Clarke, art. cit., lxi. 44–45.

[9] C. H. Cooper, ii. 161–2 and 410–12; B.M. MS. Cole xlii, fo. 290, i.e. MS. Add. 5843; C. Wordsworth, pp. 495–6.

[10] *Statutes of the Realm*, iii. 430–2—24° Hen. VIII, c. 13.

do not occur before the middle of the sixteenth century. The Act of 1533 implies that fur was used in the masters' hoods.[1]

There seems to have been no distinction between the hoods of regents and non-regents until the middle of the sixteenth century, but in 1545 'non-regent dress' is mentioned,[2] and in the statutes of Dr. Caius for his refounded Gonville Hall (1558) we notice that the hoods for regents and non-regents are to be different. In this case hoods worn by regent masters were to be lined with miniver, but those of non-regents were to be lined with silk. The colour is not mentioned, but probably lack is meant.[3] It is uncertain how long it was before the distinction between regent and non-regent hoods was accepted throughout the university, but in 1614 the black cloth hoods lined with white fur of regents and the black cloth hoods lined with black cloth of non-regents are mentioned.[4]

The practice pursued in regard to this distinction was that from the time of inception all Masters of Arts were (keeping up the fiction derived from medieval times) nominally liable to teach and were thus considered 'necessary regents', and so wore the white hood for five years after taking their degree; but after that period, unless in the meantime they had been chosen fellows or tutors, they left off the white hood and took to the black one which they henceforth always wore.[5] The use of the regent hood by all newly admitted masters is mentioned by Bedell Buck in 1665.[6] As at Oxford, in the course of the seventeenth century the use of miniver in the regent hood was gradually given up, and at Cambridge white silk was substituted for it.

In Loggan's plate (1690) the Master of Arts (No. 7) wears the square cap and gown exactly the same as those worn by the Oxford master at that time. There was one point of difference, however, although it cannot be seen here, which was that 'strings' were attached to the Cambridge gown. They consisted of two pieces of black ribbon fastened one on each side of the gown in front under the facings, and were originally used to tie up the gown.[7] 'Strings' were worn not only on masters' gowns,

---

[1] *Statutes of the Realm*, loc. cit.   [2] *Cambridge Grace Book Δ*, fo. 12 b.
[3] *Cambridge University and College Statutes*, ii. 259–60, ¶ 27 (*De Vestitu*).
[4] B.M. MS. Cole xlii, fo. 286, i.e. MS. Add. 5843.
[5] *Notes and Queries*, 2nd ser. v. 501–2.
[6] Cambridge, Univ. Libr. MS. Add. 5107, fo. 39.
[7] Cambridge, Univ. Libr. MS. Add. 2616, no. 3, fo. 144 (R. Gooch, *Collectanea*).

but on those of all other degrees. They were introduced in the sixteenth century when gowns became open. The reason for their not appearing in Loggan, Harraden, and Uwins is because from their position they could not be seen unless the wearer was in movement. The regent master (No. 8) wears a fully displayed hood with all the lining showing. It is large and descends to the liripipe in the same way as an Oxford master's hood, but has a square of material underneath the main part of the hood. On the other hand, the non-regent (No. 9) wears a plain black cloth hood which appears as a simple square of black material covering the shoulders and reaching half-way down the back.

On studying Harraden (1803) we see that at this time on informal occasions Masters of Arts wore an ordinary hat with the gown,[1] but a hat was never worn when the hood was, the square cap being then used.

By the time we reach Uwins's plates of 1815 the gown is the same as before, but the non-regent hood has become full and of the same shape as that of the regent.[2] It was silk-lined.

There were two different ways of wearing the regent hood. When worn 'squared' for ordinary occasions it appeared entirely black except for a thin edging of the white silk lining, but when 'flourished' or 'displayed' all the white showed.[3] The 'flourished' hood is thus described: 'The hood "flourished" signifies not merely that it is pendant in chance folds, but that the peaked position of the lines is folded over till it touches the flat half of the hood which covers the back; so that if the hood were applied to its original use, the frontlet of the "head gear" would be the white edging.'[4]

Masters of Surgery wore the dress of non-regents in the early nineteenth century, and presumably they did so earlier, but there is no record.

(k) Bachelors of Divinity

In the draft of regulations for the halls of Cambridge made by Hugh de Balsham, Bishop of Ely, in 1276, Bachelors of Divinity of the *studium* were expected to wear a *cappa clausa*.[5] Their dress by the fifteenth century had come to be the same as

---

[1] Cambridge, Univ. Libr. MS. Add. 2616, no. 3, fo. 144 (R. Gooch, *Collectanea*).
[2] W. Combe and T. Uwins, ii. 312–13.   [3] W. Combe and T. Uwins, loc. cit.
[4] *Notes and Queries*, 2nd ser. viii. 74–75.   [5] B.M. MS. Harl. 7032, ¶ 146.

that of Bachelors of Divinity at Oxford, and consisted of *sub-tunica*, *supertunica*, and a *cappa clausa* with two side slits. With this was worn a hood lined with white fur and a 'shoulder piece' similarly lined. They had no form of head-dress.[1]

What kind of fur was used on the dress can be seen from a clause in the royal statutes of 1415, in which Bachelors of Divinity in common with bachelors of other faculties were ordered to use only fur of inferior quality such as budge or lamb's-wool.[2] In 1494, however, they were allowed by grace to use silk for the lining of their hoods.[3]

In 1533 the Act of Parliament allowed them a scarlet lining to their *roba*, which had become the outside garment.[4] In common with others they began to wear the square cap in the reign of Edward VI, and this was confirmed in 1559.[5] According to the Elizabethan statutes ranging from 1560 to 1585 their gown was to be the same as that of Masters of Arts of either the 'priest's' or the 'Turkey' variety.[6]

By 1690 their dress with its square cap with a tuft, black gown, and black hood was exactly the same as that of the non-regent masters. They wore the non-regent hood in virtue of their being regarded as non-regents when they took this degree, more than five years always having elapsed from their being admitted to the master's degree before they could proceed to the degree of Bachelor of Divinity.[7]

By 1815 the hood was lined with black silk in conformity with the similar elaboration of the non-regent master's,[8] and so by a dissimilar process became the same as the Oxford Bachelor of Divinity hood except that it was less full.

(*l*) *Bachelors of Canon Law*

The last graduations in Canon Law at Cambridge took place in 1556.[9] There is no direct evidence for the dress of this degree,

---

[1] H. Druitt, p. 135.

[2] Cambridge, Univ. Libr. MS. Dd. 4.35, fos. 75 ff.; *Communications, Cambridge Antiquarian Soc.*, 8vo ser. iv, ¶ iii, p. 87.   [3] *Cambridge Grace Book B*, pt. i, p. 70.

[4] C. H. Cooper, i. 355.   [5] J. Heywood, p. 241, ¶ 10.

[6] C. H. Cooper, ii. 161–2 and 410–12.

[7] Compare with this the Oxford Bachelor of Divinity hood whose black lining represented the original colour of the Faculty of Theology, whereas the Cambridge non-regent hood was simply the small clerkly hood common to all members of universities in the Middle Ages.

[8] W. Combe and T. Uwins, ii. 312–13.   [9] J. Romilly, following p. vi.

and it can only be inferred that it was like that of Masters of Arts and Bachelors of Divinity.[1] In 1533 in company with masters and others of higher standing below the doctorates they were allowed a variety of furs but of secondary quality.[2]

(m) Bachelors of Laws

The dress of Bachelors of Laws was in medieval times the same as that of bachelors of the higher faculties, and followed the same changes and developments. The only departure from these principles is referred to in 1522 when Bachelors of Laws were allowed the use of silk or miniver in their hoods at the time of the disputations to complete the exercises for their degree (*tempore sue predicationis*), on condition of a certain payment to the university.[3]

The Elizabethan statutes treated them better than Masters of Arts and Bachelors of Medicine, allowing them silk or other rich stuff on their collars as well as half a yard of silk down the facings of their black or dark gowns.[4] During the seventeenth century they wore, with a Bachelor of Arts hood, a winged-sleeved gown with tufts at the top of the sleeves and four rows of button and cord braiding at the bottom of them, which appears in Loggan's costume plate as No. 6, but during the eighteenth century they seem to have taken to the plain Bachelor of Arts gown as can be seen from John Downman's chalk drawing of Charles Chadwick, LL.B. (1778).[5] By 1815, however, they had come to wear the master's gown with 'strings', and the non-regent black hood,[6] and they sometimes even attempted to assume the regent hood.[7] A tassel was added to the tump of their square cap in the middle of the eighteenth century.

(n) Bachelors of Medicine

The history and development of the dress of this degree are exactly the same as that of the Bachelor of Laws.

Apparently in Elizabethan times Bachelors of Medicine as

[1] Cf. E. C. Clarke, art. cit., l. 207–8; E. T. Beaumont, *Academical Habit*, p. 27.
[2] *Statutes of the Realm*, loc. cit.
[3] *Cambridge Grace Book Γ*, p. 199.
[4] C. H. Cooper, ii. 161–2; C. Wordsworth, p. 496.
[5] Cambridge, Fitzw. Mus., no. 1894.
[6] W. Combe and T. Uwins, ii. 312–13.
[7] *Notes and Queries*, 2nd ser. v. 501–2.

being practising physicians and so 'doctors' tried to affect the scarlet *cappa* (or Congregation) dress of Doctors of Medicine, for a clause in a university statute of 1570 orders them to wear a tabard, which they chose to interpret as a long over-garment such as the *cappa* was. In fact, 'tabard' was simply used loosely for 'gown'.[1]

In Loggan's 1690 plate (No. 6) they wear a winged-sleeved tufted and braided gown with a Bachelor of Arts hood, but they did not do so after the eighteenth century. Certainly by 1815 they were wearing the non-regent master's costume.[2]

The Baccalaureate of Surgery was always held in conjunction with this degree, and so there was no separate dress for it.

(o) Bachelors of Music

In 1502 an Oxford Bachelor of Music who wished to be incorporated as Bachelor of Music at Cambridge was allowed by grace to have the academical dress of this degree of any colour he wished.[3] It seems to have been the shape or cut of the habit which mattered as yet. By 1545 Bachelors of Music were wearing non-regent master's dress.[4] In Burghley's statutes of 1585 Bachelors of Music, together with Master of Arts and Bachelors of Laws and Medicine, were allowed silk or similar facings running part of the length of their gown.[5] In 1606 and 1616 there are references to the use of Bachelor of Arts dress by Bachelors of Music.[6] After this we hear no more of their dress for a long time, in fact until 1815, by which date they were wearing once more the costume of non-regent masters.[7]

(p) Bachelors of Arts

The dress of the degree of Bachelor of Arts is mentioned for the first time in the statutes of King's Hall (1380), and is to consist of a *roba* (i.e. *supertunica*) with a tabard suitable to the degree over it.[8]

In 1414, according to the university statutes, bachelors were ordered to wear a tabard on which there was to be no kind of

---

[1] Cambridge, Univ. Libr. MS. Mm. 4.51, § 3, fo. 383.
[2] W. Combe and T. Uwins, ii. 312–13.
[3] C. F. Abdy Williams, *Historical Account of Degrees in Music*, p. 154; *Cambridge Grace Book Γ*, p. 5.   [4] *Cambridge Grace Book Δ*, p. 28.
[5] C. H. Cooper, ii. 410–12.   [6] C. F. Abdy Williams, p. 156.
[7] W. Combe and T. Uwins, ii. 312–13.   [8] T. Rymer, *Foedera*, tom. vii, p. 242 b.

adornment of fur or silk or anything of value. On their hoods they were allowed to use only budge or lamb's-wool unless of noble family when they might use rich fur.[1] They were not to have any head-covering.[2] Thus we realize that at both Oxford and Cambridge the dress of Bachelors of Arts in the Middle Ages consisted of a *supertunica*, with a sleeved tabard over it, and presumably a 'shoulder piece' and a furred hood.

There next followed the process which has been described in the account of the dress of Oxford Bachelors of Arts, the leaving off of the tabard during the latter part of the fifteenth century with the consequent enlargement of the *roba*, which now became the outer dress with full sleeves.[3]

Bachelors of Arts gained a head-dress during the sixteenth century, for they were ordered to wear the *pileus quadratus* from 1559 onwards.[4] In 1585 Burghley ordered them to wear black or brown cloth gowns with cloth facings (the gown now being open in front), a standing collar, and a hood of the same material and colour as the gown.[5] The use of budge or lamb's-wool in the hood was still enforced, and the square cap was again enjoined as the head-dress. In 1586 they were warned against wearing silk facings on their gowns.[6]

In 1690 the bachelor's dress appears in Loggan's costume plate (No. 5) as a black square cap with a tuft, a black gown with very full and long tapering sleeves exactly the same as the sleeves of the Oxford Bachelor of Arts, and a full hood with a 'displayed' lining of white fur. John Evelyn in 1680,[7] and John Byrom in 1711,[8] mention that lamb's-skin was used for the lining. According to the university statutes of 1750 the official material for the gown was 'Prunello or Prince's Stuff'.[9]

---

[1] *Communications, Cambridge Antiquarian Soc.*, 8vo ser. iv, ¶ v, p. 89.

[2] Cambridge, Univ. Libr. MS. Dd. 4.35, § 5; Cambridge, Univ. Libr. MS. Mm. 4.47, § 176, fos. 271 (65) ff. (*De penulis et pelluris Baccalaureorum*); C. H. Cooper, op. cit. i. 156–7.

[3] G. Clinch, *English Costume*, pp. 250–1 and 253. In view of the development of all other academical costumes at this time which resulted in formal outer garments being left off and the *supertunica* taking their place, the opinion of H. Druitt (pp. 135–6), that the Cambridge bachelor's gown of modern times is the original tabard, seems untenable.   [4] J. Heywood, p. 241.

[5] C. H. Cooper, ii. 410–12.

[6] Cambridge, Univ. Libr. MS. Mm. 4.56, § 1, fo. 62.

[7] *The Diary of John Evelyn*, ed. E. S. de Beer, iv. 217.

[8] J. Byrom, *Remains*, i, pt. l, p. 17 (Chetham Soc., vol. xxxii, 1854).

[9] Cambridge, Univ. Libr. MS. Mm. 4.55, § 1, fo. 126.

From 1777 to 1780 the well-known artist John Downman stayed in Cambridge and made a good income by executing chalk drawings of members of the university, especially those who had just taken degrees. Many are in the Fitzwilliam Museum, and there are three examples of Bachelor of Arts dress, one of 1777 and two of 1778.[1]

In 1803 according to Harraden the gown was generally made of bombazine and the hood was lined with lamb's-wool, while the sleeves of the gown were the same as in 1690. The black square cap, by this time with a tassel, was used.

The dress in 1815 was the same as before except for a change in the gown's sleeves, which, although retaining the same shape as before, had now a hole in the front, through which the arms passed. This was the first change made to free the hand from the cumbrous, loose sleeve. It is important also to notice that the black 'strings' were fastened on the front in a bow,[2] as they had been in 1792.[3] Later the sleeves were split open down the seam right from the shoulder, so that they hung down free of the arm, for the sake of convenience when dining.[4] Cuff-strings were never used at Cambridge.

(q) Undergraduates

1. *Students of Civil Law.* As result of the fact that originally the standing of students of Civil Law in the Faculty of Law was considered as equivalent to that of Bachelors of Arts in the Faculty of Arts, they wore the dress of Bachelors of Arts.[5]

2. *Noblemen.* According to the enactments of the Congregation of 1414, noblemen, while they were to conform in general shape to the *talaris* dress of scholars in the widest sense of the word 'scholars', were allowed silk facings to their dress like masters gremial and beneficiaries of good position.[6] At the same time they were allowed to use rich fur in their hoods if noblemen-bachelors.[7]

---

[1] Examples of those in Bachelor of Arts dress are Francis Randolph (1777) (Fitzw. Mus. no. 1819); Thomas Mantell (1778) (Fitzw. Mus. no. 1865); and Gilbert Wakefield, Porson's enemy (1778) (Fitzw. Mus. no. 1874).

[2] W. Combe and T. Uwins, ii. p. 313.

[3] J. W. Goodison, p. 105 (portrait of Philip Francis).

[4] *Notes and Queries,* 2nd ser. viii. 74–75.

[5] *Notes and Queries,* 2nd ser. x. 160–1; *Notes and Queries,* 2nd. ser. vi. 258 a.

[6] C. H. Cooper, i. 157.

[7] Cambridge, Univ. Libr. MS. Mm. 4.47, § 176, fos. 271 (65), ff.

In the statutes of Cardinal Pole (chancellor 1556–8) noblemen and their sons were allowed to wear at the university any dress they liked since they were living at their own expense,[1] but when from 1566 onwards the university under the chancellorship of Sir William Cecil, afterwards Lord Burghley, began to legislate about academical dress,[2] their costume was brought into general line with that of other undergraduates, though it was in every way richer.

In 1588 Burghley in a letter to the university ordered that, though they must conform to the wearing of a round cap, which was to be worn by those not on foundations, noblemen might have them made of black velvet.[3] This was a reiteration of the 1585 order.[4]

By 1690 their dress had become so greatly elaborated that they wore a brocaded gown with braiding and buttons at the shoulders, and with false panel sleeves reaching to the hem of the gown decorated in two places with a square of braid.[5] The round velvet cap was still worn, but as often as not an ordinary lay hat. So popular among noblemen did the wearing of ordinary hats become that their use was given official sanction, as long as they were plain, in the statutes of 1750.[6]

In 1769 the cap of all undergraduates was changed from round to square,[7] and in Harraden's plate (1803) we find the nobleman wearing a black square cap with a gold tassel. With this he wears a long pale blue gown (the full dress) edged with gold lace, a gold embroidered coronet appearing on the train of the gown. The sleeves are winged and have false panels, and the whole dress is decorated at intervals with great double knots of gold braid sewn on. The colour of this silk gown might vary according to choice. The great Cambridge benefactor Viscount Fitzwilliam wore when a nobleman of Trinity Hall (1761–4) a red silk gown embroidered with gold lace, as can be seen from his portrait (1764) painted by Joseph Wright of Derby,[8] but blue

---

[1] J. Heywood, pp. 241–3, ¶ 10; J. Lamb, pp. 245–7.
[2] C. H. Cooper, ii. 230.
[3] H. Ellis, iii. 26; E. C. Clarke, art. cit., lxi. 44–45.
[4] E. T. Beaumont, *Academical Habit*, p. 57.
[5] D. Loggan, costume plate, no. 21.
[6] Cambridge, Univ. Libr. MS. Mm. 4.55, § 1, fo. 126.
[7] C. H. Cooper, iv. 355.
[8] J. W. Goodison, i. 89 and pl. xv, no. 127.

was the favourite colour. The undress of noblemen was a full
bell-sleeved black silk gown, and with this a three-cornered hat,
by 1803 a top-hat, was worn.[1]

3. *Fellow-commoners*. This order was the equivalent of the
Oxford gentleman-commoner (fellow-commoner, however, at
Worcester), but in earlier times it was not well defined, and
fellow-commoners were treated as members of the order of
noblemen in the statutes of Cardinal Pole.[2] In common with
them they were in 1588 allowed round black velvet caps,[3] but
they were forced to conform to the Burghley statutes as regards
a sober and clerical colour of dress. By 1690[4] they wore the
winged-sleeved gown, braided in loop and button style at the
bottom of the sleeves, on the skirt at each side, and at the back.
With this gown an ordinary lay hat was worn.

In Harraden's plate of 1803 the dress consists of a black
square cap with a gold tassel and a false panel-sleeved gown of
black Prince's stuff. The sleeves above the arms are richly
embroidered with horizontal bars of gold lace, but the panels are
plain except that very near the bottom there is one horizontal
row of gold braid. The shoulders of the gown are stuffed so as to
form a high ridge, which is also decorated with gold braid.

A distinction had been made half a century before between
two kinds of fellow-commoners. Those who were the eldest sons
of baronets and the younger sons of noblemen had in 1750[5] been
confirmed in their use of an ordinary hat instead of the square
academical one for informal occasions, and were called 'hat
fellow-commoners', but ordinary fellow-commoners had to
conform to the wearing of the square cap. For formal wear both
classes used the black velvet square one with a gold tassel,
which we know was used in 1736, as can be seen in Hogarth's
full-length portrait of this year of Thomas Western, a fellow-
commoner of Clare.[6]

Fellow-commoners of Trinity were distinguished from fellow-
commoners of other colleges, who had black gowns decorated

[1] Cambridge, Univ. Libr. MS. Mm. 4.55, § 1, fo. 126.
[2] J. Heywood, loc. cit.; J. Lamb, loc. cit.
[3] H. Ellis, iii. 26; C. H. Cooper, ii. 456.
[4] D. Loggan, op. cit., no. 4.
[5] Cambridge, Univ. Libr. MS. Mm. 4.55, § 1, fo. 126.
[6] R. B. Becket, *Hogarth*, p. 61 and pl. 80. According to the *New English Dictionary*
the term 'tuft-hunter' was first used at Cambridge in 1755.

with gold braid,[1] by having a blue bell-sleeved gown decorated down the front on each side of the opening with a zigzag line of silver braid. They wore a blue gown in virtue of the foundation statutes of their college (1546),[2] although violet appears to have been originally intended. Fellow-commoners of Trinity wore a square black velvet cap with a silver tassel.

Two water-colours by the artist Silvester Harding provide excellent illustrations of the gown of fellow-commoners of Trinity and of those of all the other colleges. His portrait of J. T. Nottidge (1794) shows him wearing the silver-laced, light blue gown,[3] while that of Marmaduke Dayrell (about 1790), a fellow-commoner of Christ's, depicts him in the black gown decorated with gold lace.[4]

In 1815 all fellow-commoners, except those of Trinity and Emmanuel, wore a black gown of Prince's stuff with a velvet 'bridge' yoke and velvet facings down the front, and false panel sleeves, together with a square black velvet cap with a gold tassel, unless 'hat fellow-commoners' who wore a top-hat. Fellow-commoners of Trinity wore blue bell-sleeved gowns decorated with gold buttons on the sleeves, and gold lace, while those of Emmanuel had their black, velvet-faced gown decorated with gold embroidery round the shoulder-ribs, on the skirts, and on the panel-sleeves in bars and squares.[5] It thus appears that between 1803 and 1815 gold braid had been left off the gowns of fellow-commoners of all the other colleges. Trinity fellow-commoners had changed from silver to gold.

4. *Pensioners*. As opposed to Oxford the dress of under-graduates at Cambridge was generally a college and not a university affair, at any rate in later times, except as regards head-dress. King's Hall seems to have been the first Cambridge body to pay special attention to dress. In 1380 its scholars were ordered to wear a long outer garment (*roba talaris*) befitting their state of being clerks.[6]

By the middle of the next century the dress of the scholars had been somewhat elaborated, as appears from the foundation statutes of King's College (1441), in which undergraduate

---

[1] R. B. Becket, loc. cit.
[2] *Cambridge University and College Statutes*, iii. 444 and 446.
[3] J. W. Goodison, i. 108.   [4] J. W. Goodison, i. 107.
[5] W. Combe and T. Uwins, ii. 313.   [6] T. Rymer, tom. vii, p. 242b.

members were bidden to use a short tabard (as an outer dress) and a cloth hood.[1]

In the foundation statutes of Trinity (1546) we find that a definite livery was intended for junior members of the college, for it was ordered that all bachelors and undergraduates of the college were to wear gowns of a violet colour. This dress, together with a head-dress, was to be used on all occasions, even more particularly in public, so that everyone might be able to admire the college's corporate qualities through such visible symbols.[2] This use of the statutory colour, which came to be blue, was maintained by undergraduates but not by bachelors. It is mentioned in 1669,[3] and in 1711.[4]

Caius at the time of his refounding of Gonville Hall in 1558 had the same idea in mind when he ordered all members of his new college to wear a *vestis,* a long gown reaching to the ankles, with full sleeves, and a standing collar, the whole to be of black or violet, or a colour in between the two.[5] This being so, it is impossible to doubt that the fellows must have known this when in 1837 the blue gown was introduced for undergraduates of Caius.[6] Although, of course, this was according to statute, until that year black seems always to have been used.

It is noticeable that so reactionary was Caius, who seems to have remained faithful to the Church of Rome, that he also ordered the *exomis* ('shoulder piece') to be worn as part of the dress, and a *tunica* or cassock under the gown whether the wearer was in Orders or not.[7] It is scarcely likely that such a rule was long obeyed. Apart from these exceptional rules the statute dress at the other colleges had become at the beginning of Elizabeth's reign a dark coloured gown with a cloth hood to match.

In 1549 scholars on the foundations of colleges were ordered

---

[1] *Cambridge University and College Statutes,* ii. 538–9, § 23 (*De habitu Sociorum et Scholarium*).

[2] Cambridge, Univ. Libr. MS. Mm. 1.40 (Baker MS., vol. 29) (*Statuta Sanctae et Ind. Trinitatis Cantabrig.*), cap. 23, fo. 159, and cap. 21, fos. 157–8; *Cambridge University and College Statutes,* iii. 444 and 446.

[3] S. Newton, *Diary,* p. 46.

[4] J. Byrom, p. 17. It is still used.

[5] *Cambridge University and College Statutes,* ii. 258–60, ¶ 27 (*De Vestitu*).

[6] A. G. Almond (*Gowns and Gossip,* p. 14) seems unaware of this and quotes Whibley's poem *In Cap and Gown* which mocks Caius for using Trinity blue.

[7] *Cambridge University and College Statutes,* loc. cit.

by the parliamentary visitors to wear square caps, but apart from the question of head-dress the university in the following years left the initiative with the colleges, and in 1559 the colleges were ordered to obey their several statutes.[1] By 1570 pensioners were wearing the dress of the character which remained theirs for nearly two hundred years, an ankle-length gown and a round bonnet with a band and a brim larger than that on the Oxford one. It did not originate as at Oxford in the apprentice's 'catercap', but in the ordinary lay hat of the period.[2] Black hats were again enjoined for the generality of undergraduates in 1576,[3] and the wearing of the round cloth cap by pensioners was again insisted on by Burghley in 1588.[4] In Jacobean times, when the gown was also elaborated, black velvet was added to the brim of the pensioner's bonnet which otherwise continued to be of black cloth lined with black silk on canvas.[5]

By the end of the seventeenth century the dress of pensioners varied, as can be realized by studying D. Loggan's plates. The gown worn at Trinity was violet and full-sleeved like a Bachelor of Arts gown;[6] at King's, Queens', Peterhouse, and Trinity Hall a plain black gown was worn, in shape like that used at Trinity but in every way shorter,[7] and as nearly all members of these four colleges were on the foundation it seems reasonable to suppose that the bell-sleeved gown which they wore was a natural development of the sleeved *supertunica*, a 'clerkly' dress. At all the other Cambridge colleges, with a few exceptions for special scholars, a lay type of gown (like that worn by Oxford commoners) had appeared during the sixteenth century. The majority of the members of those colleges were not on foundations, and so in those the lay type of gown prevailed.

This lay gown appears to have been worn as a prescribed dress for pensioners from about 1570,[8] and was further elaborated during Jacobean times. In Loggan's costume plate (figure No. 1)

---

[1] J. D. Mullinger, op. cit. ii. 392, n. 1.   [2] J. D. Mullinger, op. cit. ii. 392.
[3] C. E. Mallet, *History of the University of Oxford*, ii. 120.
[4] H. Ellis, iii. 25.   [5] C. H. Cooper, iv. 355.
[6] D. Loggan, no. 3. A miniature of John Byrom (1709), who in that year was elected to the foundation at Trinity, shows him wearing such a gown, but with the addition of large buttons like those of an overcoat (J. Byrom, op. cit., frontispiece). Buttons were sometimes used on B.A. gowns at this period (W. J. Harrison, *Life in Clare Hall, Cambridge, 1658–1713*, p. 77).   [7] D. Loggan, no. 2.
[8] J. D. Mullinger, ii. 392.

it is depicted as a long open black gown faced with black velvet half-way down the front. To these facings is joined a black velvet flap collar, and the shoulders of the gown are decorated with black velvet. Broad streamers like those on Oxford commoners' gowns hang from the shoulder to the hem, and they are decorated all the way down with small lozenges of braid. With it is worn a round bonnet bound with a cord, the bow of which hangs off at the back.

All these dresses were the same in 1803 as in 1690 except that the ordinary pensioners' gowns had lost their streamers, and all now wore the black square cap with the black silk tassel, the round cap having been abolished throughout the university in 1769 owing to an agitation against it by certain pensioners.[1] In the statutes of 1800 for the new college of Downing, the full-sleeved gown of the shape used at Trinity was to be worn by all undergraduates, but it was to be black,[2] an early indication of the change from 'curtain' to bell-sleeved gown which many colleges were to begin to adopt about thirty years later. In Harraden's book of 1803 the bell sleeves of the Trinity, Peterhouse, King's, Queens', and Trinity Hall gowns had come to be split high up the arm so that the arm was free of them. A good example of the Trinity pensioner's dress before this change is provided by Silvester Harding's water-colour (1798) of Robert Rushbrooke.[3]

In 1815[4] we find that these bell sleeves have been sewn up, the seam showing vertically running the length of the upper part of the sleeve. The Trinity pensioner's gown was now dark blue with black cloth facings of 'Prince's stuff', while Peterhouse and Queens' pensioners now wore the black bell-sleeved gown with the sleeves sewn up. Pensioners of King's wore a gown of the same shape and colour but of a special thick cloth. Those of Trinity Hall also wore the type of gown of Peterhouse and Queens', but the sleeves were fastened up at the elbow with a black button and cord. All other pensioners wore black sleeveless gowns which in the course of the eighteenth century seem to have lost their streamers. These 'curtains', as they were sometimes disparagingly called, were made of 'Prince's stuff'

---

[1] C. H. Cooper, loc. cit.   [2] *Cambridge University and College Statutes*, iii. 645.
[3] Cambridge, Fitzw. Mus., no. 622a.
[4] W. Combe and T. Uwins, ii. 313 and pls.

and were faced in front with black velvet and had black velvet flap-collars. The square cap remained as before. Never at any time were there 'strings' on undergraduate gowns.[1]

5. *Scholars and Exhibitioners.* Under this section are mentioned only such scholars and exhibitioners whose dress did not conform with that of pensioners.

Thus scholars of King's, Rustat scholars of Jesus, Patchett scholars of St. John's, and Duchess of Somerset exhibitioners of St. John's wore a full bell-sleeved black gown of fine cloth ('costume cloth'). In all these cases the arms appear through a gash in the middle of the upper part of the sleeve. Westminster scholars of Trinity wore a black bell-sleeved gown with a violet button and loop at the bottom of the forearm seam.[2]

As members on foundations scholars and exhibitioners were ordered in 1549 to wear the square cap.[3] After 1769 they were differentiated from pensioners, who in this year began to wear a square black cap with a black tassel,[4] by continuing to have on their caps the tump without the tassel.[5]

6. *Sizars and sub-sizars.*[6] The position of sizars was originally very lowly, but had greatly improved by 1730.[7] After this they began to approach more and more the position of pensioners and so came to wear the pensioners' dress except that the square cap which they began to wear in 1769 had no tassel. At those colleges at which the 'curtain' was worn they wore a plain one with no velvet on facings or collar.[8]

Until 1769 they had worn round black cloth bonnets with a brim of prunella or silk.[9]

(r) Notes

1. *Use of the chapel dress at Cambridge.* Until the Reformation the surplice had been worn in the college chapels of the universities, but in Elizabeth's reign the question of its retention came

[1] The subsequent changes in the college gowns from 1828 onwards are discussed by A. G. Almond in his *Gowns and Gossip* (1925). They are illustrated in N. Whittock's *The Costume of the Members of the University of Cambridge* (? 1847) and, showing certain modern alterations, in A. G. Almond's, *College Gowns* (2nd edn., 1926).

[2] J. R. Tanner, p. 196.   [3] J. D. Mullinger, ii. 392, n. 1.
[4] C. H. Cooper, loc. cit.   [5] J. R. Tanner, loc. cit.

[6] Sizars were the equivalent of Oxford battelars and sub-sizars of Oxford servitors. They could not take their commons in hall, but had to 'size' (i.e. bespeak and eat their meals) in their own room. *Gentleman's Magazine*, lvii, pt. 2 (1787), p. 1146.   [7] T. Hearne, *Collections*, x (O.H.S., lxvii), 281.

[8] W. Combe and T. Uwins, loc. cit.   [9] C. H. Cooper, loc. cit.

under review. Elizabeth was one of those who favoured its use, but the question of the surplice was a hotly contested one all over Europe as can be realized from the quaint book, *Responsio M. Nic. Galli et M. Fla. Illyr.* which gives both sides of the argument.[1] At Cambridge there had been trouble about the wearing of the surplice,[2] but it was finally decided that it should be worn in college chapels, at any rate on saints' days, together with a hood in the case of holders of degrees.[3] This use of the surplice was again insisted on in 1603, when in canon 17 of the Church of England canons all masters, fellows, scholars, and students were to wear a surplice in chapel on Sundays and holy days, the graduates among them to appear in the hood of their degree.[4] The use of the hood was insisted upon in college chapels and in cathedral churches to prevent the wearing of the amess which had been affected particularly by members of collegiate and cathedral institutions.[5] The use of the amess had been forbidden at Cambridge in 1571.[6]

In 1643 the Long Parliament decided that anyone might, if he wished, refuse to wear the surplice in chapel.[7] As a result it was almost entirely abandoned at Cambridge, but was ordered to be worn again at the Restoration.

2. *The mourning gown.* The mourning gown at Cambridge was of the same shape as that used at Oxford, according to Loggan's costume plate, figure No. 10.[8]

We find its origin in the statutes of 1560 in which the 'sad-colored' gown of 'priest's shape' is allowed as one of the alternatives for the ordinary dress of graduates.[9]

It was not until the Restoration that members of the university began to wear it indiscriminately. Even undergraduates wore it for the same reason as at Oxford, and it was found necessary to legislate against this abuse. Thus in 1681 it was ordered that no one below the degree of Master of Arts might wear it for any reason whatever.[10]

[1] For instance in its favour, see typographical p. A5.
[2] C. H. Cooper, ii. 217.   [3] J. Lamb, p. 324; G. Dyer, i. 196.
[4] M. E. C. Walcott, *The Constitutions and Canons Ecclesiastical of the Church of England*, p. 25.
[5] M. E. C. Walcott, p. 37, Canon 25; P. Dearmer, *Ornaments of the Ministers*, p. 5.
[6] C. H. Cooper, ii. 277.   [7] C. H. Cooper, iii. 336.
[8] Cambridge, Univ. Libr. MS. Mm. 1.53.
[9] C. H. Cooper, ii. 161–2; B.M. MS. Cole xlii, fo. 290, i.e. MS. Add. 5843.
[10] Cambridge, Univ. Libr. MS. Mm. 4.56, fos. 158–9.

The gown survived as an alternative dress to the master's gown for Doctors of Divinity, as we have seen, and it was also worn by fellows of King's.[1]

3. *Academical mourning at Cambridge.* This, besides the mourning gown which drops out of view in the late seventeenth century, was indicated by wide black ribbons drawn across the square cap from corner to corner with a black rosette of ribbon in the middle where the lines of ribbon intersected.

In the case of mourning for the chancellor or a member of the royal family bows of black ribbon called 'butterflies' were worn upon the skull-piece of the cap at the back, three in the longest part of it, two on the narrowing spaces on each side, and one each side on the narrowest part.[2]

4. *'Fathers.'* At the time of introducing their pupils for degrees 'fathers' (i.e. praelectors) wore the *cappa* (Congregation) dress with a round black velvet bonnet with a gold band.[3]

LAMBETH DEGREES

The Archbishops of Canterbury and Armagh from the time of the Reformation had the right of bestowing all degrees upon persons of their choice. The recipient of the degree thus granted wore the academical dress suitable to his degree of the university of the archbishop who bestowed it.[4] There does not, however, seem to be any authority for this custom.

III. SCOTLAND

ST. ANDREWS (1411)

At St. Andrews from the first some accepted kind of academical costume was worn, and it was of the same character as that used at other European universities.[5] We have no definite evidence as to the type of dress used, for Scotland is particularly poor in illuminated manuscripts, brasses, and glass, and the fine

---

[1] Plate in R. Harraden.

[2] J. R. Tanner, p. 194. Tanner is not explicit as to the position of these bows, but Mr. A. Rutherford Almond in a letter to me of 5 Aug. 1955 says, 'I should conclude that the three at the back would be worn vertical and so with those at the sides. The two at the front I think would have to be horizontal as there would scarcely be room for them otherwise.'

[3] Cambridge, Univ. Libr. MS. Add. 5107, fo. 31.

[4] C. Wall, art., 'Lambeth Degrees', in *British Medical Journal*, ii (1935), 854 ff.

[5] R. G. Cant, *The University of St. Andrews*, pp. 19–20.

sixteenth-century university seal does not aid us.[1] However, it is not difficult to believe that, as Scotland looked to France for political and cultural leadership till the middle of the sixteenth century, it copied the dress of its universities.[2]

Hoods were early prescribed for all graduates of St. Andrews, and we know that furred hoods were associated with the degree of Bachelor of Arts and red cloth or silk hoods with that of Masters of Arts.[3] Masters and doctors wore some form of *cappa*, perhaps a *cappa manicata*, their head-dress being the *pileus*. The *pileus* preserved at the university and still used there at the doctoral ceremony[4] was probably made for the university in 1696 on the model of earlier ones.[5]

Undergraduates do not seem to have had a special dress before the foundation of St. Leonard's College (1512), the second in age of the three collegiate foundations. In the original statutes of this college the students were ordered to wear 'gown and hood', no doubt the same kind of undergraduate dress as was worn in the Middle Ages at all European Universities, consisting of a black *supertunica* of some kind and small black cloth hood.[6]

At the Reformation the link with medieval times was suddenly broken. The Kirk looked with hostility upon such memorials of the papal world as academical dress, and for the future only during periods of episcopal rule was any attention paid to it. The custom of wearing it was not interdicted, but was simply allowed to die of neglect. All that remained in use at St. Andrews of the old dress was the rector's purple robe, and this has survived to the present day.[7] A gown of lay type was, however, from this time onwards worn by Regent Masters of Arts. It is described by Thomas Kirk, an English visitor to St. Andrews in 1677, as a black gown, 'almost such as our freshmen have at Cambridge', that is like the sleeveless 'curtain'.[8] Doctors of Laws of all Scottish universities were ordered by James VI in 1610 to wear black gowns, faced in front and on the collar with back velvet.[9]

---

[1] H. Laing, *Ancient Scottish Seals*, i. 200–1, no. 1114.
[2] The influence of the University of Paris is mentioned in T. Baty, *Academic Colours*, pp. 6 and 26; of Louvain in *Notes and Queries*, 1st ser. iii, 329.
[3] R. G. Cant, pp. 19–20, n. 1.
[4] J. Wells, *The Oxford Degree Ceremony*, p. 30, n. 1.
[5] R. G. Cant, pp. 19, n. 1, and 20.
[6] R. G. Cant, p. 19.   [7] R. G. Cant, p. 20.   [8] R. G. Cant, p. 74.
[9] Anon. art. 'Scottish Legal Costume', in *Journal of Jurisprudence*, xxviii (1884), 67.

Academical head-gear was given up at the Reformation as were hoods.[1] Hoods were not revived until the 1870's. Should head-covering be needed on account of the weather when wearing an academical gown, an ordinary hat of contemporary lay fashion was worn.[2]

All undergraduates of the university, irrespective of their college, were instructed by James VI, perhaps in the latter part of his reign, to wear a scarlet gown, as were those of the other Scottish universities.[3] Scarlet was chosen to be the colour so that students, particularly at night, could be watched and tracked down by the disciplinary officers.[4] The scarlet gown of St. Andrews was made of thin stuff, and was short and sleeveless, varying slightly for primars, secondars, and termars.[5]

In the eighteenth century Doctors of Divinity wore bands and an open gown with a very broad black velvet collar reaching over the shoulders both before and behind. It was fastened at the neck like a cloak and had false panel-sleeves; but what was chiefly remarkable about the gown was that there were decorations of cloth sewn on down the front of it on each side and on the sleeves in the form of the letter gamma and the gamma reversed, as is to be seen in Raeburn's portrait of Hugh Blair, D.D., St. Andrews (1718–1800), an interesting example of the revival of the medieval *gammadium*.[6]

GLASGOW (1451)

At the time of the foundation of Glasgow College it was decided that its dress was to be modelled on that worn at the University of Bologna,[7] but Paris academical costume also had a great influence. Dress was to be of a clerical character, full-length, closed, and girt, such as is in 1482 mentioned as a dress befitting students of Arts and of Canon Law.[8] The material of the outer dress was to be of frieze (i.e. coarse woollen cloth) as at Paris.[9]

---

[1] *Notes and Queries*, 1st ser. iii. 329; cf. *Notes and Queries*, 7th ser. xii. 241–2.
[2] R. G. Cant, p. 119 and n. 2.
[3] R. G. Cant, p. 19 and n. 4, and p. 20.
[4] Cf. C. Innes, *Fasti Aberdonenses*, p. 372, 'The Commission on Scottish Universities, 1695'.   [5] R. G. Cant, 74 and n. 2. It was altered in 1838.
[6] See A. Cardon's engraving of the original in *The Life of Samuel Johnson*, by James Boswell, ed. R. Ingpen, ii. 661.
[7] C. Innes, *Munimenta Universitatis Glasguensis*, ii. 24.
[8] C. Innes, *Munimenta*, ii. 19.
[9] D. Murray, *The Old College of Glasgow*, p. 474.

Students on ceremonial occasions were at first ordered to wear a certain form of dress, the character of which is not explained, but later the rule was relaxed, and as long as they had a seemly dress that was deemed sufficient.[1]

As regards graduates, the furred hood was the mark of the bachelor.[2] In 1452 Masters of Arts were ordered to wear a cloth *cappa*,[3] probably a *cappa manicata*. In 1463 two masters were ordered to buy for the Faculty of Arts a magistral *cappa* and four or six hoods,[4] and in the same year Patrick Linch bequeathed to the college of Glasgow a red hood lined with miniver.[5] In 1464 the office of keeper of vestments (*Custos habituum*) was established. He was to be in charge of academical dresses and to be responsible for hiring them out for degree ceremonies, for it seems that full dresses were not owned, their cost being too great to buy them. A fund was from this time worked up and the accounts were audited in 1469.[6]

From the fact that in 1490 the bursar was appointed to purchase six hoods of blue (*blodius*) cloth 'sufficiently furred' for the common use of the Faculty of Arts both regents and students, it would seem that this was the established and recognized symbol of the mastership, and that students wore such a hood at the ceremony at which they took the master's degree,[7] for from the silence about the Bachelor of Arts degree it seems that it had already died out. This hood is supposed to have been modelled on that of Bologna.[8] Graduates wore a *pileus*.[9]

The Rector in 1469 was ordered to have at least a furred hood or one lined with taffeta, and for certain feasts he was to have a richer dress still.[10]

At the Reformation the *pileus* and *birettum* and the hood were rejected,[11] but a lay Tudor bonnet was used at the doctoral ceremony and at the time of the bestowal of the degree of Master. D. Murray[12] gives examples of two kinds of bonnet. The doctor's bonnet was black and the same as the Oxford lay doctor's bonnet; the master's bonnet, also black, was larger, was flat and

---

[1] J. Coutts, *A History of the University of Glasgow*, p. 28.
[2] J. Coutts, p. 24.   [3] C. Innes, ii. 180.
[4] C. Innes, ii. 201.   [5] C. Innes, ii. 199–200.
[6] J. Coutts, pp. 28–29.   [7] C. Innes, ii. 256; J. Coutts, pp. 28–29.
[8] *Notes and Queries*, 1st ser. iii. 329.
[9] C. Innes, loc. cit.; J. Coutts, loc. cit.   [10] C. Innes, ii. 75.
[11] D. Murray, p. 473, n. 2. Cf. R. G. Cant, p. 19, n. 1.   [12] Pl. opp. p. 308.

brimless, and had a red silk lining. Otherwise, on ordinary occasions a hat of contemporary lay fashion was worn with the gown, for the square cap was not introduced until modern times.[1] Gowns, of what shape we are not told, were worn by all regents, as Andrew Melvill, who became principal of the college of Glasgow in 1574, mentions in his *Diary* under the year 1578.[2]

In 1634 Charles I ordered students to wear their gowns in Glasgow Cathedral, in the university buildings, and even in the streets of the city.[3] According to Sir William Brereton, who visited Glasgow in 1635, students wore gowns of red, grey, or other colours as they pleased,[4] from which it appears that James VI's order about the use of the scarlet gown[5] was not strictly enforced.[6]

The visitation from the General Assembly in 1642 ordered all students to have gowns,[7] while in 1664 masters and students were instructed to wear their gowns in college and in the streets.[8]

A college enactment of 1690 ordered deans to have a 'grave decent gown' for important occasions, and the rector to have 'some marks of distinction becoming a Magistrate' on his gown, which might consist of decorations of either braid or velvet.[9] Then in 1695 the visitation of the Parliamentary Commission on Scottish Universities ordered the students of Glasgow to wear the scarlet gowns as described under St. Andrews, while regents were to continue to wear black gowns.[10]

In the eighteenth century Doctors of Medicine wore a black gown with a large flap-collar and wide bell sleeves. It was open in front, and was decorated at wide intervals down the front on each side with large square braided buttonholes to each of which was attached a tassel hanging from one side.[11]

---

[1] D. Murray, pp. 473–4.
[2] J. Melvill, *The Diary* (Bannatyne Club), p. 55; J. Melvill, *The Diary*, ed. R. Pitcairn, p. 72.
[3] J. Coutts, p. 96.
[4] W. Brereton, *Travels*, p. 117 (Chetham Soc. i).
[5] Mentioned under St. Andrews.
[6] *Notes and Queries*, 12th ser. ii. 537; *Notes and Queries*, 12th ser. iii. 59; D. Murray, op. cit., p. 476.
[7] *Notes and Queries*, 12th ser. ii. 537; D. Murray, p. 475.
[8] *Notes and Queries*, 12th ser. ii. 537.
[9] C. Innes, ii. 350.
[10] C. Innes, ii. 523; J. Coutts, p. 177; D. Murray, op. cit., p. 475.
[11] See Ridley's engraving of William Cullen, M.D. of Glasgow (1710–90).

As to undergraduate dress in the eighteenth century, John Wesley on visiting Glasgow in 1753 writes: 'They' [the under-graduates] 'wear scarlet gowns reaching only to their knees . . of coarse cloth.'[1] These gowns later reached well below the knees, and a flap collar, a cape, and short false panel sleeves were added to them.[2] Although this description is based on a nine-teenth-century water-colour, it seems reasonable to suppose that the gown was then no different from what it had been in the latter part of the previous century. The thick cape was no doubt added to protect the shoulders of the wearer from rain.

ABERDEEN (1494)

In an instrument of Gavin, Bishop of Aberdeen, of 1529 there are orders addressed to Doctors of Canon Law, Medicine, and Civil Law of the University of Aberdeen concerning their dress, from which it would appear that the first two were to dress according to the use of the University of Paris, while Doctors of Civil Law were to use the dress worn by those of this degree at the University of Orléans.[3]

From the inventory of effects of the university (1542) we see that the chief features of the dress of the rector at that time were the scarlet *cappa* (*cappa lutea, vulgo* 'ane scarlat caip'), which means either a *cappa* with two slits or more likely simply a cloak, and a hood of skin and fur doubled over. Another item, which appears to have been the rector's everyday dress, was a 'French brown' *cappa* without a hood.[4] At the same time the Faculty of Arts had in its possession four *cappae rotundae*,[5] five furred hoods, a doctoral *cappa*, a small *cappa nigra*[6] without a hood, and four *epitogia* ('shoulder pieces'), three of them being red and one 'French brown'. In addition the Faculty of Arts owned four hoods, one of 'French brown', one red, and one black, and twenty-one furred Bachelor of Arts hoods.[7] These Bachelor of Arts furred hoods are again mentioned in a clause in the orders published at the time of the chancellor's visitation of 1549.[8] The

---

[1] J. Wesley, *Journal*, ii. 286.   [2] D. Murray, frontispiece.
[3] C. Innes, *Fasti Aberdonenses*, p. 87.   [4] C. Innes, *Fasti*, p. 571.
[5] This type of *cappa* was of a round cut and was in use at Paris, particularly for members of the Theological Faculty there in 1517, according to R. Goulet, *Magnificence of the University of Paris*, pp. 38 and 78.
[6] E. T. Beaumont, *Academical Habit*, pp. 20–21, calls this a sleeveless tabard.
[7] C. Innes, p. 571.   [8] C. Innes, pp. 269–70, § 44.

shape of these hoods, which were short and joined to the 'shoulder piece', is said to have been copied from those worn at Paris.[1]

This visitation caused a reform to be made in the shape of the *cappa*, hood, and 'shoulder piece' of Masters of Arts and Bachelors of Arts,[2] but we are not told what this was. Bursars (i.e. students with bursaries, or scholarships) in the Arts Faculty were at the same time ordered to wear hoods (i.e. no doubt the black cloth hoods) everywhere except in their own rooms and in church,[3] and students of the Faculty of Theology were warned that if they wished to be considered for the priesthood, they must wear round hoods and round clerical birettas.[4]

In post-Reformation times we find, as in the other universities of Scotland,[5] academical dress much neglected. In one of the few memorial brasses in Scotland, that which depicts Dr. Liddel (1613) in the Old, or West, Church, Aberdeen, there is no suggestion of academical dress. Liddel is depicted wearing an ordinary lay gown with winged sleeves decorated with buttons and braid; while his bonnet with ear-flaps suggests no more than the head-dress of a man of dignity of the day, in spite of what E. C. Clarke says about its academical character.[6]

If the Kirk did not interest itself in academical dress, Charles I and Laud, with their policy of episcopacy, did. In 1634 at the visitation of King's College, Aberdeen, the king commanded that all members of the college should use gowns according to their several degrees and faculties.[7] Hoods are not mentioned. They had apparently been abandoned too long to be successfully revived.

In 1641 at King's College the same spirit, which had been instilled by the king seven years before, prevailed, and students were ordered to wear gowns (*galerus*, *toga*) and hats in college, but they were allowed informal caps and cloaks when enjoying recreation.[8] At the same time bursars (i.e. scholars) were ordered to wear hats and gowns, and if disobedient they were as a

---

[1] *Notes and Queries*, 1st ser. iii. 329; *Notes and Queries*, 7th ser. xii. 241–2.
[2] C. Innes, p. 265, § 22.   [3] C. Innes, p. 261, § 4.
[4] C. Innes, p. 260, § 2.   [5] R. G. Cant, p. 20.
[6] E. C. Clarke, art. cit. lxi. 62. An illustration of the brass is given in C. T. Davis, art. 'Monumental Brass in the Old, or West, Church, Aberdeen', in *Archaeological Journal* li (1894), pl. opp. p. 76.
[7] C. Innes, p. 394.   [8] C. Innes, p. 233, § 11.

punishment to wear leather belts.[1] This curious punishment of having to wear a belt, which is to be considered as a sort of symbol of restraint, is again mentioned in 1659, when a bursar speaking in 'the vulgar tongue' was told to go without his gown and with a broad white leather belt.[2] In this year bursars were again ordered to use a gown and a hat at all functions.[3] Their gowns were to be black or tawny, and not red,[4] but in 1695, as we have already seen, the Commission on Scottish Universities ordered all students in all the Scottish universities to wear red gowns; while at Aberdeen as elsewhere regents and other masters were to wear black ones.[5] Even after that there seems to have been some difficulty in enforcing this, for it was found necessary in 1704 to order bursars to wear gowns.[6] Doctors of Laws continued to wear, as in 1610 they had been ordered to do in a proclamation of James VI, black gowns faced on the front and on the collar with black velvet.[7]

It has been said that the square cap was not used in Scotland until the late nineteenth century, but in J. Kay's caricature 'The Sapient Septemviri' (1786) three professors of King's College, Aberdeen, wear square black caps without tuft or tassel.[8]

From 1695 to 1860 the students of the two colleges of Aberdeen, King's (1494) and Marischal College (1593), wore slightly differing red gowns. Two water-colours of 1860[9] show what the gowns must have been like in the eighteenth century. The first shows a bajan (freshman) of King's College wearing an open red gown reaching to a little way above the knee, with a broad flap collar in two layers covering the shoulders. The sleeves have small panels, and a hole for the arm to pass through is cut above the elbow in the shape of an inverted V. There are two red buttons in front near the top of the gown. The second water-colour shows a bajan of Marischal College wearing a gown of the same length, but it is of a duller red. It is fastened high up by two red buttons, but it is open otherwise. The broad

---

[1] C. Innes, p. 237, § 45.   [2] C. Innes, p. 255, § 14.
[3] C. Innes, p. 254, § 5.   [4] C. Innes, loc. cit.
[5] C. Innes, p. 372.   [6] R. S. Rait, *The Universities of Aberdeen*, p. 185.
[7] Anon. art. cit., *Journal of Jurisprudence*, xxviii (1884), 67.
[8] J. Kay, *A Series of Original Portraits and Caricature Etchings*, i, pl. opp. p. 76, no. xxxv.
[9] W. Johnston, *The Last Bajans of King's and Marischal Colleges*, frontispiece and pl. opp. p. 1.

PLATE 16

Dress of Bajans of King's and Marischal Colleges, Aberdeen

flap collar, which is of the same shape as that of the King's College bajan, is of purple velvet. It has large false panel-sleeves, dull red as is the rest of the gown, which fall broad, flat and square over the arms and reach only to the hips (Pl. 16).

EDINBURGH (1582)

Until 1858 when all authority was taken from the Civic Council and placed in the hands of the *Senatus Academicus*, Edinburgh was a civic college.[1]

Though as early as 1583 it was decided that undergraduates should wear gowns, this was not observed, for when in 1695 the Parliamentary Commission ordered regents of Edinburgh College to see to it that the wearing of red gowns by undergraduates was put into practice, the wording implies that, as was not the case at St. Andrews, Glasgow, and Aberdeen, Edinburgh students were not in the habit of wearing gowns.[2] But Sir William Brereton in 1635 expressly mentions that Edinburgh undergraduates wore 'coloured cloaks'.[3] This may mean either that in the interval between 1635 and 1695 they had given up wearing them, or that the commissioners wished them to wear true gowns and not cloaks.

Principals of the college had no particular dress, but being generally clergy appeared in the Geneva gown.[4] Other developments belong to the nineteenth century.

In the eighteenth century the gown of Doctors of Divinity had a velvet collar, was open in front, and had large long braided buttonholes on each side, from the outer end of which hung a tassel. A clear illustration of this is to be found in the painting by D. Martin of Robert Henry (1718–90), who became a Doctor of Divinity of Edinburgh in 1774.[5] This was an adaptation of a lay fashion of the time as can be seen from the portrait by A. Carpentier of the sculptor L. F. Roubiliac. Here the loose coat which he negligently wears while busy in his studio is decorated with tassels in precisely the same way as Henry's gown.

---

[1] Anon. *Edinburgh University: A Sketch*, pp. 19 and 76–77.
[2] Anon. *Edinburgh University*, p. 4; J. Coutts, p. 179; C. Innes, *Munimenta Universitatis Glasguensis*, iii. 523; C. Innes, *Fasti*, p. 372.
[3] W. Brereton, p. 117.
[4] J. Kay, pl. opp. p. 94, no. xlii (portrait of William Robertson, principal 1762–93).
[5] There is an engraving of this portrait by J. Caldwell. Cf. p. 141, n. 11.

IV. IRELAND

TRINITY COLLEGE, DUBLIN (1591)

After several unsuccessful attempts between 1311 and 1585 to found a university in Ireland, the first stone of Trinity College, Dublin, was laid in 1591, and the first students were admitted two years later.[1]

It was from the first greatly influenced by the University of Cambridge,[2] and its academical dress was almost entirely copied from Cambridge, and in a few cases from Oxford.

Statutes about dress are few and unsatisfactory. It is first mentioned in 1637 when in the course of Charles I's statutes the provost and all graduates are ordered to wear on every feast day, presumably in chapel, a clean surplice and the hood befitting their degree.[3] Fellows, scholars, commoners (pensioners), and other students are to have gowns, which are not described, to be worn not only in college, but in the city, while boots are not to be worn and ordinary clothing is to be plain.[4] A supplement to the statutes of 1759 contains no further information, and all that is interesting in the statutes of 1760 is the reference to a custom for all recipients of degrees to pay for gloves to be distributed to the appropriate officers.[5]

The vice-chancellor's dress was copied from that of Cambridge, as can be seen from the portrait of about 1682 of Anthony Dopping in the college. As it is a portrait showing the head and shoulders only it is not as valuable for evidence as it might have been, but the red robe and the white fur 'shoulder piece' plainly appear.[6]

The 'business' (Congregation at Cambridge) dress of Doctors of Divinity, according to the portrait of William King, Archbishop of Dublin (D.D., 1689), consisted of the *cappa* costume, the same as that of a Cambridge Doctor of Divinity with a large white fur hood spread over the shoulders and a fur-lined *cappa*

---

[1] Cambridge, Univ. Libr. MS. Add. 707, fos. 2–5 and 8.

[2] For instance, the early provosts were imported from that university (J. W. Stubbs, T. K. Abbott, J. P. Mahaffy, and others, *The Book of Trinity College, Dublin*, p. 17).

[3] H. G. MacDonnell, *Chartae et Statuta*, p. 45.

[4] H. G. MacDonnell, p. 57.

[5] *The Statutes of Trinity College, Dublin*, trans. R. Bolton, p. 161.

[6] W. G. Strickland, *Pictures, Busts, and Statues in Trinity College, Dublin*, p. 13.

PLATE 17

Edmund Burke in the LL.D. Festal Dress of Trinity College, Dublin, 1795

with a wide and long opening in front.[1] The full dress was scarlet with bell-sleeves lined and faced with white silk.[2] The undress was the Master of Arts gown, the same as at Cambridge, but without 'strings'.

Doctors of Laws wore as full dress a scarlet cloth robe with salmon pink bell-sleeves, and a salmon pink hood is worn with it, incorrectly by English standards. With this costume was worn a square black cap with a black tassel, and long white bands.[3] John Hoppner's portrait of Edmund Burke (1795) (Pl. 17) shows him in this robe, but he does not wear the hood and instead of bands wears a lace fall as being an honorand.[4] There is no record of a *cappa* dress. The Master of Arts gown was worn as undress.

Doctors of Medicine wore for full dress a scarlet cloth bell-sleeved robe faced with crimson silk, and if the hood was worn it was of the same colours.[5] The head-dress was the same as for the Doctor of Laws, and the Master's gown was worn for undress.

Doctors of Music followed the Cambridge dress of that degree.[6]

The dress of a Master of Arts was the black gown, the same as the master's gown at Oxford and Cambridge and without 'strings'. The hood is given in Taylor's book as being of black silk lined with pink silk.[7] The change to dark blue lining[8] took place in the mid-nineteenth century.[9] With this the black square cap with a tassel copied from Oxford and Cambridge was worn, but no doubt it would have had a tuft and no tassel before the later eighteenth century. The shape of the master's hood was in 1850 described as being smaller in itself than those of either Oxford or Cambridge, but having a long square-ended liripipe,[10] and it had probably always been like that.

The dress of the Bachelor of Divinity and the Bachelor of

---

[1] J. W. Stubbs, T. K. Abbott, J. P. Mahaffy, and others, p. 241.
[2] W. B. S. Taylor, *History of the University of Dublin*, pl. opp. p. 530. In the nineteenth century the colour of the facings on the sleeves and the lining was changed to black (T. W. Wood, *Ecclesiastical and Academic Colours*, p. 48).
[3] W. B. S. Taylor, frontispiece.
[4] A. P. I. Samuels, *Early Life of Edmund Burke*, pl. i, opp. p. 1.
[5] T. W. Wood, p. 48.   [6] T. W. Wood, loc. cit.
[7] W. B. S. Taylor, loc. cit.   [8] T. W. Wood, loc. cit.
[9] It is worth noticing that at Trinity 'a pink' is the equivalent of the Oxford and Cambridge 'blue'.
[10] G. J. French, *Tippets of the Canons Ecclesiastical*, p. 6, fig. 16.

Laws was the same as the dress for these two degrees at Cambridge. That of the Bachelor of Medicine was the same as the Dublin master's dress, while the dress of the Bachelor of Music had a mid-blue silk hood trimmed with white fur. The hood of Masters of Surgery was copied from that of this degree at Oxford.[1]

In the 1820 plates the Bachelor of Arts wears the same square cap as those of all other degrees wear. His gown has very large bell sleeves slashed open as at Cambridge and his hood is trimmed with white fur.[2]

In the same series the junior fellow wears a long black plain open and sleeveless gown, but which has material covering the upper part of the arm as if the beginning of a master's sleeve. He wears bands, as do doctors and masters in these plates.[3]

The nobleman wears a square black cap with a gold tassel, and a long black gown adorned with thick gold braid and gold tassels on the sleeves, on the sides of the gown, and on the skirts. The decorations on the skirts and on the sides consist of two or three buttons from which small gold tassels hang, and these buttons have a connecting piece of braid between them; but the braiding on the sleeves is more elaborate and consists of five rows of three buttons with connecting braid between them and small gold tassels hanging from the outer buttons, while down the middle of all these a thick piece of braid runs vertically. One feature of this dress to be particularly noticed, since it is not found in the dress of Oxford or Cambridge, is that the sleeves end in front at the elbow and hang down behind the arms in little panels with one gold tassel on the lower outside corner.[4]

The dress of the fellow-commoner differs from that of the nobleman in that all the decorations, which are exactly the same in character as those on the nobleman's gown, are black instead of gold, and the sleeves in this case reach only to the elbow and stop abruptly there without the little panel.[5]

The foundation scholar wears a square black cap without a tassel and a full long black gown with bell-sleeves not slashed open. The upper part of the open gown is faced with mid-blue velvet and there is a mid-blue velvet stripe at the wrist on each of

---

[1] T. W. Wood, loc. cit.
[2] W. B. S. Taylor, pl. opp. p. 440.
[3] W. B. S. Taylor, pl. opp. p. 364.
[4] W. B. S. Taylor, pl. opp. p. 364.
[5] W. B. S. Taylor, pl. opp. p. 530.

the sleeves.[1] There is no illustration of the pensioner's dress, but it seems to have been (if we take into account its present appearance) the same as that of the foundation scholar except that there was no velvet on the gown, and the cap had a tassel.

In the eighteenth century sizars seem to have worn a sleeveless black stuff gown and a red cap, 'the badge of a servant'.[2] The red cap was probably round after the 'catercap' style.

[1] W. B. S. Taylor, pl. opp. p. 440.
[2] J. Forster, *Life of Goldsmith*, chap. ii.

5

I. GERMAN-SPEAKING COUNTRIES

A. GENERAL

A GERMAN professor of about 1490 wears a long and ample *supertunica* with close-fitting sleeves, and a small low hat with a turned-up brim. At his feet among the students sits second from the left a probable Bachelor of Arts, who is to be distinguished by his little low flat cap and a hood hanging behind.[1]

In a good woodcut of about 1500 showing the Emperor Maximilian I in disputation with seven professors representing the seven liberal arts we have examples of German professorial dress, particularly in that of the professor with his back full towards us. A small flat cap is worn, and the rest of the habit consists of an ample gown with openings in the glove sleeves for the arms; and a 'shoulder piece' with a very small rudimentary hood at the back of the neck. From this descends a long straight liripipe reaching nearly as far as the back of the knees.[2]

From the *Epistolae Obscurorum Virorum*, written at Erfurt and published in 1516, we learn that at this time in Germany Doctors of Theology wore black *tunicas* and large hoods with a liripipe (*nigras tunicas, et magna caputia cum liripipiis*).[3] At the same period furred *cappas* were generally associated with the dress of Doctors of Law.[4]

As to colours, during the first half of the sixteenth century, as before, persons of academical dignity in company with lawyers and schoolmasters wore a red *Sendelbinde* (*chaperon*) on the left shoulder; but Protestant members of these professions after this time discarded the *Sendelbinde*.[5] By the seventeenth

---

[1] E. Reicke, *Lehrer und Unterrichtswesen in der deutschen Vergangenheit*, p. 38, Abb. 29.
[2] E. Reicke, *Lehrer*, p. 43, Abb. 34.
[3] *Epistolae Obscurorum Virorum*, i, letter 2, p. 294; letter 26, pp. 339–40.
[4] *Epistolae Obscurorum Virorum*, i, letter 2, p. 295.
[5] F. Hottenroth, *Handbuch*, p. 597, fig. 152. 3.

century the faculty colours generally observed in Germany, though there were exceptions such as at Leipzig, Kiel, and Helmstädt, were for Theology, black; for law, red; for Medicine, blue; and for Philosophy, violet.[1] By this time the shape of the *pileus* varied at different universities.[2]

As for the academical gown it was worn closed and had a standing collar, until at the Reformation, under the much increased influence of lay fashion Protestants of academical dignity, as well as lawyers and schoolmasters of the Reformed Faith, giving up the *Sendelbinde*, took to an open black gown with a flap collar.[3] Roman Catholic lawyers continued to wear the *Sendelbinde* and the old type of closed gown.[4] The new gown was really the *Schaube*, a lay gown, which came also, but in a somewhat altered form, to be identified with the dress of the Protestant clergy.[5]

B. INDIVIDUAL UNIVERSITIES

PRAGUE (1347)

In 1367 it was ordered that at all academical Acts and on all solemn occasions Bachelors of Arts and Masters of Arts should wear a tabard or special dress suited to their standing. If they failed to do this their presence would be ignored.[6] It was found necessary to insist upon this again in 1389, when masters were particularly mentioned.[7] From these two references, and from another of 1380 of a similar character,[8] it would seem that, although other forms of *toga* were used, the tabard was the most generally accepted form of dress for graduates. Another form of dress appears in a clause of the 1380 enactment.[9] This is the *toga rugata*, a gown of many pleats or folds.[10] Candidates about to be created bachelors were especially ordered to wear this, but it was equally used by masters.[11] It was in fact some form

---

[1] A. Steger, *Dissertatio de purpura*, pp. 29–30.

[2] F. G. Struve, *De Symbolis*, p. 3a; A. Steger, p. 29; C. Biccius, *Tractatus Juridicus de Pileo*, p. 18, cap. ii. x.

[3] F. Hottenroth, p. 597, fig. 152. 3. [4] F. Hottenroth, p. 763.

[5] M. von Boehn, *Modes and Manners*, ii. 77 and 128–9.

[6] *Monumenta historica universitatis Pragensis*, i. 9. [7] Ibid. i. 10.

[8] Ibid. i. 54, § 21. [9] Ibid. i. 55, § 25.

[10] *Rugata* = *plissée*; see H. Beaune and J. d'Arbaumont, *Les Universités de Franche-Comté*, p. xlix, n. 2.

[11] W. W. Tomek, *Geschichte der Prager Universität*, p. 37.

of tabard, or perhaps simply another name for it.[1] In 1393 the tabard is again insisted on for masters.[2]

The following was the dress at this university in the Middle Ages: for students a plain, closed, sleeved *mantellum*, i.e., a short *supertunica*; and for Bachelors and Masters of Arts a much-pleated sleeveless closed *supertunica* called a tabard or *habitus*, or *toga rugata*, the two degrees being distinguished by the fact that, whereas the bachelors had no head-dress and had plain gowns, Masters of Arts not only wore the *pileus*, but were also allowed to have their dress lined with silk and trimmed with fur.[3]

As to doctoral dress at Prague it consisted of *biretta* or *pileus* (the biretta, rigid, square and four-cornered, succeeding to the *pileus* during the sixteenth century), and the 'shoulder piece' (*epomis*), worn over the *toga*, and the doctor on his creation received the ring, the book, and the kiss.[4] The biretta and *epomis* of the Faculty of Theology were purple, and those of the later Faculty of Philosophy, created from that of Arts, violet. The insignia of Doctors of Medicine were altered in 1614 to a round black bonnet and a black shoulder scarf (*chaperon*). The wearing of all doctoral insignia was abolished by imperial decree in 1784.[5]

VIENNA (1365)

In 1389 Doctors and Bachelors of Theology were ordered to wear the *cappa clausa*,[6] while in the same year Masters of Arts were required to wear dress reaching to the ankles, and Bachelors of Arts were not to make use of any fur, but noblemen and bishops were exempt from these orders.[7] In 1458 Masters of Arts are described as wearing *pallium* (a loose *supertunica*) and biretta,[8] and in 1503 they still wore the long *pallium*.[9] In 1513 academical head-dress was forbidden to Bachelors of Arts of any condition.[10]

[1] W. W. Tomek, loc. cit.   [2] *Monumenta Pragensis*, i. 96, § 6.
[3] C. Meiners, art. 'Geschichte der Trachten', in *Göttingische akademische Annalen*, i (1804), 219; A. Schultz, *Deutsches Leben*, p. 215; W. W. Tomek, p. 37.
[4] *Monumenta Pragensis*, ii. 562, n.   [5] Ibid. ii. 562.
[6] R. Kink, *Geschichte der Univ. zu Wien*, ii. 95.   [7] R. Kink, ii. 193–4.
[8] i.e. the round variety, for the square one had not yet appeared.
[9] C. Meiners, art. cit. i. 220–1; *Conspectus historiae universitatis Viennensis*, ii. 68.
[10] R. Kink, ii. 318.

As to undergraduates, in 1458 they were ordered to wear *tunicas* which were short to distinguish them from graduates;[1] while in 1503 they wore with their closed *tunica* a girdle. This girdle was worn by them as a sign that they were still apprentices bound to their university, and seems to have been a mark of their dress long before this date.[2] By the early sixteenth century they had come to wear a much longer *tunica*, dark brown or black with sleeves, and a small round brown cap (*Gugel*).[3]

At the beginning of the eighteenth century the dress of the deans of the four faculties consisted of bell-sleeved gowns, open from the waist downwards, 'shoulder pieces' divided down the front and edged with plain braid, and cylindrical caps.[4] In 1703 the rector wears a closed cassock with tight sleeves, and over this a damasked 'shoulder piece' reaching to the elbows, edged along the lower edge and probably lined with miniver. He wears white bands and has a cylindrical black velvet hat with a gold hat-band (Pl. 18 *a*).[5]

In 1752 the dress of the chancellor consisted of the 'shoulder piece' (*epomis*) with a little hood attached, a black velvet gown embroidered with gold thread and trimmed with ermine, and a black velvet gimped biretta. On occasions of mourning these articles of dress were all of red velvet. The dress of the deans was by this time the same as that of the chancellor, but less richly embroidered. Their dress was also of red velvet for mourning.[6]

When in 1773 the university applied for new dress the Empress Maria Theresa refused to comply with the request, but allowed the old to be retained on the condition that it should never be worn in her court, where university officials were warned to appear only in black suits. One can see how affairs were tending, and it is not surprising to note that on 11 November 1784, the Emperor Josef II abolished the old dress which he considered to be 'a reminder of the dark days when the Papal chair claimed the sole right to establish universities'.

[1] C. Meiners, art. cit. i. 220–1. [2] *Conspectus*, ii. 68.
[3] A. Richter, *Bilder aus der deutschen Kulturgeschichte*, ii. 349; J. von Aschbach, *Geschichte der Wiener Universität*, i. 67.
[4] E. Reicke, *Der Gelehrte*, p. 102, Abb. 88.
[5] J. R. Planché, *Cyclopaedia of Costume*, ii. 325.
[6] R. Kink, i. 112–13, n. 126.

In 1792 the chancellor and deans wore black suits with a ribbon round the neck, red for the secular and purple for the clerical members, and from the ribbon hung a medal. In 1804 gold chains were acquired instead of the ribbons with more attractive medals.[1]

ERFURT (1378)

In the late fourteenth-century seal of the university the rector, seated on the left, has a small round shallow *pileus* with a button apex, a *tunica*, and a furred 'shoulder piece' quite open in front. The doctors on the right have long closed *tunicas* with short puffed sleeves and large *pilei* with the button apex.[2] During the next hundred years a change took place in the rector's dress, for in the rectorial seal of the late fifteenth century he wears a flowing *roba* with hanging sleeves. His head-dress is the same as before.[3]

COLOGNE (1385)

In the statutes of 1392 all of whatever degree are ordered to wear clerical dress, not short, decorated, or parti-coloured.[4] At the same time the dress of the rector is mentioned, from which it appears that as yet no definite costume had been given him, for he is to wear for the present an *epitogium*, that is, a large gown with a 'shoulder piece' with a miniver hood which in summer may be of silk. If he prefers he may simply wear the dress of the degree he holds as a doctor or master.[5] Two interesting points arise from this, first, that already silk was allowed as an alternative lining for the hood forty years before it was allowed at Oxford, and secondly, that the rector, like the vice-chancellors of Oxford and Cambridge, had no special official costume.

As early as 1389 the Faculties of Theology and Arts had legislated about the dress of their members. Thus Bachelors of Theology were ordered to wear a variety of *cappa clausa*, the

---

[1] R. Kink, i. 112–13, n. 126.
[2] J. G. Hagelgans, *Orbis Literatus Academicus Germanico-Europaeus*, p. 5, top large illustration.
[3] E. Gritzner, *Die Siegel deutscher Universitäten*, Taf. 6, no. 2.
[4] F. J. von Bianco, *Geschichte der Universität und der Gymnasium der Stadt Köln*, p. 406, § 7.
[5] F. J. von Bianco, p. 416, § 42.

PLATE 18

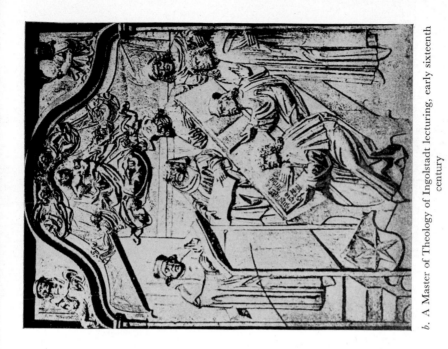

b. A Master of Theology of Ingolstadt lecturing, early sixteenth century

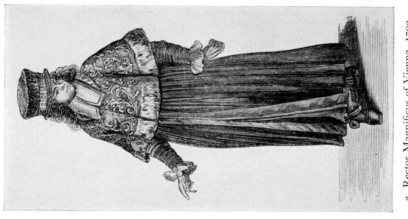

a. Rector Magnificus of Vienna, 1703

cappa rotunda as at Paris for all formal occasions,[1] while Masters of Theology were to wear the same dress as Masters of Arts. What this was is not mentioned, but Masters of both Theology and Arts were to wear the *birettum* while bachelors of both faculties, as was the case throughout Europe at this time, had no head-gear.[2] Very likely both these masters wore the *cappa clausa*. Bachelors of Arts were ordered to wear a hooded *epitogium* or a tabard, the hood either lined with miniver or with silk.[3] In 1393 members of the Faculty of Medicine were also allowed these alternative linings to their hoods.[4] In the reformed statutes of the Faculty of Arts of 1457 masters were required to wear the *epitogium*.[5]

This dress, consisting of *epitogium* and cylindrical biretta, was worn by regents in 1508.[6]

In 1516 a Master of Arts is said to have been privileged to wear a gold ring and to have a silk lining to his *cappa (sericum sub cappa)*,[7] but the latter must have been used only on formal occasions.

In the eighteenth century professors wore the *epomis* ('shoulder piece') over a black gown as at Vienna, Heidelberg, and Mainz.[8]

HEIDELBERG (1386)

In 1386 masters and bachelors of all faculties are to wear uniform *cappas* (of what kind is not stated) at all acts in the schools.[9]

In the following year there is mention of the Faculties of Arts and Theology. All that is said about the dress of Bachelors and Masters of Theology is that they are to use *cappas*,[10] but the dress of Masters of Arts is given in detail. They are to wear a dress which is a form of tabard lined with miniver or silk with two lappets *(cum duabus lingulis)*, of which there are many examples in illustrations of academical and legal persons at this time throughout Europe, worn at the neck. The tabard is either to be without sleeves or with short and close-fitting

---

[1] F. J. von Bianco, p. 456.   [2] F. J. von Bianco, p. 444.
[3] F. J. von Bianco, p. 439.   [4] F. J. von Bianco, p. 490.
[5] F. J. von Bianco, p. 501.   [6] E. Reicke, *Der Lehrer*, p. 40, Abb. 31.
[7] *Epistolae Obscurorum Virorum*, ii, letter 23, p. 442.
[8] E. Winkelmann, *Urkundenbuch der Universitaet Heidelberg*, ii. 305, § 2421.
[9] E. Winkelmann, i. 5; E. F. Henderson, *Historical Documents*, p. 263.
[10] E. Winkelmann, i. 23.

sleeves, and the head-dress is to be the biretta, that is the round one.[1] Incepting masters are to wear a black *cappa* lined with miniver or silk and are to have a biretta.[2] Bachelors of Arts had apparently dress of the same cut as masters, but except by special permission were not to have linings of either miniver or silk[3] and were presumably without a head-dress.

In 1409 the Faculty of Theology made it clear that as far as the faculty was concerned bachelors and licentiates were not to wear a head-dress, and that what was done in other faculties was no concern of theirs.[4] It seems that there was at this time a love of luxury among the clergy, and in 1411 the Faculty of Theology legislated against this abuse and refused to allow Bachelors of Theology to wear a ring unless persons of dignity.[5]

By 1444 Masters of Arts had begun to wear such unseemly dress that they had to be forbidden to wear a *pallium* open right down the side or a *tunica* too long or too short, and if they continued to disobey they were to be suspended from their functions.[6]

At length in 1469/70 came the first legislation about costume addressed to the university in general, but particularly to students of all faculties. As at Oxford in 1489 the hood is ordered to be worn fastened down to the *supertunica*.[7] After this perhaps students, deprived of the head-covering which the hood had provided, tried to wear some kind of academical cap, but in common with bachelors this was forbidden them.[8]

Regular legislation about dress ended in the sixteenth century. In 1533 there is evidence that already students had taken to Spanish fashions instead of the old long *tunica*,[9] but the little cloak then mentioned came in time to have an academical significance, and in a somewhat longer form was the only particular dress which German students had in the seventeenth century.

In 1580 the chancellor and rector were both distinguished by a velvet biretta, presumably round.[10] The type of dress worn

[1] E. Winkelmann, i. 43. [2] E. Winkelmann, i. 41.
[3] E. Winkelmann, i. 36. [4] E. Winkelmann, i. 103.
[5] E. Winkelmann, i. 106. [6] E. Winkelmann, i. 152.
[7] E. Winkelmann, i. 186; R. F. Seybolt, *Manuale Scholarium*, p. 117.
[8] E. Winkelmann, i. 198, and ii. 61, § 551. [9] E. Winkelmann, ii. 88, § 811.
[10] A. Thorbecke, *Statuten und Reformationen der Universität Heidelberg vom 16. bis 18. Jahrhundert*, p. 184, § 60.

about this time by doctors can be seen from the print of a Doctor of Theology of this university, D. Pareus (d. 1622). He wears a gown with broad plain stuff facings sewn on flat and with a large falling fur collar. The bag sleeves of the gown have wide slits for the arms to pass through, the upper part of these openings being cut in the middle in the shape of an inverted V.[1]

As the seventeenth century progressed the wearing of academical costume was less and less observed, but the authorities at first did their best to counteract this. In 1656 professors were reminded that at lectures and academical Acts they must wear a long gown,[2] and so that there should be no excuse for not having one, in 1672 long black gowns were specially made for professors at the expense of the university, and they were requested to wear them while performing academical functions.[3] This 'professorenrock' is mentioned in 1682 as if a particular form of gown common to all professors, who wore this and not the dress of their various degrees.[4]

During the eighteenth century the 'shoulder piece' (epomis) was worn by professors and doctors as is mentioned in 1750[5] and 1774.[6] From this it seems that the use of the 'professors' gown' had died out and that professors wore the dress of the doctorate which they held. Professors and doctors wore the epomis over the black gown and had a red biretta on important occasions, but on ordinary or mourning occasions they wore the black gown alone and had a black biretta.[7] In 1795 the Professor of Theology was allowed to use a particular shape of epomis unspecified such as was used at Cologne and Mainz.[8]

The ensuing political changes which affected Heidelberg no less than other towns of Western Germany seem to have led to the abandonment of old ceremonial observances in the university, and when dress is again mentioned in 1804 it appears that there had been a complete break with the past. In this year the authorities decided to revive for professors the use of suitable dress according to the spirit of a bygone age for academical occasions.[9]

---

[1] S. Clark, *Marrow of Ecclesiastical History*, p. 451.
[2] E. Winkelmann, ii. 204, § 1664.   [3] A. Thorbecke, p. 253, § 10.
[4] E. Winkelmann, ii. 215, § 1745.   [5] E. Winkelmann, i. 428.
[6] E. Winkelmann, ii. 281, § 2237; 282, § 2244; 283, § 2250.
[7] E. Winkelmann, ii. 283, § 2250.
[8] E. Winkelmann, ii. 305, § 2421.   [9] E. Winkelmann, i. 454.

WÜRZBURG (1403)

The statutes make no mention of a special academical dress before 1587, but in that year there was a complete review of the whole question. As a result the following rules were drawn up. The rector was to be distinguished by a gold 'shoulder piece' (*epomis*) and the vice-rector by a red one.[1] It is to be assumed that these were to be worn over the ordinary rectorial robe, probably a purple, bell-sleeved gown.

As the university remained loyal to the Roman Catholic Church after the Reformation, the chancellor and vice-chancellor were still priests, and when they appeared at University functions were ordered to wear surplice and stole.[2]

Doctors of Theology were to wear a black woollen 'shoulder piece' on all important occasions, while when they presided at disputations or Acts they were to wear in addition to their other dress a fur 'roller' hood close round the neck. With this was to be worn a *cappa pellita duplici*, a 'shoulder piece' lined with fur. Bachelors and Licentiates of Theology were to wear a large fur hood (*cappa pellicea maioris*) except monks, who were, of course, to wear their monastic habit.[3] Bachelors were always to appear bare-headed.[4] Doctors of Theology wore a blue silk *pileus*.[5]

In 1610 professors of the Faculty of Medicine were ordered to wear at their lectures and at all solemn Acts a black gown (*toga*), a blue 'shoulder piece' (*epomis*), and a blue biretta.[6] A non-Regent Doctor of Medicine was in 1713 commanded to wear at his investiture a gown and *pileus*,[7] from which we may infer that the 'shoulder piece' was the sign of the regent; and to this may be added the fact that in 1732 only regent doctors wore gown, 'shoulder piece' and *pileus*. The two latter garments were of the colour of the faculty to which the doctor belonged.[8]

---

[1] F. X. von Wegele, *Geschichte der Universität Wirzburg*, ii. 155, § 70.
[2] F. X. von Wegele, ii. 160, § 70.
[3] F. X. von Wegele, ii. 175–7, § 71.
[4] F. X. von Wegele, ii. 183, § 71.
[5] F. X. von Wegele, ii. 186 and 188.
[6] F. W. von Wegele, ii. 250, § 94.
[7] F. X. von Wegele, ii. 306, § 122.
[8] L. Carlier, *In Iure academico*, p. 26 (pars. i, sect. iii, 33). In 1809 lay professors were given the title of *Rath* (councillor) and were ordered to wear the military type of costume of that office, while clerical professors were to dress according to episcopal instruction (F. X. von Wegele, ii. 512).

LEIPZIG (1409)

Doctors in 1496 wore a biretta, a very large hood, a 'shoulder piece', and some form of *supertunica* not specified. The biretta appears to have been black.[1]

Members of the Faculty of Philosophy (Arts) were in 1436 ordered to wear their *pallium* closed, but without a belt, and to have a cap (*Mütze*), a 'shoulder piece', and a hood hanging down behind.[2] This dress appears on the fifteenth-century seal of the Faculty of Philosophy.[3] It seems from this that originally masters were not allowed a head-dress of distinction like a biretta, which was reserved for doctors, but something of a less dignified nature. In 1496 masters still wore a small cap, this time called a *mitra*, which was flat,[4] but by 1499 they were wearing a black (*fuscus*) biretta.[5]

Already in 1495 the authorities had had to combat the growing fondness of members of the university for lay fashions, of which the 'little winged cape' (*caputiolus petiatus*) is especially condemned.[6]

Bachelors were to assume a simple dress to reach below the knees, and they were on no account to wear the black biretta, according to an order of 1499. This was repeated in 1507 and 1512.[7] The dress of undergraduates seems to have been almost, if not the same, as that of bachelors.[8]

In the *Dritte Statutenredaction* of 1471, with additions to 1490, is a reference to the dress of deans of the Faculty of Philosophy. These officers on their election were to wear a tabard, the symbol of their office.[9]

The particular mark of the *Rector Magnificus* in 1741 was a purple silk-cloth (*pannus sericus*) cloak-gown edged with various

---

[1] F. Zarncke, *Die Statutenbücher der Universität Leipzig*, pp. 18–19, § 5, *De Habitus Honestate* (1496), and p. 456, *Vierte Statutenredaction*, viii. 10; A. Schultz, p. 212.

[2] F. Zarncke, *Statutenbücher*, p. 320, § 4, *De Palleis apertis*; A. Schultz, loc. cit., where he gives the date wrongly as 1440.

[3] J. G. Hagelgans, p. 13, small seal on lower right.

[4] F. Zarncke, *Statutenbücher*, pp. 18–19, § 5.

[5] F. Zarncke, *Statutenbücher*, p. 456, *Vierte Statutenredaction*, viii, § 10.

[6] F. Zarncke, *Die Deutschen Universitäten in Mittelalter*, p. 166, quoting the *Libellus Formularis*, § 27.

[7] F. Zarncke, *Statutenbücher*, p. 470, *Vierte Statutenredaction*, xiii, § 21; p. 477, *Vierte Stat.*, xiv, § 17, *De Habitu Baccalariorum*; p. 496, *Fünfte Statutenredaction*, i, § 19.

[8] F. Zarncke, *Statutenbücher*, loc. cit.

[9] F. Zarncke, *Statutenbücher*, p. 383, *Dritte Statutenredaction*, ii, § 12.

furs and a 'shoulder piece' with a small hood attached of the same colour and material; while Doctors of Theology and of Philosophy wore a violet biretta and a violet cape (*paludamentum*), and Doctors of Law and of Medicine a purple biretta and purple cape.[1]

GREIFSWALD (1456)

In 1456 at the time of the foundation of Greifswald University, Bachelors of Arts were ordered always to appear in a hood (*caputium cucullatum*).[2]

In the university seal, struck the same year, the *Rector Magnificus* appears wearing a 'shoulder piece', a long fur robe, and a round cap with a long 'stalk' apex, and he holds a sceptre.[3] A rector of 1522 appears on the right-hand side of his seal wearing a long sleeveless pleated tabard closed in front, a 'shoulder piece' covering his chest, and a fur bonnet which he holds in his hand.[4]

On the university seal of 1692 the rector is not dressed in the style of that year but rather of the sixteenth century. He wears a *pallium* and a 'shoulder piece' in two layers, and is bareheaded.[5]

INGOLSTADT (1472)

According to the foundation statutes of the university (1472) the rector's hood and *birettum* were to be red if he was a doctor or a prelate of the highest standing, brown if a master or a prelate of lower standing, and if a priest black.[6]

There are examples in the university archives[7] of the red hood and *birettum*, and no doubt it was nearly always a doctor or a highly placed prelate who was elected rector. From these it can be seen that over a long loose cape was worn the hood and 'shoulder piece', red in colour edged with gold braid and

---

[1] A. Steger, pp. 28–29; F. G. Struve, p. 3b.
[2] J. G. L. Kosegarten, *Geschichte der Universität von Greifswald*, ii. 309 (Stats. Fac. Arts, § 109).
[3] J. G. L. Kosegarten, ii (at end), Taf. 3, no. 15.
[4] J. G. L. Kosegarten, ii (at end), Taf. 4, no. 19.
[5] E. Gritzner, Taf. 11, no. 1; J. G. Hagelgans, p. 9.
[6] C. Prantl, *Geschichte der Ludwig-Maximilians-Universität in Ingolstadt*, i. 40.
[7] As for instance in the 'Matriculation Book', University Archives D, iv, no. 4, depicting the inauguration scene of the *Rector Magnificus* in 1589.

ermine, while the *birettum* was of the same colour and similarly adorned.[1]

In 1475 scholars, bachelors, licentiates, and secular doctors are ordered to wear *cappas*, perhaps in fact the loose capes mentioned above, at all academical functions according to the practice of other universities, after which there is no legislation about dress for a considerable time.[2]

A Master of Theology, Magister Adorf, on a tombstone of 1505 wears a fairly rigid *pileus* without an apex, but with side-pieces (Pl. 18*b*). He has a *cappa manicata*, a 'shoulder piece', and a hood with a liripipe which falls behind. The man, a Master of Arts, standing on the right behind the students has a long-sleeved gown and a long and large *chaperon* (*Sendelbinde*) on his left shoulder.[3]

Here during the latter fifteenth century the practice had arisen for all graduates to wear the *birettum* (*pileus*). Doctors of the lay faculties wore red ones, Masters of Arts dark purple ones, while graduates in Orders wore black ones.[4] Towards the end of this century, the *cingulum*, or girdle, had become an acknowledged part of the dress of Masters of Arts. This was no doubt regarded by the masters as a symbol of servitude fit only for students, for they appealed for permission to dispense with them.[5] Indeed students of Ingoldstædt did wear girdles.[6] The *cingulum* seems to have been variously regarded at different universities and at different times, sometimes being forced upon undergraduates as a sign of their inferiority, sometimes refused them and given only to graduates and even doctors as a sign of dignity.

After a very long gap dress is at length mentioned in 1642 when the rector's costume is described. By this time it consisted of the same loose cape or cloak as in the fifteenth century, decorated with buttons.[7]

MAINZ (1477)

In 1629 doctors used the ring at the ceremony of their creation, and their head-dress was the biretta (*pileus*) of the colour of the faculty to which they belonged. It was black for Masters of

---

[1] C. Prantl, i. 40, n. 13.   [2] C. Prantl, ii. 62.
[3] F. Philippi, *Atlas zur Weltlichen Altertumskunde des deutscher Mittelalters*, Taf. 117.
[4] C. Meiners, art. cit., pp. 228–9.   [5] C. Meiners, art .cit., pp. 229–30.
[6] *Conspectus*, ii. 68.   [7] C. Prantl, ii. 394.

Theology, red for Doctors of Law, and blue for Doctors of Medicine and of Philosophy. All wore the same black silk damasked gown.[1] Professors were wearing the *epomis* in 1795.[2]

TÜBINGEN (1477)

At the University of Tübingen in the sixteenth century the particular mark of the Master of Arts (Philosophy) was the round violet-blue biretta, while the Master of Theology was distinguished by the square scarlet biretta, a ring, and a 'shoulder piece'.[3] In 1525 it was ordered that all Masters of Theology and of Philosophy (Arts) must wear gowns with full sleeves, as also scholars, but ordinary students of Law and Medicine might wear the sleeves or not.[4] This last is particularly interesting as being comparable to the full sleeves of Oxford scholars, while commoners are without them.

Academical dress was, however, falling rapidly out of use, and by 1543 Doctor Leonard Fuchs when taking a degree at Tübingen simply wore ordinary dress, as he writes to a friend.[5] From the short clause, *De Vestitu*, in the revised statutes of 1601 it would seem that any fixed rules as to the wearing of academical dress had been abandoned.[6]

The ducal college. From the set of plates of the ducal college of Tübingen published about 1589 it is to be seen that, while on ordinary occasions no academical dress was worn,[7] it was worn at certain times. Thus in the quaint scene of dinner in hall[8] with the duke and his suite at high table, masters sitting at a table on the right in the foreground wear full gowns and short round hoods. They are in fact dressed for an occasion, as for dining in hall at Oxford and Cambridge (Pl. 19).

WITTENBERG (1502)

Since in the statutes nothing is mentioned about dress except sumptuary rules, one is dependent in the case of Wittenberg on odd fragments of information gathered from various sources.

[1] M. Sandaeus, *Theologia Juridia*, Comment. L, pp. 676–7.
[2] E. Winkelmann, ii. 305, § 2421.
[3] K. Klüpfel and M. Eifert, *Geschichte der Universität Tübingen*, pt. 2, pp. 18–19.
[4] K. Klüpfel and M. Eifert, pt. 2, p. 27.
[5] M. von Boehn, *Die Mode, 16 Jahrh.*, p. 94.
[6] *Statuta universitatis scholasticae Studii Tubingensis*, pp. 111–12.
[7] J. S. Neyffer and L. Ditzinger, *Illustrissimi Wirtembergici ducalis novi collegii Delineato*, pl. i.   [8] Ibid., pl. ii.

PLATE 19

Scene in the Hall of the University of Tübingen, c. 1589

Among the medallions of coats of arms in the *Lutherhaus* is a portrait of Polich von Mellerstadt, first Rector of Wittenberg. He wears a round pill-box *pileus* and a white turn-down collar. Unfortunately only the head and shoulders appear.[1]

In 1702 on the occasion of the bicentenary a festival was held. An anonymous eyewitness of the grand procession of doctors describes the colours of the birettas of the doctors of the various faculties as being black for Theology, red for Law and Medicine, and violet for Philosophy.[2]

In the seventeenth century students wore a short gown (*halb-geistliche*),[3] but at the festival of 1702 they wore what might have been a cloak-gown, for it is not described as *geistlich*[4] or even *halbgeistlich*.

FRANKFURT-ON-ODER (1506)

The statutes of Frankfurt University published at the beginning of the *Notitia Universitatis Francofurtanae* (1707) contain no reference to academical dress.[5]

All the information to be found is that provided by the print of Cornelius Boutekoe. Here is to be seen the type of gown worn in the late seventeenth century by a Doctor of Medicine. It is of the bag-sleeved variety with an opening for the arm to pass through. The upper part of this opening is cut in the shape of an inverted V. The gown has black velvet facings and a flap collar.[6]

KÖNIGSBERG (1544)

On the seal of the Faculty of Law of about 1544 the Rector of Königsberg University wears a small lace collar, a short ermine 'shoulder piece', a loose-sleeved *tunica* with an opening down the front, though it is worn closed, and a bonnet broadly edged with ermine and having a short tassel.[7] The statutes contain no relevant information.

---

[1] W. Friedensburg, *Geschichte der Universität Wittenberg*, 2nd pl. at end.
[2] K. H. Schundenius, *Erinnerungen an die festlichen Tage der dritter Stiftungsfeyer der Akademie zu Wittenberg*, p. 61.
[3] W. Friedensburg, p. 35.
[4] K. H. Schundenius, p. 60.
[5] J. C. Becmann, *Notitia Universitatis Francofurtanae*.
[6] Oxford, Ashmolean Museum (Hope Collection).
[7] J. G. Hagelgans, p. 17, top right figure.

JENA (1558)

In the fine woodcut of the sixteenth century by Hans Weiditz depicting the ceremony of the bestowal of the doctoral bonnet all the doctors and the rector wear soft bonnets, open gowns, and a *Sendelbinde*, which hangs over both shoulders and descends in front like a sling.[1]

A full-length print of a late seventeenth-century *Rector Magnificus* shows his dress to perfection. His head-dress is a round tall pleated bonnet with a hat-band of gold braid. He wears a 'shoulder piece' which covers the shoulders and the arms as far as the elbow. It is fastened vertically down the front with many small buttons, embroidered with a leaf motif, and edged with ermine at the bottom. His robe is tight-sleeved and is fairly close to the body, but has a long train, and although it is open down the front the two sides are drawn together. He wears bands.[2]

In the seventeenth and eighteenth centuries the insignia of Doctors of Law were the purple *pileus*, a purple silk gown, and a gold ring.[3]

Although students of the lay faculties, as was the case at most German universities, seem to have given up the cloak-gown in the later seventeenth century, theological students continued to wear it. In a small water-colour illustration in the university *Stammbuch* for the year 1730 a theological student is depicted at his *viva* standing before the Professors of Theology. He wears a black flap-collared cloak which hangs behind him well away from his arms.[4]

HELMSTÄDT (1575)

Information about the dress worn at Helmstädt (now Helmstedt) is meagre. According to a patent of 1644 issued by the regents, the use of the *Pennalkleidung* (i.e. any dress with winged or long and hanging sleeves) was forbidden.[5]

In 1739 a purple silk *pileus* (i.e. round bonnet) was being worn not only by Doctors of Law,[6] but by doctors of all faculties.[7] Doctors throughout the period seem to have worn a cloak with

---

[1] E. Borkowsky, *Das alte Jena und seine Universität*, p. 29.
[2] E. Borkowsky, p. 68.
[3] P. Müller, *De Gradu Doctoris*, p. 26; A. Steger, p. 31.
[4] E. Borkowsky, p. 83, upper figure.
[5] Helmstädt Univ. Archives, *Decretum in Consistorio XI Maij, 1644*.
[6] J. G. Kipping, *Oratio de Honoribus Academicis*, p. 21; A. Steger, p. 31.
[7] F. G. Struve, p. 3b.

a flap collar fastened in front with a morse. The whole cloak was edged with braid and reached half-way down the body. This dress is exemplified in the print of the first half of the eighteenth century of J. G. Pertsch, Doctor of Law.[1]

ALTDORF (1578)

The University of Altdorf is particularly rich in pictorial information, thanks to collections of engravings of portraits of professors past and present brought out in the earlier eighteenth century. One of these collections shows the dress of regents at the time of the university's foundation. It consists of a close-fitting skull-cap like a helmet and an open flap-collared gown with cord and button braiding on the sleeves.[2]

J. C. Durrius (d. 1677), Professor of Theology, wears in a print of after 1657 a flap-collared black cloak and broad white bands.[3] This may be termed academical 'undress'.

M. Koenig (1616–99), Professor of Greek and Poetry, and librarian, wears full academical dress consisting of a black cassock with many buttons down the front, over this a full black gown with hanging bell sleeves, the gown having broad facings, and large white bands.[4]

An early eighteenth-century Professor of Medicine, J. J. Baier, wears a silk 'shoulder piece' with an opening in the middle and edged at the top and bottom with broad embroidery.[5] A dean's dress of the same period is remarkable for the plain cloth 'shoulder piece' with an opening in the middle and with a thin edging of lace.[6] The gowns of all lay professors were red.[7] Professors of Theology wore black.[8] The rector wore the same as the lay professors.

STRASSBURG (1621)

At first a gymnasium, in 1566 it became a degree granting academy, and in 1621 it gained the status of university by imperial decree.[9]

---

[1] Oxford, Ashmolean Museum (Hope Collection).
[2] S. J. Apin, *Vitae Professorum Philosophiae* (Altorfinae), pl. before p. 1.
[3] G. G. Zeltner, *Vitae Theologorum Altorphinorum*, p. 344.
[4] S. J. Apin, pl. opp. p. 188.
[5] J. J. Baier, *Biographiae Professorum Medicinae . . . In Academia Altorf*, frontispiece.
[6] S. J. Apin, pl. opp. p. 300.
[7] A. Tholuck, *Das akademische Leben des siebzehnten Jahrhunderts*, p. 132, § 7.
[8] C. Meiners, art. cit., p. 252.   [9] See S. d'Irsay, *Histoire des Universités*, ii. 25.

By an order of 1604 gentlemen-commoners, noblemen, licentiates, masters, and doctors were allowed the use of velvet, silk, satin, and damask in their dress, and to wear a biretta or hood, but bachelors and all other students were forbidden these.[1] Although this indulgence was granted, dress of a military type was not to be tolerated.[2]

According to the plates in the *Speculum Cornelianum* (1618), the dress of professors consisted of a round, pleated, corded bonnet and a fur-lined, fur-faced gown with a flap collar of fur. Whether the sleeves were of a bell shape or of the character of false panels seems to have been immaterial.[3]

KIEL (1665)

Kiel University was of slight importance until it came directly under Prussia in the nineteenth century. There is no reference to dress in its statutes.

Doctors of Theology wore purple *pilei* (i.e. round bonnets) and black gowns,[4] while Doctors of Law wore purple *pilei* and purple gowns.[5]

HALLE (1694)

At the time of Halle's foundation there was much opposition to the adoption of a purple robe for the *Rector Magnificus* because of that colour's original association with the papacy, the belief being that popes had first granted the use of that colour to doctors; but owing to the influence of Christian Thomasius, the jurist, it was agreed to use it in *defiance* of the pope.[6]

A. H. Francke, a Professor of Theology, wears in a print of about 1719 a cassock, white bands, an open gown with a flap collar, and a small round loose velvet bonnet, i.e. a *pileus*.[7] In 1736 a purple *pileus* was worn by the *Rector Magnificus*, a black one by Regents of Theology, and a blue one by the Dean of the Faculty of Philosophy.[8] Further than this we know nothing,

---

[1] M. Fournier, *Les Universités françaises—Les Statuts et Privilèges*, iv. 333, Order no. 2144 (1604), ¶ 10, § 11, 9.
[2] M. Fournier, iv. 34, Order no. 1992, n. 2, Latin version.
[3] J. von der Heyden, *Speculum Cornelianum*, pls. 2, 20, and 56.
[4] J. F. Mayer, *De Doctoratu Theologico*, p. 12.
[5] A. Steger, p. 31.
[6] F. Delitzsch, *Iris*, p. 88.
[7] W. von Seidlitz, *Allgemeines historisches Porträtwerk*, pt. 12, port. of Francke.
[8] C. Biccius, p. 17, cap. ii, x.

for the short and business-like statutes contain no mention of dress.

GÖTTINGEN (1737)

Göttingen was founded in the same modern and scientific spirit as Halle, and in like manner there is no mention of dress in the statutes. However, from a pictorial source one learns that in 1747 the dress of a professor consisted of an open gown with a flap collar and probably (for the picture is under half-length) bell sleeves. The collar and the facings of the gown are decorated with velvet, and on the sleeves above the elbows is a horizontal fold of velvet.[1]

ERLANGEN (1743)

At Erlangen the King of Prussia was nominally rector, while the pro-rector carried out the functions performed by a rector in the older universities.[2] The dress of the pro-rector consisted of a purple-coloured gown (*pallium*), a gold-embroidered 'shoulder piece', and a head-dress which might be according to choice either a purple biretta or a purple four-cornered cap, presumably like the English one.[3]

Regents wore on all important occasions a long and full cloth robe faced with velvet, and a biretta or a four-cornered velvet cap as they wished. Robe and cap were of the colour of the regent's faculty. All regents were doctors. Thus Doctors of Theology wore black, those of Law red-scarlet, those of Medicine dark red, and those of Philosophy violet.[4]

C. STUDENT DRESS

This is so significant a branch of this study as regards German-speaking countries that the dress of students is worth a special review.

Although true academical student dress vanished early, there are enough examples, both descriptive and pictorial, to furnish us with information as to its original character. Thus in

---

[1] W. von Seidlitz, pts. 10 and 11, port. of J. M. Gesner.
[2] G. W. A. Fikenscher, *Geschichte der Königlich Preussischen Friedrich-Alexanders-Universität zu Erlangen*, p. 431.
[3] G. W. A. Fikenscher, p. 454; F. Delitzsch, p. 88.
[4] G. W. A. Fikenscher, pp. 455 and 468.

1436 students of Leipzig wore a closed *supertunica*,[1] in 1470 Heidelberg students had to have their hood fastened on to their *supertunica* to prevent its being worn on the head,[2] and in 1489 a student is depicted in a woodcut wearing a *tunica* reaching to a little way above his ankles, and over it a loose sleeveless mantle.[3] In 1495 students of Leipzig were ordered to wear full-length hoods and not abbreviated ones, and to go bare-headed.[4] Length of dress for students of Erfurt was insisted on in the fifteenth century.[5] In 1505 students of Ingolstadt wore closed gowns with loose sleeves.[6] At Cologne in 1516 students wore plain black hoods.[7] In 1523 students in general wore open full-sleeved gowns with ordinary hats of contemporary lay fashion,[8] while at Tübingen in 1525 they were ordered, if scholars (bursars), to wear full-sleeved gowns, but if commoners, gowns with sleeves or without them as they preferred.[9] We can see exactly what this enactment meant by looking at the plates of Tübingen scenes in Neyffer and Ditzinger's late sixteenth-century book. In the scene in the hall,[10] in which the members of the university are dining, commoners, if we are to judge from the figure near the lower table standing up near a recess with a tankard in his hand, wear a long cape with a flap collar, while servitors carrying in dishes wear the same cape with the addition of 'streamers' falling from the shoulders, exactly the same as those of Oxford commoners. Other examples of the streamer-less capes of commoners are to be seen in the plate of a lecture and that of the library.[11] A Strassburg student of 1618 who appears in a print depicting 'Thaïs', the symbolical woman who lures scholars away from their work, with her devotees,[12] wears over his ordinary dress a cloak with a flap collar. The cloak is of moderate length and is drawn over the arms to below the elbow, but what is chiefly remarkable about his dress is his head-dress which is a trencher cap with a tump like the English one.

---

[1] F. Zarncke, *Statutenbücher*, p. 350.   [2] E. Winkelmann, i. 186.
[3] F. Philippi, Taf. 62, '*Studente*, 39' (*Des Dodes Danz*, Lübeck).
[4] R. F. Seybolt, p. 118, n. b.   [5] C. Meiners, art. cit., pp. 227–8.
[6] F. Philippi, Taf. 117.   [7] *Epistolae Obscurorum Virorum*, i, letter 39, p. 366.
[8] H. Peters, *Der Arzt in der deutschen Vergangenheit*, p. 25, Abb. 24.
[9] K. Klüpfel and M. Eifert, pt. 2, p. 27.
[10] J. S. Neyffer and L. Ditzinger, pl. ii.
[11] J. S. Neyffer and L. Ditzinger, pls. iii and iv.
[12] J. von der Heyden, pl. 56.

The story of the students' opposition to the *geistliche Kleide* begins at Leipzig as early as 1412 when it was found necessary to order students not to carry weapons. This seems to have been obeyed, for in 1440 the university felt strong enough to forbid Bachelors of Arts and students to wear a cloak or to gird their *tunica*. In the same year they were told to wear large hoosp on festive occasions.[1] This seems to have met with only slight response, for in 1458 legislation was directed against foppish dress, and the close, tight-sleeved *tunica* was still insisted on. The answer of the students to this was to ignore the order and later to rip the document off the church door and tear it up. In 1500 there was further legislation, of the success of which we hear nothing;[2] but no wonder action was necessary, for in 1482 Leipzig students had worn hats with high plumes and the rich dress of courtiers.[3] At Leipzig throughout the sixteenth century the lamentation goes up that so scandalously slack is the regard that is had to appearances that one cannot tell a doctor or a master from a shopkeeper. In 1570, it seems, not only students but doctors and masters went about armed.[4]

Throughout the fifteenth century members of the University of Vienna had been exceptionally orderly in their dress, which remained clerical and accorded with the statutes; but in 1503 a fight took place between the students and the vintners of the suburbs, and so hard pressed were members of the university that the authorities allowed the students to leave off their *tunicas*, which must have greatly impeded them in fighting, and allowed them to wear ordinary dress for the time of the emergency. After the trouble had passed the authorities realized too late that they had given away their powers of discipline, and the Faculty of Philosophy sought to repair the damage by ordering the students to resume the *tunica* and to give up their arms. Indignant at this the students refused to comply and presented their case to the Emperor Maximilian, who referred them to his Governor of Austria, and he took the side of the students.[5] For some years the students enjoyed their freedom to dress as they wished and to carry arms, until in 1516 with the help of the church authorities the regents forced them to

---

[1] A. Schultz, p. 210.
[2] A. Schultz, p. 212.
[3] C. Meiners, art. cit., p. 232.
[4] A. Schultz, pp. 213 14.
[5] C. Meiners, art. cit., pp. 238–40.

give up arms and to wear open cloaks of the colour of the faculty to which they belonged.[1]

The sixteenth century, an age of violence, contributed still further to the laying aside of students' academical dress, but this was far more widespread in the Protestant universities than in the Roman Catholic ones. There was less discipline in the Protestant bodies where the college system had entirely broken down,[2] and where there was no discipline such rules as those which entailed the wearing of academicals could least of all be enforced, especially as the students were living in lodgings spread all over university towns. In some cases the authorities themselves may have discouraged the wearing of the old dress as 'papistical'.

By 1558 the short Spanish cloak was worn generally by the students of Wittenberg,[3] and in 1562 their dress was described as consisting of a velvet bonnet, wide Spanish breeches, a jacket, and a cloak trimmed with velvet and silk,[4] a costume inspired by the modes of Spain, the great military power of the age, whose influence could be felt even in Germany.

On the other hand the authorities of certain universities opposed this military fashion. For instance, at Tübingen an ordinance of 1525 prohibited the wearing of an imitation of military dress. Students were to use not a lay hat, but a plain biretta without plumes (though noblemen-students were allowed plumes), and long dress. It appears that by this time it was too late to forbid swords, so the authorities contented themselves with ordering that short swords (which no doubt would be less dangerous) alone might be used.[5] Legislation involving the same prohibitions appeared at Ingolstadt in 1556.[6] At Heidelberg no less the wearing of military dress by students was increasing during the sixteenth century, and in 1558 it was found necessary to legislate against it.[7] At this time, however, there was an exception to this state of affairs at Prague where students seem to have worn on special occasions national costumes,[8] and there is no mention of military dress in the university statutes.

[1] C. Meiners, art. cit., p. 240.   [2] C. Meiners, art. cit., p. 245.
[3] C. Meiners, art. cit., pp. 241–2.   [4] *Leges academiae Witebergensis*, p. 24.
[5] K. Klüpfel and M. Eifert, pt. 2, p. 27.   [6] C. Prantl, ii. 225.
[7] A. Thorbecke, p. 30, § 28, iv, and p. 151, § 153, 13.
[8] V. de Viriville, *Histoire de l'Instruction Publique*, pl. opp. p. 193 (no source).

In 1572 a Leipzig student depicted in a water-colour in an album wears a black velvet cap with a red feather, a pleated lace ruff and a tight red jacket and baggy red breeches of Spanish style, while over this he has a scarlet cloak, and at his left hip a long sword with a basket-hilt.[1] In 1618 a student wears a hat with two tall plumes in front,[2] while a student of Jena of 1621 in a quaint picture of that year showing him in his study wears the ordinary lay fashion of the day.[3]

If the sixteenth century has seen the introduction into the German universities of Spanish court fashions,[4] the Thirty Years War of the following century (1618–48), when nearly every student took to arms, increased the tendency towards military dress. In 1635 a certain Professor Gerhard in an inaugural lecture mentioned the change in respect of dress which this war has brought about,[5] and Meyfart, another professor, describes the sword, feathers, boots, and spurs of the student of that time.[6] But if commoners, who could pay for it, adopted such dress, servitors were dressed in rags.[7]

All that was left of any kind of academical dress for students by this time was the short cloak with a flap collar (*Mantel*). Most universities during the greater part of the seventeenth century insisted that students should wear it on formal occasions. These black cloaks were to be seen at important functions about 1655,[8] and in 1678, or the following year, students of Jena were severely reprimanded for coming before the rector without them.[9] The University of Frankfurt-on-Oder still ordered students to wear the cloak in the presence of the chancellor in 1683,[10] and in the same year the students of Heidelberg were instructed to wear it when attending Communion.[11] Although, as we have noticed above[12] all students of Wittenberg wore the cloak in 1702 and the theological students of Jena in 1730, the diarist Veltheim was in 1696 writing as if

[1] R. and R. Keil, *Geschichte des Jenaischen Studentenlebens*, p. 55.

[2] F. Hottenroth, *Handbuch*, p. 763, fig. 218, no. 7.

[3] Jena Univ. Bibl., *Stammbuch*, Nr. 7, Bb. 272v—'Ein Jenaischer Student von Jahre 1621, in seinem Zimmer.'

[4] R. and R. Keil, loc. cit.

[5] A. Tholuck, p. 259. [6] A. Tholuck, p. 134.

[7] R. and R. Keil, p. 98. [8] C. Meiners, art. cit., p. 247.

[9] R. and R. Keil, p. 99; A. Tholuck, p. 134.

[10] C. Meiners, art. cit., pp. 247–8.

[11] E. Winkelmann, ii. 217, § 1763. [12] See under Wittenberg and Jena.

it had been disused for years.[1] This was probably the case in most universities then.

In 1642 students of Ingolstadt were ordered to wear a *pallium* over their other dress for lectures.[2] There are no means of telling what this was like, and it is not referred to again. Although this may merely mean a cloak-gown it may have been a real gown of medieval character, still preserved in the Roman Catholic university.

In 1665 on the occasion of the opening of the University of Kiel students appeared in ridiculous (*lächerlich*) costumes,[3] and this was a foretaste of what was to come. By the beginning of the eighteenth century the state of the dress of students had grown from bad to worse. In 1702 it was found necessary to legislate against the wearing of dressing-gowns and night-caps and of smoking pipes at lectures.[4] Leipzig, Jena, and Halle were particularly noted for this kind of behaviour. At Leipzig the practice was three times condemned between 1702 and 1719,[5] at Jena it was prohibited and finally stopped in 1750,[6] but at Halle it lasted into the 1820's.[7]

On the other hand there were fashionable students who wore full-bottomed wigs and assumed red cloaks exactly the same as those cloaks used at some universities by the professors on festal occasions.[8] The days when the first student to wear a wig at Altdorf had it torn to pieces by his fellows (1671) were long since past.[9] The fop was well established, although the ordinary student probably wore dress unobtrusive enough.[10]

There is much evidence as to students' dress during the course of the eighteenth century. The plates by P. J. Leidenhoffer in J. F. Leopold's *Academia* (about 1720) provide examples of the typical student of various universities. Thus the Leipzig student wears beautiful laced clothes, the Giessen student carries a muff, but the Tübingen student is sombrely dressed. In each case the inevitable sword is to be seen. A

---

[1] A. Tholuck, p. 135; R. and R. Keil, p. 99.
[2] C. Prantl, ii. 403 (Caput 13, no. 2).
[3] H. Ratjen, *Geschichte der Universität zu Kiel*, p. 59 (n. 5, 'Bericht von den Processionen, Schleswig, 1665').
[4] A. Tholuck, p. 134.   [5] A. Tholuck, loc. cit.
[6] R. and R. Keil, p. 158.   [7] A. Tholuck, op. cit., loc. cit.
[8] C. Meiners, art. cit., op. cit., p. 248.
[9] C. Meiners, art. cit., op. cit., loc. cit.   [10] R. and R. Keil, op. cit., p. 156.

satirical article of 1736 on the eve of the university's incorpora-
tion, mocked both the over-rich and the over-mean dress of
the students arriving at Göttingen.[1] In the engraving above the
title of F. W. Zachariä's *Poetische Schriften* (1765) we see his
Renommist (Braggart) wearing dress of a military cut, with a
very large hat, square in shape and cocked on one side. He has
boots or gaiters reaching to the knee, a riding-whip, and a large
sword. In 1775 the student of Giessen 'does not spend much
money on his dress', writes the theological student Laukhard.
'On Sundays or on weekdays alike he wears the same dress;
a coat (*Flausch*) of thick stuff, or an overcoat (*Rock*), breeches,
and boots.'[2] The fashion for extravagant head-dress with plumes
is ridiculed in 1780.[3] K. A. Kortum in his mock heroic, *The
Jobsiad* (1784), describes his comic hero arriving home from
the university wearing 'a very large hat with a feather, breeches,
a waist-coat of yellow leather, a short cape of grey cloth, a huge
sword . . . large and pointed'; while C. J. Weber in *Demokritus*
writes that even boys at school during their last year wore care-
fully blacked boots, and gloves like courtiers.[4] The authorities
did nothing to put a stop to this, and at Heidelberg in 1775
foreign students were even allowed by statute to wear gold-
laced or silver-laced clothes.[5]

In the latter part of this century at Tübingen only sons of
the nobility and of officers might use powder, and it was especially forbidden to beneficiaries (holders of scholarships and
other grants of money).[6]

The French war which began in 1792 gave an impetus to
the students' associations (*Landsmannschaften*), but in the earliest
stages of the war they, as champions of liberty, supported the
revolutionary armies, the very opposite of the attitude that the
student-bodies later took. It was during the Thirty Years War
that members of most universities in Germany had divided
themselves up into military groups, according to nation, each
nation having its own uniform. Particularly noticeable features

---

[1] F. C. Neubur, art. 'Kleidung der Studirenden auf der Universität Göttingen'
in *Der Sammler*, v. Stück, pp. 33–35.
[2] Letters from Dr. A. Roth of Baden-Baden.
[3] M. Schluck, *Dissertatio de Norma Actionum Studiosorum*, p. 18.
[4] Letter from Dr. A. Roth.
[5] E. Winkelmann, op. cit. ii. 284, § 2256.
[6] M. von Boehn, *Modes and Manners*, iv. 244.

of the dress were the coloured ribbons, variously coloured for each nation, tied to the sword-hilt.[1] After the Thirty Years War these ribbons are lost sight of for a long time, but in an album in which A. B. Filzhofer collected poems, quotations, sketches, and water-colours contributed by his friends from his student days onwards is to be found a water-colour dated 1727. It depicts Altdorf students sitting at a table, one of whom wears a plain red ribbon slung across his chest.[2]

In the last decade of the eighteenth century arose a new style of military dress for students, from which was derived at the time of the War of Independence (1813) the dress of the new *Burschenschaften*, popular bodies which came into being in opposition to the old exclusive *Landsmannschaften*.[3]

In the 1790's it was at Jena that the *Landsmannschaften* particularly flourished. Here the students' everyday dress consisted of a coat of military cut and breeches, with a plumed leather helmet and a sword, while on Sundays and on festal occasions they wore a *Stürmer* dress, which consisted of a three-cornered hat decorated with braid, tassels, and coloured plumes, a gold-embroidered uniform jacket with silver or gold epaulettes, or sometimes a short jacket with facings of a different colour. At the end of the century the round coloured pill-box hat took the place of the three-cornered one.[4] Two silhouettes of 1795 (Pl. 20) show what the students' head-dress was like at Jena. One wears a helmet with a plume falling forward. The other has a cocked hat and a pig-tail.[5]

Of the student dress of Halle, where he was from 1804 to 1806, Ludwig Börne the publicist says that it consisted of such items as large boots called *Kanonen*, and leather helmets with plumes of the colours of the particular *Chore* to which the student belonged. The senior members of the corporations always wore their *Stürmer* hat and their sword.[6]

In the earlier period of the French war the authorities looked askance at all manifestations of sympathy with the new liberty. This seems to have been especially the case at the University

---

[1] R. and R. Keil, op. cit., p. 122.
[2] B.M. MS. Eg. 1425, fo. 88ᵛ (Album of A. B. Filzhofer, 1719–71).
[3] F. Paulsen, *The German Universities*, p. 372.
[4] R. and R. Keil, op. cit., p. 303.
[5] E. Borkowsky, op. cit., ills. on p. 134.
[6] R. and R. Keil, op. cit., pp. 303–4.

PLATE 20

Silhouettes showing Students' head-dress at Jena, 1795

of Würzburg, where in 1799 Bishop Georg Karl decreed that no students were to wear the French tricolour on their collars.[1] This Roman Catholic university continued to hold out against the wearing of military fashions, and in 1805 the use of coloured cockades and cords, and of masks and uniforms was forbidden.[2] At Heidelberg in 1800 students were ordered not to wear *sansculotte* dress.[3]

Certainly during the eighteenth century what little remained of the true forms of academical dress of the German student was destroyed. 'The recent revolutions and developments in our own lifetime', writes C. Meiners in 1804,[4] 'have abolished them completely.'

II. THE LOW COUNTRIES

A. HOLLAND

Until the provinces began their fight for national freedom under William the Silent there were no universities. The first was Leyden, founded in 1575.

LEYDEN (1575)

At Leyden until the end of the seventeenth century professors of the university wore cloth cloaks, without sleeves and with flap collars, of the colour of their faculty; white for Arts (Philosophy), red for Law, green for Medicine, and orange (the national colour) for Theology.[5] The flap collar with gatherings on the shoulder appears in the portraits of Leyden professors in the *Academia Lugd-Batava Virorum Icones* (1613). In a series of prints of the city of Leyden in 1625 this cloak can be seen, particularly in the illustration of the university garden.[6] Here a figure in the left foreground wears such a cloak, which has a flap collar, falls over the shoulders, but leaves the arms quite free. It falls behind in slight, wide pleats, and reaches to the heels, but in front it is wide open and does not cover any part

---

[1] F. X. von Wegele, op. cit. ii. 450.
[2] F. X. von Wegele, op. cit. ii. 489, § 183 (*h*).
[3] E. Winkelmann, op. cit. ii. 323, § 2532.
[4] C. Meiners, art. cit., op. cit., p. 201.
[5] T. Baty, *Academic Colours*, p. 76.
[6] J. Meursius, *Athenae Bataviae*, p. 31.

of the body. An ordinary hat of the lay fashion of the period is worn with it. But there are examples[1] of a much shorter garment, in reality a gown with short sleeves fairly close to the arm and reaching a little way below the elbow, which at the end of the century in a somewhat altered form succeeded the cloak as academical wear. A Professor of Theology as early as 1625 was wearing a gown in preference to the cloak. This was Andreas Rivetus, Professor and Doctor of Theology, who appears in his print in the Meursius book in an open gown with a flap collar, with black silk facings down the front, and with hollow sleeves with gashes, the upper part of the gashes being cut upwards in the middle in the shape of an inverted V.[2] The lay hat was not invariably worn, for a Doctor of Medicine, Petrus Forestus, wears a round bonnet with a cord,[3] which seems to have become the formal doctoral head-dress. There is in the Rijksmuseum, Amsterdam, a painting of 1655-60 by Hendrik van der Burch of a graduation ceremony at Leyden. The picture has darkened, but it can be seen that all wear black gowns with ordinary black felt, high-crowned hats with wide brims except the new doctor who wears a small soft round black bonnet.[4]

By the late seventeenth century the cloak had been superseded by a full, wide-sleeved gown, open in front, the arm coming through a slit in the sleeve. The gown was of the appropriate faculty colour and had a square flap collar decorated with velvet.[5] J. Perizonius, Doctor of Law (d. 1710), wears such a gown in his portrait in the Senate Room of the University of Leyden.[6] The slit in the sleeve was generally given up in the earlier eighteenth century. A Doctor of Medicine, B. S. Albinus (1697-1770), wears a bell-sleeved gown with velvet facings and velvet flap collar, as is to be seen in J. J. Haid's engraving after the painting by C. de Moor.[7] A later example of this gown is to be found in the portrait of the famous classical scholar David Ruhnken of Leyden, painted by J. Pothoven in 1791.[8] There is,

[1] For example, J. Meursius, p. 36, 'The University Library'.
[2] J. Meursius, p. 314.   [3] J. Meursius, p. 96.
[4] W. R. Valentiner, *Pieter de Hooch, with Appendix on Hendrik van der Burch's Art*, ill. on p. 228.   [5] T. Baty, pp. 75-76.
[6] See the reproduction in A. Gudeman, *Imagenes Philologorum*, p. 14, no. 4.
[7] Oxford, Ashmolean Museum (Hope Collection).
[8] J. E. Sandys, *A History of Classical Scholarship*, ii. 458; A. Gudeman, p. 16, no. 1.

however, one notable exception to this style of gown. An engraving after J. M. Quinkhard's painting of P. van Musschenbroek (Doctor of Medicine of Leyden and professor there, 1692–1761) shows him wearing a winged-sleeved gown decorated with gimp, exactly like the Bachelor of Civil Law type of gown at Oxford.[1]

Early in the eighteenth century the colour of the Faculty of Theology was changed from orange to white and that of the Faculty of Arts from white to blue, but the colours for Law and Medicine remained the same as before. On formal occasions a stiff black velvet cylindrical cap was worn by professors.[2] White bands, some being very large and lying in double or triple layers, were worn by all regents. J. Perizonius (seventeenth century) and H. D. Gaubius, Professor of Medicine in the mid-eighteenth century, both wear very large bands which flow out in four folds to a great broadness.[3]

In 1699 the secretary of the university was given an allowance to buy a gown (tabbaart) for himself.[4] It is not described.

FRANEKER (1586)

In the foundation statutes of Franeker (1586) professors were advised to wear some dress befitting their dignity, and to avoid one of a military type. A gown (toga) was considered the best costume for them, but it does not seem to have been regarded as academical, merely a sober form of lay dress.[5]

UTRECHT (1636)

At Utrecht the faculty colours were copied from those of Leyden, but when in the early eighteenth century changes were made for the colours of Theology and Arts, Utrecht accepted the alteration of the Arts colour, but still kept the original orange for Theology.[6]

In the second half of the seventeenth century Professors of

[1] Oxford, Ashmolean Museum (Hope Collection).
[2] T. Baty, pp. 75–76.
[3] A. Gudeman, p. 12, no. 2; print of H. D. Gaubius after the portrait (1741) by H. van der Mij (Oxford, Ashmolean Museum (Hope Collection)). There are besides several examples among the portraits in the Senate Room at Leyden.
[4] Cambridge, University Library, MS. Add. 105, fo. 25ᵛ.
[5] *Statuta et Leges Fundamentales Academiae Frisiorum quae est Franequerae*, pp. 12–13, § xxxv.
[6] T. Baty, pp. 75–76.

Theology wore long black closed gowns with full hanging sleeves.[1] By 1764, as James Boswell on a visit to Utrecht noticed, professors only wore their gowns on special occasions.[2]

OTHER UNIVERSITIES

Of the other Dutch universities founded before 1801, Groningen (1614) was of no account until the nineteenth century, and there is no mention of dress in its meagre statutes. The same is the case with Harderwijk (1648).

DRESS OF STUDENTS

Sir William Brereton on his visit to Holland in 1634 found little outward sign of academical life at Leyden. Only divinity students went 'in the habit of scholars', which must mean that they wore black cloaks. Otherwise students dressed as they pleased.[3]

In 1743 an English traveller, J. Knapton, noticed that Dutch students in all the universities he visited wore 'morning gowns' (i.e. dressing gowns) and swords.[4] This was a slovenly habit introduced from Germany and should not be confused with the wearing of 'studying gowns'.[5,6]

B. BELGIUM

LOUVAIN (1426)

The constitutions of the University of Louvain were modelled on those of the universities of Paris, Vienna, and Cologne, each

---

[1] A. Tholuck, *Das akademische Leben des siebzehnten Jahrhunderts*, p. 134.

[2] *Boswell in Holland, 1763–4*, ed. F. A. Pottle, p. 134.

[3] W. Brereton, *Travels* (Chetham Soc. i), pp. 39–40.

[4] [J. Knapton], *Description of Holland*, pp. 334, 337, and 338.

[5] 'Studying gowns', worn by many academical persons old and young, especially in the seventeenth century, were not academical gowns. They were simply used in order to keep warm when sitting in libraries, and so on. They were long and voluminous with straight sleeves. There is a good example of this gown in the oil-painting, 'Scholar and Youth in a Library' by Caspar Netscher (1639–84) in the possession of Messrs. Thomas Agnew & Sons (reproduced in R. Edwards, *Early Conversation Pictures*, no. 37).

[6] In the early nineteenth century Dutch students copied the German students in wearing peaked caps, but whereas the latter wore *Chore* ribbons on their caps, Dutch students wore caps of the colour of the faculty to which they belonged (T. Baty, pp. 75–76).

PLATE 21

Brass of Jacob Schelewaerts of Louvain, 1483

of which had influence in various ways.[1] At first there were three faculties, those of Theology, Law, and Medicine, the last of these being a lay faculty.[2] A Faculty of Arts was formed in 1429, at which time an iron mace washed over with silver was made for it. It is still preserved. In the niches on it are figures, among them Aristotle and Boëthius, dressed as Masters of Arts. Both wear a loose, pleated *cappa rugata*, and Aristotle wears in addition a 'shoulder piece' (*epitogium*).[3]

In 1450 it was ordered that all, whether clerical or lay, should wear a long dress befitting learned men, and this was repeated in 1455 and at other times in the following years.[4]

The fine brass of Jacob Schelewaerts (d. 1483) in Bruges Cathedral[5] gives us a good idea of the academical dress of Louvain in the fifteenth century (Pl. 21). In it Schelewaerts, who was a Doctor of Theology and from 1472 to 1476 was Professor of Theology at this university, is seen giving a lecture to a class of seven. He wears a *cappa* with side slits through which his arms appear, and wears on his head a hood, under which is a skullcap. As to his audience, not one of them are exactly pupils, but are rather senior members of the university doing him homage as a great teacher, for their faces are those of mature men, and they all have a head-dress, which no undergraduate in Europe would have been allowed. Of the three closest figures, the first (left foreground) has a *chaperon* falling scarf-wise over his left shoulder. His gown is narrow and bell sleeved, and his head-dress is a *pileus*. He is probably a Master of Arts if we are to judge by the prominence of his *chaperon*. The figure in the middle foreground with a large round *pileus* with a button on top of it and a short round hood without a liripipe is perhaps a licentiate of a higher faculty; while the figure in the right foreground who wears a *pileus*, a hood with a rounded liripipe, and a miniver 'shoulder piece' is likely to be a Bachelor of Theology, if we take into consideration the fact that he wears miniver. None below the degrees of Bachelor of Theology and

[1] P. F. X. de Ram, *Considérations sur l'histoire de l'Université de Louvain*, p. 10; P. Delannoy, *L'Université de Louvain*, p. 24.

[2] V. Andreas, *Fasti Academici Lovaniensis*, p. 241.

[3] P. F. X. de Ram, *Analectes*, no. 33, p. 28.

[4] V. Andreas, pp. 338-9.

[5] A reproduction of this brass is given in W. F. Creeny, *A Book of Fac-similes of Monumental Brasses on the Continent of Europe*, p. 44.

Master of Arts, according to medieval statutes generally, were allowed so rich a fur, and the rounded liripipe was a feature of the hood of Bachelors of Theology of Paris at this period. It was probably copied at Louvain.

It is worthy of notice that Schelewaerts, although a Doctor of Theology, wears not the *cappa clausa* but a less formal variety of *cappa*. That the *cappa clausa* was the full dress of Doctors of Theology at Louvain at this time can be seen from the fact that the four figures in the four corners of the brass representing the Four Doctors of the Church are shown wearing it. We must suppose some latitude at ordinary university functions such as lectures, while on the most solemn occasions, for Doctors of Theology at any rate, the *cappa clausa* would still be insisted on, unpopular as it was.

In 1430 it is stated that the biretta was for doctors and masters only and not for bachelors,[1] which must mean Bachelors of Arts, for bachelors of the higher faculties must have been allowed them if we compare the practice at other universities. In 1481 these birettas are described as being 'double', that is, of two parts sewn together.[2]

Nothing more is heard of dress until the middle of the sixteenth century. In 1565 the existing statutes were codified and new ones were made,[3] and it was ordered that the rector should be distinguished by a scarlet 'shoulder piece' lined with fur.[4] At the end of the century (the date is not known) students were instructed to wear as a fitting dress a *tunica* reaching to the knee, and not to go out without an over-gown and cap.[5]

A print (1606) of the *Halle*, the Cloth Hall of the city of Louvain used by the university for its assemblies, shows what the dress of the regents was at this time. It consisted of a rigid biretta with a tump, and a black gown open in front with bell sleeves reaching to the waist and black velvet facings down the front.[6] This dress was still worn in 1752 as the portrait of a Regent Doctor of Medicine, H. J. Réga (1690–1754), shows. The original oil-painting was destroyed with the Cloth Hall in 1914.[7]

[1] V. Andreas, p. 241.   [2] V. Andreas, p. 149.
[3] P. Delannoy, p. 27.   [4] P. Delannoy, p. 28.
[5] P. F. X. de Ram, *Analectes*, no. 22, p. 105, n. 1, § *De moribus scholarium*; P. Delannoy, p. 144.
[6] P. Delannoy, ill. opp. p. 192.   [7] P. Delannoy, ill. opp. p. 156.

The rector's dress in 1741 was the same as in the sixteenth century, and consisted of gown, *pileus*, and a red 'shoulder piece' edged and lined with fur.[1] In the reformed statutes for the university granted by Maria Theresa in 1755 the bonnet is mentioned as being the head-dress of the chancellor and rector.[2]

The university was dispersed in 1797.[3]

DOUAI (1560)

All the information which can be gained about dress at the University of Douai is that in the year of its foundation the rector was ordered to wear a bonnet, a *roba*, and a large 'shoulder piece' with a hood (*caputium*) attached to it.[4]

III. SWITZERLAND

The only two Swiss universities which had a prescribed dress were the University of Basel and Calvin's Academy of Geneva.

BASEL (1460)

In the year of the foundation of Basel University its members were ordered to wear a closed *pallium* of proper length, and over this on important occasions a *Schaube* (*zschupparum*), a black closed bell-sleeved gown such as was worn by the older and graver sort of citizen of the day. Over this members were to wear a 'shoulder piece' with a hood and liripipe (*capucium et lyripipiatum*). No one unless a bishop, a Doctor of Law or Medicine, a canon of the cathedral, a nobleman, or those who held the combined degree of Doctor of Philosophy and Master of Arts might wear the round red bonnet (*birettum rotundum*).[5] This *Schaube* dress, but not the 'shoulder piece', liripipe, and hood, continued to be worn after the Reformation. Felix Platter, as he mentions in his diary, wore in 1557 when he took the degree of Doctor of Medicine at Basel a *Schaube* guarded with velvet.[6] In an engraving Johann Buxtorf (1564–1629),

[1] A. Steger, *Dissertatio de purpura*, p. 28.
[2] *L'annuaire de l'Université de Louvain*, p. 197.
[3] P. F. X. de Ram, *Considérations*, p. 52.
[4] G. Cardon, *La Fondation de l'Université de Douai*, p. 225.
[5] W. Vischer, *Geschichte der Universität Basel*, pp. 133, n. 46, and 214. Doctors and masters were called the *Birretati*.
[6] M. von Boehn, *Modes*, ii. 155–6.

Professor of Oriental Languages at Basel, wears a plain open *Schaube* pleated at the shoulders.[1] By 1617 it had a standing collar and fairly close sleeves with turned-back cuffs, and was open in front. The doctor who wears this dress in a woodcut in a book published that year has a biretta, a rigid form of the original *birretum rotundum*.[2]

In 1465 the rector's dress was ordered to consist of a red 'shoulder piece' with hood attached made of fine cloth lined with miniver, worn over a *Schaube*, and a red bonnet double-lined with fur.[3]

GENEVA (1559)

At the Academy of Geneva at the time of its foundation all regents wore the *Schaube*; but by the seventeenth century, as is to be seen in the fine print of F. Spanheim, D.Th. (1647), this has been changed to a gown with false panel sleeves, very broad black silk facings, and a very large flap collar.[4] By the early eighteenth century all wore a flap-collared cloak without sleeves except for Doctors of Theology, who continued to wear the full gown.[5] Later in the century, however, they also took to the cloak.[6] Sumptuary rules for the dress of students were framed in 1640, 1652, and 1670.[7]

IV. SCANDINAVIA

A. DENMARK

The early statutes of the University of Copenhagen (1478) contain only one reference to dress, when it was ordered that all members of the university were to wear dark dress of seemly cut. They were at the same time forbidden to use chains and buckles. Later statutes concerned with dress are all of a sumptuary nature.[8]

---

[1] D. Herrliberger, *Schweitzerischer Ehrentempel*, pl. 2. For another good example of the *Schaube* see J. F. K. Johnstone, *Alba Amicorum*, pl. xvii (lower).

[2] L. Kunning von Basel, *Stambuch der Jungen Gesellen*, pl. 56.

[3] W. Vischer, p. 116.

[4] C. Borgeaud, *Histoire de l'Université de Genève*, i, pl. opp. p. 352.

[5] C. Borgeaud, pl. opp. p. 504 (2), portrait of Gabriel Cramer, and pl. opp. p. 530, portrait of B. Pictet (1707).

[6] C. Borgeaud, pl. opp. p. 558, portrait of J. Vernet (1785).

[7] C. Borgeaud, p. 453.

[8] H. Matzen, *Kjøbenhavns Universitets Retshistorie*, ii. 151.

The only other information which can be found is hidden away in an academical dissertation of 1694. From this it appears that at that time Doctors of Theology wore a black four-horned biretta (*quadratus cornutus*), while the birettas of doctors in the other faculties were of the same shape but purple.[1]

B. SWEDEN

There are no records about academical dress in Sweden before the eighteenth century, and it would seem that no illustrative material before this period exists. No doubt, as can be seen in such a work as the mural, 'The Gathering of the Manna', by Albert the Painter, in Härkeberga Church, Uppland (about 1480), which shows civilian dress of the time, it was the same as that worn in other parts of Europe. In Post-Reformation times it would have followed the developments of academical dress in north Europe.

Then suddenly in 1778 the existing dress of professors was abolished and instead they wore the costume of members of the Swedish Academy, which King Gustav III himself designed. It consisted of a black suit with a standing collar, a broad red sash over the right shoulder and coming down over the chest, and red rosettes at the knees and on the shoes.[2] At Uppsala in 1784 a black cloak was worn with this uniform, and a traveller of this year says that regent-doctors (i.e. professors) wore silk hats of the colour of the faculty to which they belonged. Doctors of Theology wore black hats, Doctors of Law white ones, Doctors of Medicine green, and it would appear, although the author writes that Doctors of Medicine wore hats of green *or* sky-blue silk, that the last were worn by Doctors of Philosophy, as conformable with the German practice.[3] In 1784 students' dress still consisted of a black silk flap-collared cloak, but it was worn only on very special occasions and was rapidly disappearing.[4] At Lund in the early nineteenth century a gold buckle was introduced on the front of the silk hats of Doctors of Law and of Medicine.[5] This was undoubtedly the result of a

---

[1] S. P. Glud, *Dissertatio de Gradu Magisterii*, p. 64.
[2] E. Bergman, *Nationella Dräkten*, p. 111, fig. 29, 'Professor C. P. Thunberg (1743–1828) I svart akademiuniform (1808)'. This dress for professors died out about 1830.   [3] W. Coxe, *Travels*, iv. 147.   [4] W. Coxe, loc. cit.
[5] D. J. Cunningham, *The Evolution of the Graduation Ceremony*, pp. 39 and 51; J. E. Sandys, art. 'Ancient University Ceremonies', in *Fasciculus*, p. 237.

late eighteenth-century lay fashion. The familiar student's cap of Scandinavian universities was introduced from Germany in the early nineteenth century.

C. FINLAND

The University of Åbo was founded in 1640. The old dress of the Rector of Åbo, revived when the university was moved to Helsingfors in 1827, was a red velvet mantle with a white silk lining. Doctors of Arts (Philosophy) and Doctors of Medicine wore a black cylindrical hat decorated with gold emblems, while Doctors of Law had red cylindrical hats similarly decorated.[1] These were also revived on the move to Helsingfors. Otherwise at Helsingfors all wore the military type of dress prescribed in 1817. The lyre motif on the cap of students was introduced at this date.[2]

D. NORWAY

No university existed in Norway before the nineteenth century.

V. HUNGARY

This section has been written with the help of a monograph specially composed for me by Dr. Csizmadia Andor, University Lecturer at Budapest University, and dated 6 June 1957.

There is no reference before the eighteenth century to any particular academical dress being worn except by students at any Hungarian university. The statutes of the three old universities, Pécs (1367), Óbuda (1389), and Pozsony (1467) are almost entirely lost, and such as remain provide no information to the purpose.

If one is to judge by the earliest portrait remaining of an academical person, that of István Huszthy, the great Hungarian jurist of the seventeenth century, and the first Professor of Law at the Bohemian Academy of Eger, it will be seen that his full dress is simply Hungarian national costume.

It is not until 1759 that we hear of any true academical dress

[1] T. Baty, p. 81.
[2] Letter from Helsinki University with information extracted from the archives, 28 Feb. 1955.

being worn by regents. In that year, as can be realized from the story of Miklós Székely, a dismissed professor, who tried to join in a procession wearing one, regents of the Law Faculty of the University of Nagyszombat (later Budapest) wore a cloak-gown.[1]

Apparently before 1784 rectors and regents wore with this black gown on important occasions a 'shoulder piece' with hood attached falling behind (*epomis*), for in that year Josef II put a stop to the wearing of all such costume in Hungary as in Austria. This dress was sold by public auction at Pest and Pozsony.[1] The members of the University of Budapest are said to have been pleased to be rid of academicals except for regents of the theological faculty. In order to satisfy the latter they were allowed to wear with their canonicals a red cincture and a ring, old symbols of the doctorate in many European countries, to distinguish them among the rest of the clergy. The full professors of the other faculties were given the title of 'royal councillor'.[3] They would thus wear a form of court dress.

The picture of the ceremony held at the opening of the University of Buda in 1780 is lost, and unfortunately the repro-duction of it in *The History of Hungarian Culture*[4] is not clear enough for one to be able to see what dress was worn.

The first mention of the dress of students occurs in 1621 in the statutes of the Calvinist and Lutheran College of Sárospatak, but this was only a sumptuary measure and gives no positive information.

There is, however, a detailed description of the dress of students of the Calvinist College of Debrecen, which in 1624 György Rákóczy, the Governor of Transylvania, ordered them to wear. This consisted of an ankle-length dolman (i.e. like a cassock) fastened by means of hooks and eyes, and over that a green gown (*tóga*) with yellow facings and with an embroidered eagle on one side of the facings. The head-dress consisted of a high fur hat decorated on top with pieces of green stuff.

This remained the dress of students at Debrecen until 1774 when under the influence of Josef II it was altered. The dolman

[1] F. Eckhart, *The History of the Faculty of Law*, p. 22.
[2] Hungarian Public Record Office, nos. 14/127/1784 and 7235/1785 (Orders of the Council of Governor-General).
[3] T. Pauler, *The History of the Hungarian Royal University of Budapest*, i. 201.
[4] iv. 468.

remained as before, but the colour of the gown was changed
from green to black, and a three-cornered hat took the place
of the high one. In 1775 the gown was given up, and in summer
the dolman was worn alone or with an ordinary cloak over it if
the weather was bad; but in winter a short coat lined with fox
fur was worn over the dolman. In 1776 the black gown was
reintroduced, but was given up again in 1780 when the fox fur
coat reappeared.[1] The two kinds of dress are shown in the
drawings of students of 1774 and 1803 reproduced in *A History
of the Royal Free Town of Debrecen.*

The dress of the *Rector Magnificus* dates only from the nineteenth century.[2]

There is no record of students of other colleges and universities wearing a particular costume.

VI. POLAND

The University of Cracow, the only old one in Poland, was
recognized by the papacy in 1362, but was in a poor condition
until refounded by Vladislas Jagellon, Duke of Lithuania, in
1400.[3] It consisted of three colleges, the *Jagellonicum*, commonly
known as the Greater College or the College of Artists; the
Collegium Minus; and the *Collegium juridicum.*[4]

Tabards seem to have been the ordinary dress worn by
regents, for in 1429 new regent-masters of the *Jagellonicum* were
ordered to procure and wear them.[5] Again in 1449 it was
enacted that no one would be elected to the staff of the regent-
masters of the *Jagellonicum* unless he had a tabard. This was also
insisted upon in the *Collegium Minus*, where failure by regents
to procure a tabard would mean a loss of salary.[6] At the end of
the same year it was enacted that no one should be elected to
the post of Dean of the Faculty of Arts unless he possessed a
good tabard to be worn to do honour to the faculty he represented.[7] Just over a week later it was decided that it was neces-

---

[1] *History of the Royal Free Town of Debrecen,* iii. 926–7.
[2] T. Baty, p. 79.   [3] S. d'Irsay, *Histoire des Universités,* i. 184.
[4] *Statuta nec non Liber Promotionum Jagellonica, 1402–1849,* ed. J. Muczkowski,
p. 444.
[5] *Statuta antiqua Collegii Majoris,* p. 13, § 29, *De habitu magistrali* (*Archiwum do
Dziejów Literatury,* i).   [6] *Stat. ant. Coll. Maj.,* p. 17, § 43.
[7] *Statuta nec non Liber Promotionum Jagellonica,* pp. xxviii–xxix.

sary to renew the university's tabards, and allowances of cloth for these garments were voted to be given to the regents to divide amongst themselves.[1] A large hood was regarded as the particular mark of the master's degree in 1491.[2]

As to the dress of Bachelors of Arts at this time, it consisted, as we see from an inventory of the goods of Johannes de Olomucz (1490), of a yellow gown (*schuba*), lined with wolf-skin, brown *tunica*, biretta, two cassocks, and padded cloak (*puluilotega*).[3] Two points arise from this, the first being that bachelors had already come to wear the much-coveted biretta of the masters;[4] and the second, the bright colour of the *schuba*. This need not surprise us. As in all universities before the middle of the sixteenth century great latitude as to colour was allowed.[5] It was the cut rather than the colour that was considered all-important for distinguishing the different degrees. But bachelors had to be careful not to be too free with their dress, for one who continually wore a *tunica* of too good a black cloth and a gown (*palium*) with large sleeves decorated with purple was condemned to some punishment not specified in 1473.[6]

Only in the Faculty of Theology was the *cappa clausa* preserved. In the revised statutes of the Faculty of Theology (1521), Masters (Doctors) of Theology and Bachelors of Theology were ordered to wear the *cappa* on solemn occasions.[7]

By 1533 the undress of Masters (Doctors) of Theology and the dress for all occasions of doctors in the lay faculties and for Masters of Arts had come to consist of a long closed narrow-sleeved *tunica* and a round biretta.[8] The biretta of Masters of Theology was black, and red for the lay doctors.[9]

In 1537 and 1538[10] Masters of Arts were once more ordered to wear a tabard; but later in the century they had returned to the dress which they had worn in 1533. Thus in 1572 at a Convocation of the university they were forbidden to wear the

[1] *Statuta Jagellonica*, n. p. xxix.
[2] *Acta Rectoralia Cracoviensis*, i, § 1406 (Year 1491).
[3] *Acta*, i, § 1343 (Year 1490).   [4] Cf. *Acta*, i, § 2299 (Year 1514).
[5] Cf. *Acta*, i, § 2799 (Year 1524).
[6] *Acta*, i, § 293 (Year 1473).
[7] *Stat. ant. Coll. Maj.*, p. 81.
[8] *Acta*, i, § 3195 (Year 1533).
[9] *Acta*, i, § 3189 (Year 1533).
[10] *Acta*, ii. 27, § 88 (Year 1537) and ii. 47, § 129 (Year 1538).

dress of lay doctors, that is, a tight-sleeved *tunica*, and a doctoral *pileus* or biretta,[1] or a cap with ear-flaps (*auriculatus*), and if they continued to do so they were not to be admitted to the higher faculty to which they aspired.[2] In 1601 a new Master of Arts on taking the oaths at the time of the ceremony of his admittance was ordered to promise to wear at his public lectures a gown with side sleeves.[3] From this it may be seen that the difference in dress between lay doctors and Masters of Arts at this period was that the doctors wore a tight-sleeved *tunica* and the masters a wide-sleeved gown.

We know that by 1547 gloves had come to be considered as part of the doctoral dress.[4] In 1579 a festal dress for lay doctors is first mentioned, and reference is again made to it in the following year.[5] This festal dress—it is interesting to notice that festal dress was introduced at Oxford and Cambridge almost at the same time—consisted of a blue damask gown (*subba*, i.e. *schuba*). In 1579 it is referred to as the festal dress of doctors generally, but in 1580 it is described as worn by a Doctor of Law. In spite of this reference to an exclusive use of the blue *schuba*, the 1579 statute was no doubt observed, and all doctors used it.

Students seem to have been left to their own devices as long as their dress was modest. In the early days the authorities seem to have found nothing in the students' costume to which to take exception, but in the later fifteenth century it began to run to extravagance. In 1473, 1493, and 1533 the dress of students is mentioned only to condemn its richness or its too blatant lay character. Thus in the first of these years the wearing of a black *tunica* of very good cloth (*Astrodomensis*, Astrakhan), or a gown with sleeves decorated with purple is condemned,[6] as is the wearing of green boots;[7] while by 1533 it had become necessary to legislate against a short dress of a lay character.[8]

During the course of the sixteenth century the disturbances and changes in Europe made it more and more necessary, as

---

[1] Cf. the ceremony of the creation of doctors described as *Ad Biretti Impositionem* (*Statuta nec non Liber Promotionum Jagellonica*, footnote, pp. cxxxiv–cxxxvi).

[2] *Statuta Jagellonica*, p. lxviii.   [3] *Statuta Jagellonica*, p. lxxvii.

[4] *Acta*, ii. 139, § 326 (Year 1547).

[5] *Acta*, ii. 324, § 623 (Year 1579), and 331, § 635 (Year 1580).

[6] *Acta*, i, § 290 (Year 1473).

[7] *Acta*, i, § 1594 (Year 1493).   [8] *Acta*, i, § 3197 (Year 1533).

elsewhere, for the authorities at Cracow to keep watch over the dress of members of the university. Thus in 1537 the rector took action against tailors who cheated members of the university and encouraged them to spend their money freely in buying rich cloths. The legislators looked with particular disfavour upon the grey-blue cloth (*szupyczka*) very popular at this time.[1] There were also offences of another kind, as when in 1580 Laurencius Gadomski, a Bachelor of Arts, was punished for appearing in a *pileus*, although in 1514 this had been allowed.[2]

The Deans of the Faculty of Philosophy wore from 1601[3] until about 1778, at their installation, an *epomis* (cloak) once worn by St. Joannes Cantius (d. 1473), a former professor at Cracow. It was kept in the church of St. Anna at Cracow, and was only brought out on these special occasions.[4]

In the eighteenth century regents wore the *palliolum*, a loose and ample cloak; while an order of 1765 demanded that prodeans should wear a purple *epomis*, a garment which was shorter and less full than the *palliolum*. Deans had a similar dress, but it was richly braided, while ex-deans were to wear black silk cloaks or mantles decorated with purple and edged with a narrow line of silver.[5]

---

[1] *Acta*, ii. 21, § 68 (Year 1537).
[2] *Acta*, ii. 324–5, § 625 (Year 1580). Cf. *Acta*, i, § 2299 (Year 1514).
[3] Probably earlier.
[4] *Statuta Jagellonica*, pp. lxxvii–lxxviii and 445.
[5] *Statuta Jagellonica*, p. cci.

GLOSSARY

Du Cange's *Glossarium Mediae et Infimae Latinitatis*, originally published in 1678, remains, in the Benedictine edition(10 vols., 1883–7), unsurpassed for giving exact meanings of Latin terms of dress, although even so there are some examples which leave one in doubt as to the exact nature of certain articles mentioned in medieval statutes and other manuscripts. Sometimes the same word is used in a different sense in different passages, and sometimes one finds more than one word used for the same dress. By closely comparing many passages I have sought to reach definite conclusions. J. H. Baxter and C. Johnson's *Mediaeval Latin Word-List* (1955) is most useful, but in itself is not always sufficient to solve these difficulties. Other works such as V. Gay's *Glossaire archéologique* (2 vols., 1887–1928) are not enough specialized to be of use. The terms in the list which follows are used continually throughout the book.

The writers on monumental brasses, from whom general readers usually gain their knowledge of medieval academical and legal dress, have unfortunately no systematic terminology. H. Haines in his *Manual of Monumental Brasses* (1861) did pioneer work in this way and with much success, and H. Druitt, whose *Manual of Costume as illustrated by Monumental Brasses* appeared in 1906, is on the whole a very accurate writer on this subject; but F. E. Brightman in his valuable introduction to R. T. Günther's article on the brasses in Magdalen Chapel (*Magdalen College Register*, N.S., vol. viii (1915)) rightly complained of the often inaccurate explanations of articles of dress by this class of writer. How this inaccuracy persists can be seen for instance in the old mistake about the word 'tippet' still to be found in the 1953 edition of H. W. Macklin's *Monumental Brasses*.

APEX. The point, often like a stalk or button on the top of the *Pileus*, which later reappeared on the biretta, and as a tump or tuft on the *Pileus Quadratus* (Fig. 6).

ARMELAUSA (MANTLE). An outer garment open right down one side and closed on the other. Originally a late Western Roman and Byzantine dress, it was worn (as the *manteau*) by French *Chevaliers*, and soon became the recognized full dress of judges in northern Europe (Fig. 1).

BIRETTA, BIRETTUM and other spellings. Used for the horned and rigid variety of *Pileus* (Fig. 2).

CAPPA CLAUSA. A voluminous dress, sleeveless and reaching to the feet, with one slit in the middle front for the passage of both arms, or with two side slits (Figs. 3*a*, *b*).

1. Armelausa (Mantle)

2. Biretta

Flap collar

False sleeve

7. Flap-collared, false-
sleeved gown

3a. Cappa Clausa
with one slit

3b. Cappa Clausa
with two slits

4. Chaperon

5. Hood showing
liripipe

9. Gown with glove
sleeves

6. Pileus with
apex

8. Gown with winged sleeves

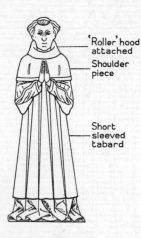

'Roller' hood
attached

Shoulder
piece

Short
sleeved
tabard

10. Sleeved tabard showing
various features common to
medieval academical dress

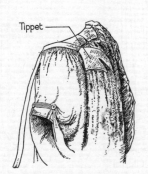

Tippet

11. Gown with tippet

12. Tunica

CAPPA MANICATA. A closed dress, shorter than the cassock (*Subtunica*) with full sleeves reaching to a point behind. F. E. Brightman in his Preface to the *Magdalen College Register*, N.S., viii, p. vi, calls the *Cappa Manicata* a Chimere with long sleeves. T. A. Lacey, describing the two forms of *Cappa*, compares the *Cappa Manicata* with the ecclesiastical Chimere and the Italian *Zimarra*, but he fails to see that it is the *Cappa Clausa* with two slits with which the Chimere should be compared (T. A. Lacey, art. 'The Ecclesiastical Habit in England' in *St. Paul's Ecclesiological Society*, iv, pt. ii, pp. 128–9). N. F. Robinson realizes this. See his article in *St. Paul's Ecclesiological Society*, iv, pt. iii, pp. 189 and 192. See TABARD.

CAPPA NIGRA. This was the same as the *Cappa Clausa* with side slits.

CAPPA ROTUNDA. A full, round form of *Cappa Manicata*. Though this is not anywhere specified, it was probably cut round at the neck and shoulders.

CAPE-GOWN OR CLOAK-GOWN. A Spanish lay fashion which appeared in the sixteenth century and was soon copied throughout Europe. It had a collar with a square flap which fell behind the neck. It hung down at the back, free of the arms.

CHAPERON (CHAUSSE). 'Chaperon' is the preferable term. It was a broad band of stuff lying on one shoulder, and was originally used as a band to which a hat was fastened so that it could be thrown off the head to hang down behind. The BOURRELET was a padded cap joined to the Chaperon (Fig. 4).

COLLAR (FLAP). The square collar falling below the neck on 'lay' gowns. A sixteenth-century fashion. L. H. D. Buxton and S. Gibson (*Oxford University Ceremonies*, p. 37) are wrong in stating that it is a modern addition (Fig. 7).

COLLOBIUM. Used in some works for the Tabard (e.g. E. C. Clarke, art. in *Archaeological Journal*, l. 139–40; V. Gay, *Glossaire archéologique*, ii. 365a, s.v. TABART, XVᵉ s.).

EPITOGIUM. In medieval manuscripts this usually means 'Shoulder Piece' but it is sometimes used for a gown with a large 'Shoulder Piece' and hood placed above it.

EPOMIS. A 'Shoulder Piece'. At Cracow the term appears to have been used for 'Cloak' (J. Muczkowski, *Statuta nec non Liber Promotionum Jagellonica*, pp. lxxvii, cci, and 445).

LIRIPIPE. The piece of material at the end of the hood used originally for pulling it on and off the head (Fig. 5).

MINIVER. A loose term for varieties of fur used in ceremonial costume. Sometimes different varieties sewn together were used at the same time, and were disguised to look like expensive fur. Marten's fur was often used.

PALLIUM. A plain, closed, and sleeveless garment which was worn over the *Supertunica* (*Roba* or *Toga*) (E. C. Clarke, art. in *Archaeological Journal*, l. 101–2; S. Gibson, *Statuta Antiqua*, pp. 39–40. Stat. of before 1350). By the fifteenth century it had come to be no different from the sleeveless

Tabard. After the Middle Ages the word *Pallium* lost the force of its particular meaning and when used meant no more than 'gown'. This has nothing to do with the ecclesiastical dress of the same name (Oxf. Bodl. Libr. MS. Rawl. B. 461 (*in fine*)).

PILEUS. Used of the round cap in its various stages of development before its squareness appeared in the sixteenth century. Although medieval legislators as often as not use BIRETTUM (particularly outside England), I employ in the earlier stages the word *Pileus* according to the above definition to avoid any confusion, the word *Birettum* being so much associated with the modern ecclesiastical hard square biretta. The biretta and the English square cap were two forms of the sixteenth-century *Birettum*. The APEX was a point or button on the top. It later reappears as a tump or tuft on the *Pileus Quadratus*.

PILEUS QUADRATUS. Used generally for the square cap, at first soft and afterwards rigid with horns, which originated at Paris about 1520. See BIRETTA and PILEUS.

ROBA. In medieval times this was the middle dress worn under such outer dress as the *Cappa*, the *Pallium*, or the *Tabard*, and above the cassock (*Subtunica*). The *Roba* or *Toga* was known as the *Supertunica*.

ROBE AND GOWN. I use the word 'Robe' only for the academical festal robe of scarlet or for the scarlet robes of judges, in the sense of a dress of particular dignity, also for such official dress as that worn by the Lord Chancellor in England. The word 'Gown' I use in its modern sense of a black outer garment. According to J. Strutt (*Dresses and Habits of the English People*, ii. 357) the word was first applied (as *Gunna*) to the *Supertunica* of certain religious orders in the thirteenth century. It was afterwards used for the upper garment of burghers and magistrates of corporate towns and cities, and lastly became a common appellation for a garment substituted for the *Supertunica*.

ROLLER' HOOD. The medieval hood proper resting upon the 'shoulder piece' and surrounding the neck. The liripipe fell over it behind (Fig. 10).

'SHOULDER PIECE.' The lower part of the medieval hood, usually of a piece with it, and covering the shoulders and chest. The 'roller' hood was the upper part (Fig. 10).

SLEEVES (GLOVE AND FALSE PANEL). Long, hanging sleeves, hollow inside, e.g. M.A. sleeves in England. Before they reached the full length of the gown in the seventeenth century they were sometimes called Bag-sleeves. These are the Glove-sleeves. The False panel Sleeves, which are of much the same character, were hanging bands of stuff, either free of the arms or hanging over them, flat and sewn up, so that they were not hollow (Figs. 7 and 9).

SLEEVES (WINGED). Usually on gowns with a flap collar. Open above the elbow in the shape of an inverted V, then cut away horizontally on each side of the elbow to meet the flat lower part of the sleeve behind (Fig. 8).

SUBTUNICA, SUPERTUNICA. E. C. Clarke (article in *Archaeological Journal*, I. 94) calls the *Subtunica* the tight tunic worn under the cassock and the *Supertunica* the cassock itself; but F. E. Brightman (Preface to *Magdalen College Register*, N.S., viii, p. iv) calls the *Subtunica* the cassock and the *Supertunica* the *Roba* or *Toga*. I believe that Brightman is right, for, as he says, one could hardly call a dress underneath the cassock a particular dress at all. See also TUNICA.

TABARD. It was long but not full, sometimes with short pointed sleeves and sometimes without sleeves (Fig. 10).

TIPPET. Only used of such pieces of material as were fastened to the shoulder of gowns and robes. These Tippets represent the remnant of the scarf which held the *Bourrelet*. Other uses of this term are incorrect (Fig. 11).

TOGA. In late medieval times this meant the same as *Roba*. From the sixteenth century the term was used loosely for 'Gown'.

TUNICA. Used of a closed, plain, often pleated outer dress, usually girded, and with close sleeves, in those cases when it cannot be called either a *Supertunica* or a *Subtunica* (Fig. 12).

CRITICAL BIBLIOGRAPHY

A. MANUSCRIPTS

Baden-Baden
  Letters from Dr. A. Roth on German academical costume. 15 August 1952 and 2 September 1952.

Budapest
  Monograph on the academical and legal dress of Hungary by Dr. Csizmadia Andor. 6 June 1957.

Cambridge
Fitzwilliam Museum
  Maclean 173. Petrarcha, *Canzone* (probably Bolognese). Fourteenth century.
  Maclean 180. Orosius, *Historiarum adversus Paganos Libri VII* (Spanish). 1442.
  James 251. Bartholomaeus Anglicus, *De Proprietatibus Rerum*, French translation by Jean Corbechon (miniatures of the style of the Boucicault master). Early fifteenth century.
  Chalk drawings by John Downman. 1777–80.
  Water-colours by Silvester Harding. 1794–8.
St. John's College
  James 182. *Alchemica* (English). 1479.
Sidney Sussex College
  James 76. *Psalterium cum Canticis. c.* 1340.
University Library
  Dd. 4.35 [*Universitatis Cantabrigiensis*] *De antiquis consuetudinibus* (a very important contemporary document). Fifteenth century.
  Mm. 1.40. Miscellaneous transcripts including statutes of Trinity Hall, and papers on Gonville and Caius College. Eighteenth century.
  Mm. 1.53. Miscellaneous papers including one on university ceremonies. Eighteenth century.
  Mm. 4.47, 51, 55, 56 Transcripts of the statutes of the University of Cambridge (of great value). 1758–78.
  Mm. 5.50. Customs and ceremonies of the University of Cambridge (Adam Wall MS. vol. l). Eighteenth century.
  Add. 105. A description of the University of Leyden with an account of its internal government. *c.* 1700.
  Add. 707. J. Barret, Historical collections concerning Trinity College, Dublin. Eighteenth–nineteenth centuries.
  Add. 2616. R. Gooch, *Collectanea* (important transcriptions of sometimes lost MSS.). 1821–37.
  Add. 5107. J. W. Clark, Mr. Buck's Book (the famous Bedell's Book). Nineteenth century.

Coniston, Lancs.
Collection of Mrs. R. A. Parsons. The diary of Dr. Thomas Fry. 1768–72.

Helmstedt
University Library. University Archives. *Decretum in Consistorio, xi Maij, 1644.* 1644.

Helsinki
Extracts relating to academical dress from the university archives. 28 February 1955.

Jena
University Library. Stammbuch, Nr. 7. Seventeenth century.

Karlsruhe
Badische Landesbibliothek. Cod. St. Peter, perg. 92. Life and works of Raymond Lull. *c.* 1320.

London
British Museum.
Arundel 484. *Justiniani Imperatoris Digestum vetus,* with glosses of F. Accursius (German). Thirteenth century (miniatures 1399).
Harley 2887. A collection of theological orations (English). *c.* 1475.
Harley 7032. Various papers including transcripts of: *Statuta antiqua Academiae Cantabr.; Statuta vetera Domus S. Petri Cant. (Peterhouse);* and *Miscellanea quaedam circa domum S. Petri,* viz. de Hugone de Balsham (Baker MSS., vol. i). 1707.
Egerton 1191. Album of Sigismund Ortelius of Padua, &c. 1573–9.
Egerton 1192. Album of P. Behaim of Nuremberg. 1574–80.
Egerton 1264. Album of Georg von Holtzschuher of Giessen, Bourges, &c. 1621–4.
Egerton 1425. Album of A. B. Filzhofer. 1719–71.
Additional 5843 (Cole Collections, vol. xlii). Antiquarian matter relating to Cambridge, including royal visits. Eighteenth century.
Additional 5845 (Cole Collections, vol. xliv). Antiquarian matter relating to Cambridge, including royal visits. Eighteenth century.
Additional 25693. *Le Chappelet de Jhesus et de la Vierge Marie.* Sixteenth century.
Additional 25695. *Horae Beatae Mariae Virginis* (French). Late fifteenth century.
Additional 25885. The first part of *Ludolphi de Saxonia Carthusianorum Argentinensium Prioris, Vita Christi* (German). Fifteenth century.
Victoria and Albert Museum
Drawer 53. Diploma of Doctorate of Law of Padua granted to Quintilio Carbo (coloured engraved portrait of later date). 1627.

Malta
Valletta. Royal University Library
1343. *Costituzioni per i nuovi Studi dell' Università e per il Collegio di Educazione di Malta.* 1769.
Correspondence Reg. No. 389/54. Letter from Librarian, 12 September 1955.

Oxford
Ashmolean Museum
Hope Collection of engraved portraits. Sixteenth–eighteenth centuries.
University Archives
Hypomnemata Antiquaria B.11. Inventories BR–C. Seventeenth century.
Hypomnemata Antiquaria B.18. Inventories R–S. Seventeenth century.
Registrum A, fo. 13. Illumination of King Edward III and the university
chancellor. 1375.
Registrum T. Convocation Register. 1647–59.
Bodley's Library
Digby 233. *De Regimine Principum. c.* 1408.
Douce 244. Album of R. Rhetinger (or Rechtinger). 1598–1610.
G.A. Oxon. a. 72. Various illustrations including H. Overton, *Habitus
Academici in Universitate Oxoniensi*; and coloured plate of William Miller.
c. 1730, 1805.
Top. Gen. a. 36. Miscellanies including R. Sayer, *Oxonia Illustrata. c.* 1700.
Top. Oxon. c. 16. Miscellaneous illustrations, the set used being 25
engravings of university costumes by C. Grignion after drawings by
Huddesford and Taylor to illustrate the requirements contained in the
statutes of 1770. 1770.
Top. Gen. c. 25. J. Aubrey, Antiquities and miscellanies (Miscellanies,
pt. II). Seventeenth century.
Top. Oxon. d. 58. J. Roberts, Water-colours of the academical dresses of
Oxford (this unique collection is the finest of all illustrative material).
1792.
Top. Oxon. d. 130. T. Uwins, Pencil drawings of academical dress for
R. Ackermann's 'Oxford'. 1813–14.
Rawlinson D 413. Constitutions of the College of Civil Law, Bologna.
Eighteenth century.
Rawlinson Letters 108, fo. 279. Letter of J. Wildgoose to T. Tanner. 1701.
Twyne 2, fos. 101–3. The colleges of Paris. Seventeenth century.
Twyne 17, fos. 147 ff. (i.e. 1–43). Oxford entertainments: royal visits to
1636. Seventeenth century.
Wood 276 A. Printed mandates of the University of Oxford. [1689].
Wood 276 B. G. Edwards, *Omnium Ordinum Habitumque Academicorum
Exemplaria* (a set of 10 plates similar to those in the above work was
published *c.* 1680 as *Habitus Academicorum Oxoniensium a Doctore ad
Servientem* by I. Oliver, Ludgate Hill). 1674.
Wood F 27. Miscellaneous papers including note on collectors, 1656.
Seventeenth century.

Paris
Bibliothèque nationale. Département des Estampes Oa 10. J. Gaignières,
*Recueil des portraits des roys et reynes de France, des princes, princesses, seigneurs
et dames et des personnes de toutes sortes de professions.* 1581.

Rome
Biblioteca Angelica. 569. A. da Butrio, *Commentariorum super Libro II
Decretalium* (Italian). Second half fifteenth century.

Vienna
  University Library. University Archives. Matriculation Book of the
  University of Ingolstadt, D. IV. 1589.

B. PRINTED BOOKS

ABDY WILLIAMS, C. F., *A short Historical Account of the Degrees in Music at Oxford and Cambridge* (1894).
Acta Rectoralia almae Universitatis studii Cracoviensis, 2 vols. (vol. 1 ed. by W. Wisłocki, vol. 2 ed. by S. Estreicher), 1893–1909.
ALMOND, A. G., *Gowns and Gossip*, 1925.
—— *College Gowns*, 2nd edn., 1926.
ANCONA, P. D', and AESCHLIMANN, E., *Dictionnaire des miniaturistes*, 1949.
ANDREAS, V., *Fasti Academici Lovaniensis*, 1650. (The best work on the subject for Louvain.)
APIN, S. J., *Vitae Professorum Philosophiae* (Altorfinae), 1728. (The prints, of course, lack colour and are limited in value by being half-length.)
ARCO, R. DEL, *Memorial de la Universidad de Huesca* (Colección de Documentos de la Historia de Aragón, tom. viii). n.d. (Full documents.)
ASCHBACH, J. VON, *Geschichte der Wiener Universität*, 3 vols., 1865–88.
ASHDOWN, C. H., *British Costume during Nineteen Centuries, Civil and Ecclesiastical*, 1910.
BAIER, J. J., *Biographiae Professorum Medicinae qui in Academia Altorf unquam vixerunt*, 1728.
BARCKHAUSEN, H., *Statuts et Règlements de l'ancienne Université de Bordeaux (1441–1793)*, 1886.
BARETTI, J., *A Journey from London to Genoa, through England, Portugal, Spain, and France*, 3rd edn., 4 vols., 1770.
BATY, T., *Academic Colours*, 1934. (Contains correspondence with university registrars.)
BEAUMONT, E. T., *Ancient Memorial Brasses*, 1913.
—— *Academical Habit illustrated by Ancient Memorial Brasses* (typescript), 1928. (Not a scholarly work, but a very full one on its subject. The only copy is in the Bodleian.)
BEAUNE, H., and ARBAUMONT, J. D', *Les Universités de Franche-Comté: Dôle, Besançon*, 1870.
BECK, S. W., *Gloves: their Annals and Associations*, 1883.
BECKET, R. B., *Hogarth*, 1949.
BECMANN, J. C., *Notitia universitatis Francofurtanae*, 1707.
BERGMAN, E., *Den svenska dräkten. Nationella Dräkten: En studie Kring Gustaf III:s dräktreform 1778*, 1938.
BERRY, W., *Encyclopaedia Heraldica*, 3 vols., 1828–40.
BIANCO, F. J. VON, *Geschichte der Universität und der Gymnasien der Stadt Köln*, 1833.
BICCIUS, C., *Tractatus Juridicus De Pileo*, 1736. (An important academical dissertation.)
BISHOP, W. J., art. 'Notes on the History of Medical Costume', in *Annals of Medical History*, N.S., vol. vi, no. 3, May 1934, pp. 193–218.

BLOXAM, M. H., *Companion to Gothic Architecture*, 1882.

BOEHN, M. U. VON, *Die Mode: Menschen und Moden in 16. Jahrhundert*, 1923.
—— *Modes and Manners*, 4 vols., 1933–5.

BONANNI, P., *Ordinum religiosorum in ecclesia militanti catalogus*, 3 vols., 1722–3.

BONNEROT, J., *L'Université de Paris du moyen âge à nos jours* (1933).

BORGEAUD, C., *Histoire de l'Université de Genève*, vol. i, 1900. (Good collection of portraits.)

BORKOWSKY, E., *Das alte Jena und seine Universität*, 1908.

BOSWELL, J., *The Life of Samuel Johnson*, ed. R. Ingpen, 2 vols., 1925.

BOURMONT, A. DE, art. 'La Fondation de l'Université de Caen et son organisation au XVᵉ Siècle', in *Bulletin de la Société des Antiquaires de Normandie*, t. xii (1884), pp. 293–622.

BOXHORNIUS, M. Z., *Monumenta illustrium virorum, et Elogia*, 1638.

BRADFORD, W., *Sketches of the Country, Character and Costume in Portugal in 1808–9*, n.d.

BRAGA, T., *Historia da Universidade de Coimbra*, vols. i–iii, 1892–8. (Full documentary evidence.)

Brasenose College, Quatercentenary Monographs, vol. ii (O.H.S., vol. liii), pt. 1, 1909.

BRERETON, W., *Travels in Holland. The United Provinces England Scotland and Ireland M. DC. XXXIV–M. DC. XXXV*. Ed. E. Hawkins (The Chetham Society, vol. i), 1844. (Some account of student dress. Eyewitness.)

BRIGHTMAN, F. E., Preface to R. T. Günther's article, 'Description of the Chapel Brasses', in *Magdalen College Register* (ed. W. M. Macray), N.S., vol. viii, 1915. (A scholarly study. Very valuable for the use of a correct terminology.)

BROOKE, I., *Western European Costume*, 2 vols., 1939–40.

BROOKS, E. ST. J., *The Life of Sir Christopher Hatton*, 1946.

BRUCK, R., *Die Malereien in den Handschriften des Königreichs Sachsen*, 1906.

BURIUS, G., *Onomasticon Etymologicum*, 1751.

BUXTON, L. H. D., and GIBSON, S., *Oxford University Ceremonies*, 1935.

BYROM, J., *The Private Journals and Literary Remains*, ed. R. Parkinson, vol. i, part 1 (The Chetham Society, vol. xxxii), 1854.

CABROL, F., and LECLERCQ, H., *Dictionnaire d'archéologie chrétienne et de liturgie*, t. iii, 1911.

Calendar of Papal Registers, ed. J. A. Twemlow, *Papal Letters*, viii (1427–47), 1909.

Cambridge Grace Books: *B*, pt. 1, ed. M. Bateson, 1903; *Γ*, ed. W. G. Searle, 1908; *Δ*, ed. J. Venn, 1910.

Cambridge University and College Statutes, printed for the Royal Commission, 3 vols., 1852.

CANT, R. G., *The University of St. Andrews: a Short History*, 1946. (Contains various useful items of information.)

CARDON, G., *La Fondation de l'Université de Douai*, 1892.

CARLIER, L., *In Iure academico (Wirceburgense)*, 1732.

CARLYLE, T., *Miscellaneous Essays*, vol. ii (Chapman and Hall's Stereotype edition, 1888).

Ceremonias y costumbres usadas y guardadas en colegio mayor de S. Clemente, Bolonia, 1660.

Chartularium Studii Bononiensis, 2 vols., 1909–13. (Contains useful material.)

CLARK, A., *Register of the University of Oxford*, vol. ii, 1571–1622, pt. 1 (Introduction) (O.H.S., vol. x), 1887.

—— *The Life and Times of Anthony à Wood*, 5 vols. (O.H.S., vols. xix, xxi, xxvi, xxx, and xl), 1891–1900.

CLARK, S., *The Marrow of Ecclesiastical History*, 1675.

CLARKE, E. C., art. 'English Academic Costume', in *The Archaeological Journal*, vol. l (1893). (Generally speaking the most complete article in existence.)

——, art. 'College Caps and Doctors' Hats', in *The Archaeological Journal*, vol. lxi (1904) (A useful work. The best on the subject in spite of some faults.)

CLINCH, G., *English Costume from Prehistoric Times to the End of the Eighteenth Century*, 1909.

COLLE, F. M., *Storia scientifico-letteraria dello Studio di Padova*, vol. i, 1824.

COMBE, W., *A History of the University of Cambridge* (Ackermann), vol. ii, 1815. (Contains the costume plates by T. Uwins.)

——, *A History of the University of Oxford* (Ackermann), vol. ii, 1815. (Contains the costume plates by T. Uwins.)

Communications addressed to the Cambridge Antiquarian Society, 8vo series, vol. iv (1854), pp. 85–93. (Edition of Cambridge University Library MS. Dd. 4.35.)

Conspectus historiae universitatis Viennensis, 3 vols., 1722–5.

КОНСТАНДСКІЙ СОБОРЪ 1414–1418. *Concilium Constantiense* (Société archéologique russe), 1874.

Constituciones, Estatutos, y Privilegios de la Universidad Luliana de Mallorca, 1698.

Constituiones et statuta coll. maj. Sanctae Crucis oppidi Vallisoletani, 1727.

Constitutiones insignis Collegii S. Ildephonsi, ac per inde totius almae Complutensis academia; and *Reformacion en la Universidad de Alcalá de Henares* (2 vols. bound in 1), 1716.

COOMBS, H., and BAX, A. N. edd., *The Journal of a Somerset Rector*, 1930.

COOPER, C. H., *Annals of the University of Cambridge*, 5 vols., 1842–53. (Particularly valuable for the sixteenth century.)

CORSINI, A., *Il Costume del medico nelle pitture fiorentine del Rinascimento*, 1912.

COTMAN, J. S., *Sepulchral Brasses of Norfolk and Suffolk*, 2 vols., 1839/8.

COUTTS, J., *A History of the University of Glasgow*, 1909.

COX, G. V., *Recollections of Oxford*, 1868.

COXE, W., *Travels into Poland, Russia, Sweden, and Denmark*, vol. iv, 1787.

CRAWFURD, R., *The Last Days of Charles II*, 1909.

CREENY, W. F., *A Book of Fac-similes of Monumental Brasses on the Continent of Europe*, 1884.

CRÉVIER, J. B. L., *Histoire de l'Université de Paris*, 7 vols., 1761. (The chief source for Paris from 1673 to 1761. Before that uncritically reliant on Du Boulay.)

CROSSLEY, F. H., *English Church Monuments*, 1921.

CUNNINGHAM, D. J., *The Evolution of the Graduation Ceremony*, 1904.

CUNNINGTON, C. W. and P., *Handbook of Mediaeval Costume*, 1952.

DAVIS, C. T., art. 'A Monumental Brass in the Old, or West, Church, Aberdeen', in *The Archaeological Journal*, vol. li (1894), and pl. opp. p. 76.

DEARMER, P., *The Ornaments of the Ministers*, revised edn., 1920.

Debrecen, The History of the Royal Free Town of, 1871.

DE CAUMONT, A., *Cours d'antiquités monumentales,* vol. vi, 1841.

DELANNOY, P., *L'Université de Louvain,* 1915. (Photographs of portraits destroyed in 1914. Only one of these is really useful for this subject.)

DELITZSCH, F., *Iris,* 1889.

DENIFLE, H., and CHATELAIN, E., *Chartularium Universitatis Parisiensis (1200–1452),* 4 vols., 1889–97.

—— and EHRLE, F., *Archiv für Literatur- und Kirchen- Geschichte des Mittelalters,* Banden iii (1887) and vi (1892). (Band iii particularly contains much information, period fourteenth century.)

DIDEROT, D., and D'ALEMBERT, J. LE R., *Encyclopédie,* 35 vols., 1751–77. (Valuable contemporary articles.)

DRUITT, H., *A Manual of Costume as illustrated by Monumental Brasses,* 1906. (A competent study.)

DUBARLE, E., *Histoire de l'Université de Paris,* 2 vols. in 1, 1844.

Dublin, The Statutes of Trinity College, trans. R. Bolton, 1760 (with a supplement, 1759). (The only systematic collection, but with little information on the subject.)

DU BOULAY, C. E., *Historia Universitatis Parisiensis,* 6 vols., 1665–73. (Much out-of-the-way information. Best for contemporary facts. In the earlier period much romancing.)

—— *Remarques sur la dignité du recteur de l'Université de Paris,* 1668.

DU CANGE, C. D., *Glossarium Mediae et Infimae Latinitatis,* 10 vols., 1883–7.

DUGDALE, W., *Origines juridiciales,* 1671.

DU MOLINET, C., *Figures des differents habits des Chanoines,* 1666.

DUPONT FERRIER, G., *Du Collège de Clermont au Lycée Louis-le-Grand (1563–1920),* 1922.

DYER, G., *Privileges of the University of Cambridge,* 1824.

Edinburgh University: a Sketch of its Life for 300 years, 1884.

EDWARDS, K., *The English Secular Cathedrals in the Middle Ages,* 1949.

EDWARDS, R., *Early Conversation Pictures,* 1954.

EELES, F. C., art. 'The Clavering Glass', in *Transactions of the Essex Archaeological Society,* vol. xvi, pt. 2 (1922).

ELLIS, H., *Original Letters illustrative of English History,* vol. iii, 1824.

Epistolae Obscurorum Virorum, ed. and trans. F. Griffin Stokes, 1909.

ESDAILE, K., and SITWELL, S., *English Church Monuments, 1510–1840,* 1946.

Estatutos da Universidade de Coimbra, 3 vols., 1772. (Pombal's reforms.)

Estatutos de la Universidad de Valladolid, 1651.

EVELYN, J., *The Diary of John Evelyn,* ed. E. S. de Beer, 5 vols., 1955.

FABRONIUS, A., *Historiae Academiae Pisanae,* 3 vols., 1791–5. (A solid work.)

FACCIOLATI, J., *Fasti Gynmasii Patavini* (2 pts. in 1 vol.), 1757.

FAVA, D., ed., *Tesori delle Biblioteche d'Italia: Emilia e Romagna,* 1932.

FÉLIBIEN, M., and LOBINEAU, G. A., *Histoire de la Ville de Paris,* 5 vols., 1725.

FERRARIO, G., *Le Costume ancien et moderne,* 1827 (various volumes). (Fine plates of the latter period.)

FIKENSCHER, G. W. A., *Geschichte der Königlich Preußischen Friedrich-Alexanders-Universität zu Erlangen,* 1795.

FORSTER, J., *The Life of Oliver Goldsmith* (Hutchinson edn., 1905).

FOURNIER, M., *Universités françaises — Les statuts et privilèges*, 4 vols., 1890–4. (Invaluable for the whole of the medieval period. It is to be regretted that it does not extend to the Revolution.)

FRANKLIN, A., *La Vie privée d'autrefois. Arts et métiers, modes, mœurs, usages des Parisiens*, vols. x–xii, 1892–3.

FRANKLYN, C. A. H., and ROGERS, F. R. S., art. 'The Dress of the Clergy', in *Parson and Parish*, 6 pts., 1951–3.

FRENCH, G. J., *The Tippets of the Canons Ecclesiastical*, 1850.

FRIEDENSBURG, W., *Geschichte der Universität Wittenberg*, 1917.

FRIEDLAENDER, E., and MALAGOLA, C., *Acta Nationis Germanicae Universitatis Bononiensis*, 1887.

FUENTE, V. DE LA, *Historia de las Universidades de Enseñanza en España*, vols. i–iv, 1884–9.

GABRIEL, A. L., *Student Life in Ave Maria College, Mediaeval Paris: A History and Chartulary of the College*, 1955.

GADAVE, R., *Les Documents sur l'histoire de l'Université de Toulouse, 1229–1789*, 1910.

GALLUS, N., and FLACIUS ILLYRICENSIS, M., *Responsio*, ?1550.

GANDILHON, R., *Sigillographie des Universités de France*, 1952.

GASPAR, C., and LYNA, F., *Bibliothèque Royale de Belgique — Principaux Manuscrits à Peintures*, vol. i (Text) and vol. i (Plates), 1937.

GERMAIN, A., art. 'L'École de Droit de Montpellier, 1160–1793', in *Académie des Sciences et Lettres de Montpellier* (Section des Lettres, vi, 1874–9).

——, art. 'Notice sur le cérémonial de l'Université de Médecine de Montpellier', in *Académie des Sciences et Lettres de Montpellier* (Section des Lettres, vi, 1874–9).

——, art. 'La Faculté des Arts et l'Ancien Collège de Montpellier, 1242–1789', in *Académie des Sciences et Lettres de Montpellier* (Section des Lettres, vii, 1882–6). (Germain's three articles are undoubtedly the best *studies* of the provincial universities. The best *sources* are to be found in Fournier.)

Gentleman's Magazine, vol. lvii, pt. 2, 1787.

GHERARDI, A., and MORELLI, C., *Statuti della Università Fiorentina*, vol. i (*Documenti di Storia Italiana*, vol. viii, 1881). (The only good collection of Florence statutes.)

GIBSON, S., *Statuta Antiqua Universitatis Oxoniensis*, 1931. (The documentary corner-stone.)

GLASSON, E. D., art. 'Les Origines du costume de la magistrature', in *Nouvelle Revue historique de Droit français et étranger*, 1884.

GLUD, S. P., *Dissertatio de Gradu Magisterii*, 1695.

GODLEY, A. D., *Oxford in the Eighteenth Century*, 1908.

GOLDONI, C., *Memoirs* (English trans.), 1926.

GOODISON, J. W., *Catalogue of Cambridge Portraits* (vol. i, The University Collection), 1955.

GOULET, R., *Compendium on the Magnificence of the University of Paris in 1517*, trans. R. B. Burke, 1928.

[GREEN, J. R.], *Oxford during the Last* (i.e. eighteenth) *Century*, n.d.

GRITZNER, E., *Die Siegel deutscher Universitäten.* (In J. Siebmachers *Wappenbuch*, Bd. i.8. Heft 1 (1904).)

GUDEMAN, A., *Imagines Philologorum*, 1911.

GUNNING, H., *Ceremonies observed in the Senate House at Cambridge*, 1828.

GYLLENE BÖCKER, *Nationalmuseum, Stockholm. Illuminierade medeltida hand-skrifter i dansk och svensk ägo*, 1952.

HAGELGANS, J. G., *Orbis Literatus Academicus Germanico-Europaeus*, 1737. (Perhaps the engravings leave something to be desired, but they are clearer than those of Gritzner.)

HAINES, H., *A Manual of Monumental Brasses*, 1861.

HARRADEN, R., *Costumes of the University of Cambridge* (1803). (Useful but crudely executed plates. Often wrongly dated 1805.)

HARRISON, W. J., *Life in Clare Hall, Cambridge, 1658–1713*, 1958.

HARTLEY, D. R., *Mediaeval Costume and Life*, 1931.

HASKINS, C. H., *The Rise of Universities*, 1923.

HASSALL, W. O., *The Holkham Bible Picture Book*, 1954.

HEARNE, T., *Collections*, vol. x (1728–31), ed. H. E. Salter (O.H.S., vol. lxvii (1915)) and vol. xi (1731–5), ed. H. E. Salter (O.H.S., vol. lxxii (1918)).

HENDERSON, E. F., *Select Historical Documents of the Middle Ages*, 1910.

HERMANN, H. J., *Die Italienischen Handschriften des Dugento und Trecento*, 2 vols., 1928–9. (Pictorial sources for Bologna.)

HERRLIBERGER, D., *Schweitzerischer Ehrentempel*, 1748. (Of pictorial value.)

HEYDEN, J. VON DER, *Speculum Cornelianum*, 1618; facsimile reprint, ? 1879. (Illustrative material for the early seventeenth century.)

HEYWOOD, J., *A Collection of Statutes for the University and Colleges of Cambridge*, 1840. (The fullest collection.)

HOBHOUSE, E., ed., *The Diary of a West Country Physician*, 1934.

HOLLIS, T. and G., *The Monumental Effigies of Great Britain*, 6 pts., 1840–2.

HOPE, W. H. ST. J., *The Seals of the University of Cambridge* (1883).

HOTTENROTH, F., *Handbuch der Deutschen Tracht*, 1896. (Unfortunately sources for the figures are not given.)

HURTAUT, P. T. N., and MAGNY, ., *Dictionnaire historique de la ville de Paris*, 4 vols., 1779.

INNES, C., *Fasti Aberdonenses: Selections from the Records of the University and King's College of Aberdeen, 1494–1854* (Spalding Club), 1854.

——, *Munimenta Universitatis Glasguensis, 1450–1727*, vol. ii (Maitland Club), 1854.

IRELAND, J., and NICHOLS, J., *Hogarth's Complete Works*, 3 vols., 1883.

IRSAY, S. D', *L'Histoire des Universités françaises et étrangères à nos jours*, 2 vols., 1933–5.

JAMES, M. R., *The Chaundler Manuscripts* (Roxburghe Club), 1916. (Contains account of the most important pictorial evidence of the Middle Ages.)

JAMESON, A. B., *Legends of the Monastic Orders*, 1850.

JOHNSTON, W., *The Last Bajans of King's and Marischal Colleges, 1859–60*, 1899.

JOHNSTONE, J. F. K., *The 'Alba Amicorum' of George Strachan, George Craig, and Thomas Cumming*, 1924.

JOURDAIN, C., *Histoire de l'Université de Paris au XVIIe et au XVIIIe siècles*, 2 vols., 1888.

Kay, J., *A Series of Original Portraits and Caricature Etchings*, 2 vols., 1838. (Some information to be derived from these.)

Keil, Ri. and Robt., *Geschichte des Jenaischen Studentenlebens (1548–1858)*, 1858. (An important contribution to the study of university life, others such being by Reicke, Tholuck, and Zarncke.)

Kibre, P., *The Nations in the Mediaeval Universities*, 1948.

Kink, R., *Geschichte der Kaiserlichen Universität zu Wien*, 2 vols., 1854.

Kipping, J. G., *Oratio de Honoribus Academicis* (Helmstädt), 1744.

Klüpfel, K., and Eifert, M., *Geschicht und Beschreibung der Stadt und Universität Tübingen*, 2 pts., 1849. (Pt. 2 deals with the university and is by Klüpfel.)

[Knapton, J.], *Description of Holland*, 1743.

Knox, V., *Essays Moral and Literary*, vol. i, 1784.

Kortum, K. A., *Jobsiade*, 1784.

Kosegarten, J. G. L., *Geschichte der Universität von Greifswald*, 2 vols., 1857/6.

Kunning von Basel, L., *Stambuch der Jungen Gesellen*, 1617; Facsimile reprint, ?1879.

Lacroix, P., *The Eighteenth Century, France, 1700–89. Its Institutions, Customs, and Costumes*, 1876.

——, *XVIIe Siècle. Institutions, usages et costumes, France, 1590–1700*, 1880.

Laing, H., *Ancient Scottish Seals*, 2 vols., 1850–66.

Lamb, J., *Documents relating to the University of Cambridge*, 1838. (Useful but too selective.)

Launoy, J., *De vera causa de secessu Brunonis*, 1662.

——, *Regii Navarraei Gymnasii Parisiensis Historia*, 2 vols., 1677.

——, *Epistolae Omnes*, 1689.

Leach, A. F., *The Schools of Medieval England*, 1916.

Le Couteur, J. D., *English Mediaeval Painted Glass*, 1926.

Leges academiae Witebergensis, 1607.

Lénaudière, P., *De Privilegiis Doctorum*, 1584. (In *Tractatus Universi Iuris*, tom. xviii.)

Lens, L. de, *L'Université d'Angers du XVe siècle à la Révolution française* (T. i. Faculté des Droits), 1880.

Leopold, J. F. and Leidenhoffer, P. J., *Academia*, ?1720.

Loggan, D., *Oxonia Illustrata*, 1675. (The first of the collections of engravings.)

——, *Cantabrigia Illustrata*, 1690. (The finest pictorial evidence of the post-medieval period which we possess.)

Loiseleur, J., art. 'L'Université d'Orléans pendant sa période de décadence' in *Mémoires de la Société d'Agriculture d'Orléans*, t. xxv, no. 3 (1885).

Louvain, L'Annuaire de l'Université de, 1847.

Loyseau, C., *Traité des ordres*, 1610.

Lübke, W., *Ecclesiastical Art in Germany during the Middle Ages*, 1870.

Lyell, J. P. R., *Early Book Illustration in Spain*, 1926. (Pictorial sources for Salamanca.)

Macalister, R. A. S., *Ecclesiastical Vestments*, 1896.

[MacDonnell, H. G.], *Chartae et Statuta collegii Sacrosanctae et individuae Trinitatis reginae Elizabethae juxta Dublin*, 1844.

Macklin, H. W., *Monumental Brasses*, revised by C. Oman, 1953.

MACRAY, W. M., ed., *Register of the Members of Magdalen College, Oxford*, N.S., vol. i, 1894.

MAGRATH, J. R., *The Flemings in Oxford*, 3 vols. (O.H.S., vols. xliv, lxii, and lxxix), 1904–24.

MAISONNIER, J., *La Faculté de droit de l'Université de Pau (1726–93)*, 1902.

MALLET, C. E., *A History of the University of Oxford*, 3 vols., 1924–7.

MALLIOT, J., and MARTIN, P., *Recherches sur les costumes*, 3 vols., 1809. (Contains valuable information.)

MALAGOLA, C., *Statuti delle Università e dei Collegi dello Studio bolognese*, 1888. (The fullest and best collection of Bologna statutes.)

——, *Storiche sullo Studio Bolognese*, 1888.

MARRIOTT, W. B., *Vestiarium Christianum*, 1868.

MARTIN, C., *Civil Costume in England*, 1842.

MARTIN, E., *L'Université de Pont-à-Mousson (1572–1768)*, 1891.

MATZEN, H., *Kjøbenhavns Universitets Retshistorie, 1479–1879*, vol. ii, 1879.

MAXWELL LYTE, H. C., *A History of the University of Oxford from the earliest times to the year 1530*, 1886.

MAYER, J. F., *De Doctoratu Theologico*, 1699.

MEINERS, C., art. 'Kurze Geschichte der Trachten und Kleide-Gesetze auf hohen Schulen', in *Göttingische akademische Annalen*, i, 1804. (Particularly trustworthy for German student dress.)

MELVILL, J., *The Diary of Mr. James Melvill, 1556–1601* (The Bannatyne Club), 1829.

MEURSIUS, J., *Athenae Bataviae*, 1625.

MONTFAUCON, B. DE, *Les Monumens de la monarchie françoise*, 5 vols., 1729–33.

Monumenta historica universitatis Carol. Ferdinandeae Pragensis, 2 vols., 1830–2. (A much better collection than more modern ones of its kind.)

MORAZZONI, G., *La moda a Venezia nel secolo XVIII*, 1931.

MORÓNI, G., *Dizionario dell' erudizione*, s.v. Z, ciii, 1861.

MOTTA VEIGA, M. E. DA, *Esboço Historico-litterario da Faculdade de Theologia da Universidade de Coimbra*, 1872.

MÜLLER, P., *De Gradu Doctoris*, 1687.

MULLINGER, J. D., *A History of the University of Cambridge*, 3 vols., 1873–1911.

MURRAY, D., *Memories of the Old College of Glasgow*, 1927.

NADAL, J. C., *Histoire de l'Université de Valence*, 1861.

[NEUBUR, F. C.], art. 'Kleidung der Studirenden auf der Universität Göttingen', in *Der Sammler*, 1736.

NEVEUX, P., and DACIER, E., *Les Richesses des bibliothèques provinciales de France*, 1932.

NEWTON, S., *The Diary of S. Newton, Alderman of Cambridge, 1664–1717*, ed. J. E. Foster, 1890.

NEYFFER, J. S., and DITZINGER, L. *Illustrissimi Wirtembergici ducalis novi collegii Delineato*, 1626. (Valuable contemporary engravings.)

NORRIS, H., *Costume and Fashion*, 3 vols., 1924–7.

——, *Church Vestments*, 1949. (A book to be used with great caution.)

Notes and Queries, 1st series, iii. 329; 2nd series, iii. 115–17 and 275–7; v. 501–2; vi. 211 and 258a; viii. 74–75; x. 160–1; 7th series, xii. 241; 12th series, ii. 537; iii. 59.

PANTIN, W. A., *Chapters of the English Black Monks (1215–1540)*, vol. ii (Camden Society, 3rd series, vol. xlvii (1933)).
——, *Canterbury College*, vol. i (Inventories) (O.H.S., N.S., vol. vi (1947)).
PANZIROLUS, G., *De Claris legum interpretatibus*, 1721.
PARNELL, H., *The College of Vicars Choral, Wells*, 1927.
PASQUIER, E., *Les Recherches de la France*, 1621.
PATIN, G., *Lettres choisies*, 1683.
——, *Nouvelles lettres*, 2 vols., 1718.
PATINUS, C., *Lyceum Patavinum*, 1682.
PAULSEN, F., *The German Universities*, 1906.
PEACOCK, G., *Observations on the Statutes of Cambridge*, 1841.
PÉRIES, G., *La Faculté de droit dans l'ancienne Université de Paris, 1160–1793*, 1890.
PERRAULT, C., *Les Hommes illustres qui ont paru en France*, 2 vols., 1696.
PETERS, H., *Der Arzt und die Heil und die Heilkunst in der deutschen Vergangenheit (15–18. Jahrh.)*. (In G. Steinhausen, *Monographien zur deutschen Kulturgeschichte*, Bd. iii, 1900.)
PHILIPPI, F., *Atlas zur Weltlichen Altertumskunde des deutscher Mittelalters*, 1924. (Some good pictorial evidence taken from woodcuts and other sources.)
PIC, P., *Guy Patin*, 1911.
PITON, C., *Le Costume civil en France du XIIIe au XIXe siècle*, n.d.
PLANCHÉ, J. R., *Cyclopaedia of Costume*, 2 vols., 1876–9.
POOLE, Mrs. R. L., *Oxford Portraits, a Catalogue*, 3 vols. (O.H.S., vols. lvii, lxxxi, and lxxxii (1911–26)).
POPE, W., *The Life of Seth [Ward]*, 1697.
PORT, C., *Les Statuts des quatre facultés de l'université d'Angers, 1464–94*, 1878.
POTTLE, F. A., ed., *Boswell in Holland, 1763–4*, 1952.
POWELL, A., *John Aubrey and his Friends*, 1948.
PRANTL, C., *Geschichte der Ludwig-Maximilians-Universität in Ingolstadt, Landshut, München*, 2 vols., 1872.
QUICHERAT, J., *L'Histoire du costume en France*, 1875. (The best study of French professional costume.)
RAIT, R. S., *The Universities of Aberdeen. A History*, 1895.
RAM, P. F. X. DE, *Analectes pour servir à l'histoire de l'Université de Louvain*, Nos. 1–43, 1838–78. (Some of the analectes are important for the purpose.)
——, *Considérations sur l'histoire de l'Université de Louvain (1425–1797)*, 1854.
RASHDALL, H., *The Universities of Europe in the Middle Ages*, ed. F. M. Powicke and A. B. Emden, 3 vols., 1936.
RATJEN, H., *Geschichte der Universität zu Kiel*, 1874.
REICKE, E., *Der Gelehrte in der deutschen Vergangenheit (15–18. Jahrh.)*. (In G. Steinhausen, *Monographien zur deutschen Kulturgeschichte*, 1900.)
——, *Lehrer und Unterrichtswesen in der deutschen Vergangenheit (15–18. Jahrh.)*. (In G. Steinhausen, *Monographien zur deutschen Kulturgeschichte*, Bd. ix, 1901.)
RENAN, A., *Le Costume en France*, 1890.
RENAZZI, F. M., *Storia dell' Università di Roma*, 4 vols., 1803–6. (Dry but reliable.)

REPTON, J. A., art. 'Observations on the various Fashions of Hats, Bonnets, or Coverings for the Head', in *Archaeologia*, xxiv (1832), 168–89.

REYNIER, G., *La Vie universitaire dans l'ancienne Espagne*, 1902. (Particularly important for Salamanca.)

REYNOLDS, J. S., *The Evangelicals at Oxford, 1735–1871*, 1953.

RICHTER, A., *Bilder aus der deutschen Kulturgeschichte*, 2 vols., 1882.

ROBINSON, N. F., art. 'The Black Chimere of Anglican Prelates', in *Transactions of St. Paul's Ecclesiological Society*, vol. iv (1898).

———, art. 'The *Pileus Quadratus*', in *Transactions of St. Paul's Ecclesiological Society*, vol. v, pt. 1 (1901).

ROMILLY, J., *Graduati Cantabrigienses*, 1846.

ROSENBERG, A., and TILKE, M., *The Design and Development of Costume*, 5 vols., 1925.

RYMER, T., *Foedera*, tom. vii (1373–97), 1709.

SAINT, L. B., and ARNOLD, H., *Stained Glass of the Middle Ages in England and France*, 1913.

SALMI, M., *La Miniatura Italiana*, 1956.

SALTER, H. E., ed., *Registrum Annalium Collegii Mertonensis, 1483–1521* (O.H.S., vol. lxxvi (1921)).

———, *Registrum Cancellarii*, vol. i (O.H.S., vol. xciii (1932)).

SAMUELS, A. P. I., *The Early Life and Correspondence and Writings of the Rt. Hon. Edmund Burke, LL.D.*, 1923.

SANDAEUS, M., *Theologia Juridica*, 1629.

SANDYS, J. E., *A History of Classical Scholarship*, vol. ii, 1908.

———, art. 'Ancient University Ceremonies', in *Fasciculus Ioanni Willis Clark dicatus*, 1909.

SAVIGNY, F. K. VON, *Histoire du droit romain au moyen âge*, 4 vols., trans. Guenoux, 1839.

SCAPPUS, A., *De Birreto Rubeo*, 1592.

SCHACHNER, N., *The Mediaeval Universities*, 1938.

SCHLUCK, M., *Dissertatio de Norma Actionum Studiosorum, seu von dem Burschen-Comment*, 1780.

SHULTZ, A., *Deutsches Leben in 14–15. Jahrhunderts*, 1892.

SCHUNDENIUS, K. H., *Erinnerungen an die festlichen tage der dritter stiftungsfeyer der Akademie zu Wittenberg*, 1803.

'Scottish Legal Costume', art. in *The Journal of Jurisprudence* (Edinburgh), xxviii (1884), 62 ff. and continued pp. 124 ff.

SEIDLITZ, W. VON, *Allgemeines historisches Porträtwerk*, 12 pts. (6 vols.), 1884–90.

SEYBOLT, R. F., *The 'Manuale Scholarium'*, 1921.

SITWELL, S., *Conversation Pieces*, 1936.

Somerset Mediaeval Wills, ed. F. W. Weaver (Wills, 1531–58) (Somerset Record Society, vol. xxi), 1905.

Spectator, The, Routledge edn., 4 vols., 1860.

Statuta almae universitatis Patavini gymnasii, 1570. (Good collection of documents.)

Statuta almi et perinsignis Collegii maioris Sancti Clementis Hispanorum Bononiae conditi, 1648.

Statuta almi Pisani studii sumpta ex originalibus per Iulianum Lupium, 1621–2 (*Annali delle università toscane*, tom. xxx), 1911. (Some information of value.)

Statuta antiqua Collegii Majoris (*Cracow*) (in *Archiwum do Dziejow Literatury i Oświaty w Polsce*, vol. i), 1878.

Statuta et Leges Fundamentales Academiae Frisiorum quae est Franequerae, 1647.

Statuta et privilegia almae universitatis iuristarum gymnasii Bononiensis, 1561. (The best of the old collections.)

Statuta nec non Liber Promotionum Jagellonica (*Cracow*), *1402–1849* ed. J. Muczkowski, 1849.

Statuta universitatis scholasticae Studii Tubingensis, 1602. (A good example of a valuable old collection.)

Statutes of the Colleges of Oxford, printed for the Royal Commission, 3 vols. 1853.

Statutes of the Realm, vol. iii, 1817, and vol. iv, 1819.

STEGER, A., *Dissertatio de purpura*, 1741. (An excellent monograph.)

STEPHENSON, M., *A List of Monumental Brasses in the British Isles*, 1926.

STRICKLAND, W. G., *Pictures, Busts, and Statues in Trinity College, Dublin*, 1916.

STRUTT, J., *Dresses and Habits of the English People*, 2 vols., 1796–9.

STRUVE, F. G., *De Symbolis quae in promotionibus doctorum adhibentur*, 1739.

STUBBS, J. W., ABBOT, T. K., MAHAFFY, J. P. and others, *The Book of Trinity College, Dublin, 1591–1891*, 1891.

Studia Gratiana, ed. J. Forchielli and A. M. Stickler, 3 vols., 1953–5.

SUFFLING, E. R., *English Church Brasses*, 1910.

TANNER, J. R., *The Historical Register of the University of Cambridge*, 1917.

TAYLOR, W. B. S., *A History of the University of Dublin*, 1845. (Crudely executed, but invaluable plates.)

Testamenta Eboracensia, vols. iv, v, vi (Surtees Society, vols. liii, 1868; lxxix, 1884; and cvi, 1902).

THIERS, B., *L'Histoire des Perruques*, 1777.

THOLUCK, A., *Das akademische Leben des siebzehnten Jahrhunderts*, 1853.

THORBECKE, A., *Statuten und Reformationen der Universität Heidelberg, vom 16. bis 18. Jahrhundert*, 1891. (A good example of sound editing.)

THORNDIKE, L., *University Records and Life in the Middle Ages*, 1944.

TOMASINI, J. P., *Gymnasium Patavinum*, 1654. (Good illustrations.)

TOMEK, W. W., *Geschichte der Prager Universität*, 1849.

TURNER, J. HORSFALL, *The Coats of Arms of the Nobility and Gentry of Yorkshire*, vol. i, 1911.

UWINS, T. see COMBE, W.

VALENTINER, W. R., *Pieter de Hooch, with appendix on Hendrik van der Burch's Art* (1931).

VECELLIO, C., *Habiti Antichi e Moderni*, 1590.

——, *Habiti Antichi et [sic] Moderni di tutto il Mondo* (1598).

VELÁZQUEZ DE FIGUEROA, V., and others, *Anales universitarios. Historia de la Universidad de Valladolid*, tom. i, 1918. (More reliable than the old collections, although these contain more information for the purpose.)

VIDAL Y DIAZ, A., *Memoria Histórica de la Universidad de Salamanca*, 1869. (Contains full statutes of Salamanca.)

VIERO, T., *Raccolta di 126 Stampe che rappresentano Figure ed Abiti di varie Nazioni*, vols. i and ii, 1783–5.

VILLANUEVA, J., *Viage Literario a las Iglesias de España*, t. xvi, 1851.

VILLAR MAIOR, J., *Exposição succinta*, 1877.

VIOLLET-LE-DUC, E. E., *Dictionnaire raisonné du mobilier français*, vol. iv, 1873.

VIRIVILLE, V. DE, *L'Histoire de l'instruction publique*, 1849.

VISCHER, W., *Geschichte der Universität Basel von der Gründing 1460 bis zur Reformation 1529*, 1860. (Important early statutes printed here.)

WALCOTT, M. E. C., *The Constitutions and Canons Ecclesiastical of the Church of England*, 1874.

WALKER, J., *Oxoniana*, 4 vols., 1808.

WALL, C., art. 'Lambeth Degrees', in the *British Medical Journal*, ii (2 Nov. 1935), 854 ff.

WALLER, J. G. and L. A. B., *A Series of Monumental Brasses from the Thirteenth to the Sixteenth Century*, 1864.

WARD, G. R. M., ed., *Oxford University Statutes* (vol. i: *Caroline Code, or Laudian Statutes, 1636*; vol. ii: *University Statutes, 1767–1850*), 2 vols., 1845–51. (A serviceable collection of modern statutes.)

WARD, R. SOMERSET, *Robespierre*, 1934.

WEBB, W. M., *The Heritage of Dress*, 1912.

WEGELE, F. X. VON, *Geschichte der Universität Wirzburg*, 1822. (One of several good examples of painstaking German scholarship, others such being by Tomek, Kink, and Bianco.)

WELLS, J., *The Oxford Degree Ceremony*, 1906. (Mediocre work.)

WESLEY, J., *The Journal of the Rev. John Wesley, A.M.*, 4 vols., 1830.

WHITE, J. B., *The Life of the Rev. Joseph Blanco White written by himself; with portions of his Correspondence*, ed. J. H. Thom, 3 vols., 1845.

WHITTOCK, N., *The Costumes of the Members of the University of Oxford* (1840).

——, *The Costumes of the Members of the University of Cambridge*, ?1847.

——, *A Topographical and Historical Description of the University and City of Oxford*, 1828.

WILKINS, D., *Concilia Magnae Britanniae et Hiberniae*, vols. i and ii, 1737.

WINKELMANN, E., *Urkundenbuch der Universitaet Heidelberg*, 2 vols. (in 1), 1886. (Excellent edition of documents.)

WOOD, T. W., *Ecclesiastical and Academic Colours* (1875).

WOODFORDE, J., *The Diary of a Country Parson*, vol. i, 1758–81, ed. J. Beresford, 1925.

WORDSWORTH, C., *Social Life at the English Universities in the Eighteenth Century*, 1874.

ZACHARIÄ, F. W., *Poetische Schriften*, 1765.

ZARNCKE, F., *Die Deutschen Universitäten in Mittelalter*, 1857.

——, *Die Statutenbücher der Universität Leipzig*, 1861. (Useful edition of statutes.)

ZELTNER, G. G., *Vitae Theologorum Altorphinorum*, 1722.

INDEX

Aberdeen, University of, 142–5.
Åbo, University of, 184.
Academical dress, origins of, 4–6; attempt to abolish at Oxford, 106; abolition of insignia of doctors at Prague, 152; abolished at Vienna, 153; abolition of academical dress at Budapest, 155.
Ad Clerum habit, 109 f.
Adorf, Magister, 161.
Agrégés (assistant professors), of all higher faculties, at Montpellier, 51; at Orléans, 52; of Law, at Paris, 46 f.; at Pau, 59; of Medicine, at Montpellier, 50; at Nancy, 58; stipendiary doctors at Bordeaux, 55.
Aix, University of, 53 f.
Albanensis, A., 22 n. 4.
Albert the Painter, 183.
Albinus, B. S., 176.
Alcalá, University of, 31 f.
Aldrovandi, U., 17.
Altdorf, University of, 165, 172, 174.
Amess (Almuce), worn by Doctors of Theology, Padua, 20; Chancellor of Oxford, 60 f.; Ecclesiastical Amess, 70 n. 7, 136.
Ancharano, P., 15.
Andreae, J., 14.
Angers, University of, 53.
Antécesseurs (professors), of all faculties, at Montpellier, 51; Orléans, 52; of Law, at Paris, 46 f.; Pau, 59; of Medicine, at Nancy, 58.
Apex, described, 190; illust., 192. For instances *see* references under *Biretta* and *Pileus*.
Aristotle, 38, 179.
Armagh, Archbishop of, 137.
Armelausa, see reference under Mantle.
Arnauld, A., 45 n. 6.
Aubrey. J., 10 n. 3, 97.
Autun, Collège de, Paris, 42.
Ave Maria College, Paris, 39.
Avignon, University of, 51 f.
Aylworth, A., 76.

Bachelors, in general, 2; at Bologna, 16 f.; Florence, 24; Coimbra, 32 f.;

Malta, 34; Montpellier, 51; Avignon, 51 f.; Angers, 53, Caen, 55; Pont-à-Mousson, 57; Oxford, 85, 103; Cambridge, 124; Trinity College, Cambridge, 132; Glasgow, 140; Prague, 151; Heidelberg, 155; Leipzig, 159; Ingolstadt, 161; Strassburg, 165 f.
Bachelors of Arts, in France, 3; Germany, 3, 150; at Vienna, 4, 152, 155; Paris, 36 f., 38, 41, 48; Oxford, 88–91, 96; Cambridge, 126–8; St. Andrews, 138; Glasgow, 140; Aberdeen, 142 f.; Trinity College, Dublin, 148; Prague, 151 f.; Heidelberg, 156; Greifswald, 160; Leipzig, 169; Cracow, 187, 189.
— of Canon Law: at Paris, 41; Oxford, 84, 103; Cambridge, 124 f.
— of Civil Law: at Oxford, 61, 84–86, 104.
— of Divinity: at Oxford, 82 f., 103; Cambridge, 112, 123 f.; Trinity College, Dublin, 147 f.
— of Law(s): at Vienna, 4; Paris, 47; Toulouse, 49; Montpellier, 49; Poitiers, 54; Nantes, 56 f.; Cambridge, 123, 126; Trinity College, Dublin, 147 f.
— of Medicine: at Vienna, 4; Paris, 37, 47; Angers, 53; Oxford, 76, 86 f.; Cambridge, 125 f.; Trinity College, Dublin, 148.
— of Music: at Oxford, 87 f.; Cambridge, 126; Trinity College, Dublin, 148.
— of Philosophy: at Pont-à-Mousson, 58.
— of Surgery: at Cambridge, 126.
— of Theology: at Vienna, 4, 152; Paris, 41, 43, 46, 179; Nantes, 56; Pont-à-Mousson, 58; Cologne, 154 f.; Heidelberg, 155 f.; Würzburg, 158; Louvain, 179 f.; Cracow, 187.
Baier, J. J., 165.
Bailey, W., 76.
Bajan (freshman) at Aberdeen, 144 f.
Baker, T., 91.
Balandran, 32.

PRINTED IN GREAT BRITAIN
AT THE UNIVERSITY PRESS, OXFORD
BY VIVIAN RIDLER
PRINTER TO THE UNIVERSITY